THE SECOND AVENUE DELI COOKBOOK

Recipes and Memories
from
Abe Lebewohl's
Legendary Kitchen

VILLARD ♦ NEW YORK

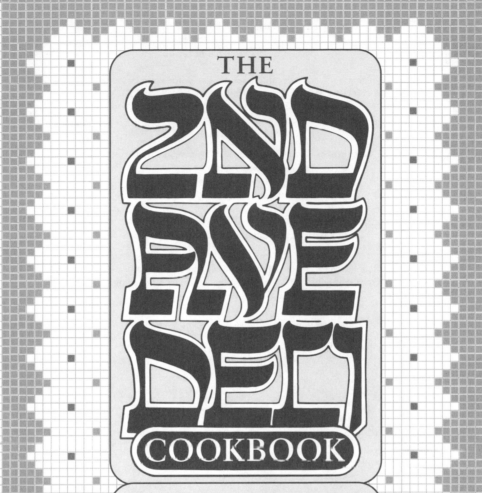

THE 2ND AVE DELI

COOKBOOK

SHARON LEBEWOHL
AND
RENA BULKIN

All rights reserved under International Pan-American Copyright
Conventions. Published in the United States by Villard Books,
a division of Random House, Inc., New York, and
simultaneously in Canada by Random House of
Canada Limited, Toronto.

VILLARD BOOKS and colophon are registered trademarks
of Random House, Inc.

All uncredited photographs are courtesy of
the Second Avenue Deli

Library of Congress Cataloging-in-Publication Data
Lebewohl, Sharon.
The Second Avenue Deli cookbook: recipes and memories
from Abe Lebewohl's legendary kitchen/Sharon Lebewohl
and Rena Bulkin.
p.   cm.
ISBN 0-375-50267-X (alk. paper)
1. Cookery, Jewish.   2. Second Avenue Deli (New York, N.Y.)
I. Bulkin, Rena.   II. Second Avenue Deli (New York, N.Y.)
III. Title.
TX734.L348   1999
641.5′676—dc21   99-14156

Random House website address: www.atrandom.com

Printed in the United States of America on acid-free paper

2 4 6 8 9 7 5 3

FIRST EDITION

Book design by Carole Lowenstein

This book is dedicated to
Eleanor Lebewohl
and in loving memory
of her husband
Abe Lebewohl

FOREWORD

MY BROTHER ABE'S great passion in life was his restaurant. "The store," as he always called the Deli, was his second home, his employees a second family. Abe loved good food, and he loved people; he was fortunate enough to have a profession that combined both of his great enthusiasms. When he wasn't at the Deli, he was visiting other restaurants under the guise of "doing research." He never went on these fact-finding missions alone. A large clique of close friends, relatives, and employees were regular diners-out on his circuit.

As a social occasion, a restaurant meal with Abe was a somewhat jarring experience, in which the flow of conversation was repeatedly interrupted at a moment's notice. For one thing, even at the fanciest restaurants, he considered the seat nearest the kitchen the best seat in the house. From that vantage point, he could occasionally sneak a peek at what was happening behind the scenes. Every time the kitchen's swinging doors flew open, his attention would become riveted on the frenzy of food preparation therein, and conversation would come to an abrupt standstill, sometimes in midsentence. Further interruptions occurred because, as a well-known New York personality, he was frequently recognized and approached, not only by other diners but by the chef. Adding to the chaos were continual calls from "the store" (Abe loved his cell phone), because he encouraged his staff to consult him about even the most minor decisions. It was his loving hands-on perfectionism and involvement in every detail that made the Deli great. And sometimes those calls were from me; we regularly spoke on the phone four or five times a day.

Like everyone who's passionate about food, Abe was forever trying to lose a little weight. After he was shot, when the family was sitting shiva, one of his regular dining companions came up to me and said, "I had lunch with Abe the day before he died. It's such a pity; he was on a diet, and he hardly ate anything. I know he would have wanted his last meals to be spectacular." I told him not to feel too bad. He was the fourth person to tell me he had had lunch with Abe that day. And I believe every one of them was telling me the truth.

Abe's death was devastating to me; he was not only my brother but my closest and dearest friend. After he died, I felt bound by three major mandates to honor his memory. The first, of course, was to keep the restaurant

open and maintain the legendary quality he had worked so hard to achieve. The second was to renovate the interior, a project that was very much on Abe's agenda at the time of his death. And the third was realizing his dream of creating a Second Avenue Deli cookbook.

When his daughter, Sharon, his close friend Rena Bulkin, and I sat down to plan this book, we all agreed we wanted it to be not just a compendium of the Deli's famous recipes but a tribute to Abe's life and generosity of spirit. For those of you who knew him—and I know he touched thousands of lives—our cookbook will rekindle many warm memories. For those of you who never had the good fortune of having Abe in your lives, we'd like you to meet him. And for Abie, my dear brother, who I'm sure is looking down at us from Heaven, this book is for you.

JACK LEBEWOHL

CONTENTS

Abe with Eleanor.

INTRODUCTION

THE SECOND AVENUE DELI COOKBOOK is more than a collection of a legendary New York restaurant's cherished recipes. For many years, the Deli's founder, Abe Lebewohl, talked about revealing the secrets of his traditional Jewish specialties—chicken soup with matzo balls, hearty cholent, grandmotherly gefilte fish, stuffed cabbage, and all the rest. But, tragically, in 1996, before he ever got the project under way, Abe was brutally murdered as he prepared to deposit the previous day's earnings in an East Village bank.

Abe was an exceptional person—exuberant, funny, compassionate—a brilliant businessman and a great humanitarian. His death generated national television and radio coverage, as well as dozens of heartfelt editorials and obituaries in New York City newspapers. And his funeral was so widely attended that the Community Synagogue on East Sixth Street, where it took place, was filled far beyond its fifteen-hundred-seat capacity. The hundreds of people who could not even find standing room in the shul filled the entire street, building to building, between First and Second Avenues. Traffic had to be rerouted by police barricades, and every stoop and fire escape was crowded with mourners. Unable to hear the funeral service inside, they stood in silence for its duration to honor him.

Abe—who fed every homeless person who walked into the Deli hungry—has been called "the Jewish Mother Teresa." At his death, even those who knew and loved him best learned for the first time just how many people his life had touched. Because Abe never spoke about it, no one will ever know the extent of his charity, which embraced not only Jewish causes but also almost any person or group who ever asked for his help. Among the funeral mourners, we heard nuns telling a reporter, "He was so good to us." Abe's legendary generosity manifested itself in every conceivable arena. A tremendous enthusiast for any cause that moved him, he gave away mountains of food to politicians he supported, fed striking workers (when there was a strike at NBC in 1987, he provided sandwiches to the picketers every day for twenty-one weeks), and delivered trays of free food to a local Ukrainian travel agency in celebration of the Ukraine's independence from the Soviet Union. Whenever anything moved or excited him, Abe sent food.

In his restaurant, both customers and employees were treated like family.

No one—not even a busboy—ever called him Mr. Lebewohl; he was always Abie, always warm, caring, and accessible.

So though this book is primarily a restaurant cookbook filled with wonderful recipes, it is also something more: a tribute to the beloved Abe Lebewohl, whose life was an inspiration to everyone who knew him.

Dozens of his famous customers, who were also his friends—politicians, media people, top New York chefs, actors, and others—have joined us in this tribute. You'll find their loving reminiscences of Abe, along with their favorite recipes, throughout this book.

In further tribute, we'd like to share with our readers the history of the Second Avenue Deli, which is integrally entwined with the history of the Lebewohl family.

A Dollar and a Dream

Abe Lebewohl once said he came to America in 1950 at the age of nineteen "with a dollar and a dream." Actually, the dollar was questionable, but the dream—of a successful life in America—was empowered by the rigors of his childhood (which he wished to put behind him), by a family tradition of courage in the face of adversity, and by his own immense vitality. The story of the Lebewohl family—a remarkable story, but one shared by thousands of immigrants who rebuilt Diaspora-shattered lives in America—is a testament to the ever-hopeful human spirit, sustained in the face of the most daunting prior experience.

Born in Lvov, Poland, in 1931 to a comfortable middle-class family, Abe's briefly secure life was shattered in 1939, when Stalin joined forces with Hitler, Poland was divided, and Lvov became part of the Soviet Union. A year later, Abe's father, Efraim, owner of a small lumber mill, was condemned as a capitalist, arrested, and sentenced without trial to ten years' hard labor in Siberia. The business was seized by the government, and, a week later, Abe and his mother, Ethel—forced to leave all their possessions behind—were taken to the railway station, herded into cattle cars, and deported to Kazakhstan in Central Asia.

Thousands of miles away, in Siberia, Efraim was put to work as a logger, enduring long hours balancing on rolling logs in freezing waters. A fall from the logs—not an uncommon occurrence among prisoners—meant instant death; before a man even had a chance to drown, he'd be crushed by the oncoming logs. It was a job for a young, athletic man in excellent condition, not a middle-aged businessman debilitated, emotionally and physically, by cold, hunger, and despair. Efraim later told Abe that his intense desire to reunite with his family focused his concentration and kept him from falling to his death.

Similarly, Ethel Lebewohl—devastated by the soul-numbing loss of everything she held dear, and unsure if she'd ever see her husband again—had to rally immediately in order to survive. She found work in a restaurant, and sent Abe to a local school. When school let out every afternoon, she'd seat him at an inconspicuous table in the restaurant and sneak him nourishing food while he did his homework.

In 1941, fate favored the Lebewohls; the Russians granted amnesty to all Polish political prisoners, and Efraim was released from the labor camp. A fellow prisoner he had befriended in Siberia, future Israeli prime minister Menachem Begin, wanted Efraim to accompany him to Palestine via Iran, but Efraim's first goal was to find his family. By the time he located Abe and Ethel, it was too late to get out of the country. The Lebewohls had to remain in Kazakhstan through the remainder of the war, scrounging at odd jobs to keep food on the table. When the war ended, they returned to Lvov, to see if they could find any of their relatives alive. Everyone—grandparents, uncles, aunts, cousins, friends—had been killed by the Nazis. Ironically, Efraim's arrest, and his family's forced deportation, had saved their lives.

The small group of surviving Jews in Lvov (most of whom had been hidden by Gentiles) were given a choice: they could become either Russian or Polish citizens. The Lebewohls chose Poland and were sent to Waldenburg, a new territory the Poles had reacquired from East Germany when Europe was reconstituted after the war. All the Germans living there were expelled, and their homes were given to Jews. After years of horror, the family enjoyed a brief respite from danger. But when, eight months later, forty Jews were killed by Polish anti-Semites in a bordering town, they decided to leave Waldenburg and settle in Palestine. Since the British were allowing very few Jews to enter, it was necessary to emigrate illegally. The family made its way to Italy, where they planned to board a ship for Palestine. At the last minute, however, Ethel Lebewohl had a change of heart: having survived the Holocaust, she could not bear to risk her son's life in the Israeli fight for independence. Efraim agreed, and despite strong protests from the young Abe, a fervent Zionist, the family decided to stay put until they could emigrate to

Jack taking a chicken soup break in the Molly Picon Room.

America. For several years, they were forced to reside in a displaced-persons' camp in Barletta, Italy, under the auspices of the United Nations. Abe's brother, Jack, who today runs the Deli, was born in that DP camp in 1948. Abe was then seventeen, and more than half his life had been spent fleeing persecution. The Lebewohls remained in the camp until 1950, when they were given the opportunity to come to America. The Hebrew Immigrant Aid Society found them housing on Lafayette Street in Manhattan, in the building that is today Joseph Papp's Public Theater.

Becoming an American

Nineteen-year-old Abe, desperate to make a success of himself in America, immediately began to study English. His teacher—also a greenhorn, but one who had arrived a few years earlier—tried to pass along the rudiments of American culture with the language. He told the class that all Americans chewed gum and were fanatical about baseball, so Abe chewed gum and memorized baseball stats and lore. A more realistic view of American life came from his daily reading—dictionary in hand—of every word in *The New York Times,* a habit that lasted a lifetime, eventually, of course, without a dictionary. Efraim found a menial job polishing display fixtures in a factory, and Ethel went to work for a tie manufacturer. Both of his parents wanted Abe to go back to school, but he insisted on working as well.

His first job was in a Coney Island deli, where he was employed as a soda jerk. During lunch breaks, he volunteered to help out behind the counter, where he could better observe the restaurant's operation. He soon graduated to the coveted position of counterman. Over the next few years, he worked in a number of deli kitchens, gleaning the secrets of superlative pastrami and other traditional Jewish delicacies.

In 1954, with a few thousand dollars he had miraculously managed to set aside, Abe took over a tiny ten-seat luncheonette on East Tenth Street—the nucleus of the Second Avenue Deli. Working around the clock for years—often filling in as cook, counterman, waiter, and even busboy—he put all his time and energy into making a success of his tiny establishment. (When he started dating his wife, Eleanor, in 1957, Abe told her he owned a restaurant. One day, she traveled down from her Bronx home to see it for herself. When she walked in and saw him sweeping up, she thought he'd lied to her. Only after she asked someone who the owner was, and they pointed to Abe, did she believe the restaurant was actually his.) For the first decade, the entire enterprise was touch-and-go. Bankruptcy often loomed; when money was tight, Abe moonlighted at other jobs to keep the restaurant going. He frequently despaired that he was taking in less money than his dishwasher. In 1957, however, he felt secure enough to marry Eleanor. By 1960, they had two baby daughters, Sharon and Felicia. Abe combined business with family life, closing the Deli every Monday and making after-school family outings of trips to suppliers, food vendors, and the bakery. After all the business was completed, the weekly ritual would end with a family dinner at an

Abe with legendary Yiddish actress Molly Picon,
for whom he named a dining room.

inexpensive restaurant. Having a family depending on him made the precariousness of business even more anxiety-producing; however, it also strengthened Abe's passionate determination to succeed. Like his father on the logs, he somehow managed to stay afloat.

Driven by Abe's love, perfectionism, and showmanship (*The New York Times* once called him "a significant performer in what might be the last Jewish stage setting for Second Avenue"), the Deli prospered and expanded. In 1980, he acquired an adjoining storefront in order to add the Molly Picon Room, honoring the great Yiddish actress and upping his seating capacity to 250. And, in 1985, he created a Walk of Stars outside the Deli, commemorating the most noted actors of the Jewish stage that once dominated this stretch of Second Avenue.

Jack with Yiddish actor Fyvush Finkel,
at the installation of his star on the
Deli's Walk of Stars.

The Jewish Rialto

ABE LEBEWOHL chose downtown Second Avenue as the site for his restaurant because he treasured the neighborhood's Jewish heritage—especially its connection with the Yiddish theater. In the early decades of the twentieth century, New York's Jewish population grew and prospered. Between 1881 and 1903, more than a million Yiddish-speaking Jews arrived in New York, and most of them settled on the Lower East Side. Second Avenue, between Houston and Fourteenth Streets became a cultural hub, lined with Yiddish bookstores, lively cafés, and playhouses. Every night, stars of the Yiddish stage strode the boards in melodramas (often with immigrant-makes-good themes), comedies, and serious theatrical productions. Tragedian Jacob Adler (famed for his moving portrayals of Shylock and Lear) and matinee idol Boris Thomashevsky—who yearned to raise the intellectual quality of Yiddish plays—adapted Shakespeare and Goethe for the Jewish stage. Edward G. Robinson, Steve Lawrence (whose father was a cantor), Paul Muni, Leonard Nimoy, impresario Joseph Papp, and director Harold Clurman all began their careers in the Yiddish theater.

The Jewish Rialto was already on the wane when the Deli opened in 1954, and today most of its venues have been torn down. The old Moorish-motif Yiddish Art Theatre on Twelfth Street and Second Avenue (built in 1926 by the great Yiddish actor/director Maurice Schwartz) is now a multi-screen movie house. And a Japanese restaurant across the street occupies the site of the old Café Royale (celebrated fictionally in Hy Kraft's 1942 comedy *Café Crown*). The Royale was once the meeting place for Jewish entertainers and intelligentsia. Charlie Chaplin, George Jessel, Fanny Brice, Eddie Cantor, Moss Hart, and Rachmaninoff—not to mention non-Jewish Village writers like e.e. cummings and John Dos Passos, who found the Royale scene colorful—were among its habitués. They gathered there to discuss art, literature, and socialism over blintzes washed down with glasses of tea.

The Café Royale had closed its doors a few years before Abe arrived on Second Avenue. As a tribute, he wanted to call his establishment the Royale Deli, but the café's owner wanted a $2,000 royalty, which, at that time, might have been $2 million. Still, the idea of honoring the Yiddish theater stuck in Abe's mind.

In the Deli's second major expansion, he dubbed his new dining area the Molly Picon Room and covered its walls with film and theater posters of

Picon in roles ranging from *Yiddle and His Fiddle* to *Fiddler on the Roof*. At an opening-night party to inaugurate the room, the famous eighty-two-year-old actress (who once sang a Yiddish ballad called "The Rabbi's Melody" so soulfully she made Al Capone cry) was once again applauded by her fellow thespians. Even Mayor Ed Koch stopped by to kiss the guest of honor and nosh a little chopped liver. Molly was a regular customer during her lifetime; her favorite dish was chicken in the pot.

In 1985, further warming to his theatrical theme, Abe created a Hollywood Boulevard–like Walk of Stars outside the Deli, with thirty-one granite stars commemorating fifty-eight luminaries of the Jewish stage. A special star pays tribute to Abraham Goldfaden, "the Father of Yiddish theater." Though Jewish theater actually harks back to the sixteenth century (rooted in Purim plays, it was the Jewish counterpart of Christian passion plays), it was Goldfaden, in the 1870s, who wrote, composed music and painted scenery for, and produced the first professional Yiddish dramas and comedies. His first performance, in a wine garden in Jassy, Romania, was such a flop that the audience not only booed but physically attacked him. The experience taught him two things: that he was a lousy actor and that his material had been too highbrow for the public taste. But instead of nurturing contempt for his unsophisticated audience, he began to use his plays as a forum to educate—to wean his fellow Jews from fanatic traditionalism and cultural isolation. He went on to shape a Yiddish theatrical tradition that, if not subtle or profoundly intellectual, was emotionally stirring and boisterously comical.

As continuing immigration brought thousands of Jews to New York, the Yiddish theater flourished, freed from fear, censorship, pogroms, and persecution. People who lived in dire poverty—who spent their days laboring in sweatshops and their nights in shabby, overcrowded tenements—managed to set aside a little money from their meager earnings for tickets. A link with their heritage and an island of comfort in a baffling new world, Yiddish plays were as nourishing and vital to them as food and drink. The Jewish stage prospered through the 1940s, when it fell victim to assimilation and the diminishing number of Yiddish-speaking Jews.

In the early 1990s, inspired by perestroika, Abe developed a new passion: to open the first kosher restaurant in Moscow. Robbed of his childhood by the rise of Communism, he enthusiastically hailed its demise. His intention was to begin restoring to Russian Jews—via matzo ball soup, chopped liver, and potato latkes—their long-lost heritage. The profits from the restaurant—which was to be called Rishon (Hebrew for "First")—would be donated, in his parents' name, to a Russian yeshiva. Abe made many trips to

Moscow trying to set things up. In the end, however, a combination of bureaucratic mire and Russian corruption (thugs demanded under-the-table payments for "security") put an end to this cherished project. Though deeply disappointed, Abe soon put Moscow behind him and returned his focus to the Deli, which by now had attained the status of a Big Apple landmark.

After decades of struggle, Abe's dream of success in America was a reality—a reality that he enjoyed tremendously until the last moment of his life. He loved people, he loved food, he loved his restaurant, and he loved New York, especially his East Village neighborhood. The Second Avenue Deli has long been the anchor of that neighborhood, its glowing neon sign the symbol of a vibrant community of successful businesses, shops, restaurants, and cafés. During his lifetime, other businesspeople in the area dubbed Abe "the Mayor of Second Avenue."

If Abe had been aware of his own violent death, he would have seen it as an anomaly, not as a sign that crime was rampant on the city streets. He was always upbeat about New York. And he would have wanted his restaurant to continue to flourish and feed the public. Soon after Abe's death, his widow, Eleanor, and his brother, Jack, reopened the Deli. They knew Abe would have wanted it that way. Under their loving stewardship, the kitchen has maintained its excellence and authenticity, while continuing to experiment and evolve. The same waitstaff is on hand to warmly welcome customers. And a final dream of Abe's has also been realized: in 1997, a sparkling new interior and façade were created by one of America's most prominent restaurant designers, Adam Tihany, who breathed new life into our surroundings without sacrificing the Deli's all-important traditional *gemütlichkeit*.

Every night, people still form long lines outside the Deli's doors, waiting to savor its peerless pastrami and incomparable chopped liver. When there are especially large crowds, waiters come out with platters of hors d'oeuvres to stave off the pangs of hunger. The Second Avenue Deli remains a vibrant New York institution that we hope will survive forever as a loving tribute to its founder, Abe Lebewohl.

ABOUT THIS COOKBOOK

IN THE COMING PAGES, you'll learn the secrets of all the Second Avenue Deli's classic creations—our award-winning chopped liver, Old World cholent, fork-tender brisket of beef, and crisp potato latkes.

Our traditional fare is the ultimate expression of comfort food. Dripping in schmaltz and nostalgia—and as diverse as the nations of the Diaspora—it's redolent of Jewish culture and history; almost every dish evokes a holiday ritual. But Abe's eclectic enthusiasms couldn't be contained even in the wide spectrum of Jewish cuisine. If he especially liked something he ate, Abe wanted it served in his restaurant, Jewish or not. Hence, our menu—and the recipes in this book—include such unexpected items as spicy barbecued chicken, buffalo wings, a California-style bow tie salad with sun-dried tomatoes, chicken cacciatore, and even vegetable lo mein!

Every year, the Deli caters hundreds of parties, bar mitzvahs, weddings, board meetings, seminars, and political events. It's a big part of our business, and, in compiling recipes, we've included many items from our catering menus that are not offered in the restaurant itself.

Abe, ever a Zionist, made many trips to Israel and loved its cuisine: so we've presented such traditional Middle Eastern fare as baba ganoush, hummus, tahini, tabbouleh, and the best falafel you've ever had.

Other wonderful recipes (all fully tested by us) were provided by Lebewohl family members and friends.

Julia Child once offered this bit of culinary comfort: "Don't be afraid of cooking. . . . What's the worst that could happen?" What's more, she added, "It's important to remember you can fix almost anything." We agree with Julia, and we've worked hard to make our recipes easy to understand so that cooking will be fun, not frightening. Hopefully, you won't even need to "fix" anything.

What's Kosher? What's Pareve?

The Jewish ritual dietary laws of kashruth—which include detailed instructions for the proper selection, slaughtering, cooking, and eating of all foods—were handed down to Moses on Mount Sinai along with the Ten

Commandments. A covenant with God, kashruth teaches reverence for life and perpetuates Jewish identity among a dispersed people.

The Second Avenue Deli is a kosher restaurant. In accordance with one of the most fundamental tenets of kashruth—which forbids combining any dairy foods with meat or poultry—we specialize in meat, fish, and poultry dishes. We serve no dairy items—no milk, butter, cheese, or derivatives thereof—and use no dairy items in food preparation. Our delicious mashed potatoes, for instance, are whipped with schmaltz (rendered chicken fat, flavored with onions), not cream and butter.

Frequently throughout this book, you'll see the word *pareve,* which means "made without milk or meat products." Fish, eggs, grains, herbs and spices, fruits, vegetables, and nuts are all pareve—neutral foods that can be eaten in combination with meat or dairy. At the Deli, our nonmeat dishes are all pareve. Hence, in our kitchen, even traditionally dairy items, such as blintz crêpes, are prepared with nondairy creamer and margarine instead of milk and butter and filled with potatoes or fruit, not cheese (though we do have faux cheese blintzes made with Tofutti cream cheese). And they're served with applesauce, not sour cream.

Because you'll be preparing these recipes at home, where even the most observant Jews are set up for both meat and dairy preparation (with separate dishes and cooking and eating utensils), we've also included some of our favorite recipes that are strictly dairy, such as cheese blintzes, challah bread pudding, and a matzo-apple kugel that contains butter and cream cheese. Wherever possible, we also offer pareve versions of dairy fare (especially desserts). That's because even though observant Jews can eat dairy, they have to wait six hours after a meat meal to do so; and we think six hours is a long time to wait for dessert!

THE JEWISH PANTRY
Step into Our Kitchen

IN THE OLD DAYS—and up to a few decades ago—the kitchen was the heart and hearth of a Jewish home, the stove the place you were most likely to find your mom. Coming home from school, you'd toss your books on the table, fling your coat on the banister post (though you'd been told a million times to hang it in the closet), and head straight to the kitchen, lured by the tantalizing aromas and warmth of cooking food and Mom's two daily questions: "So, how was your day?" and "Are you hungry?" A little nosh from the stove—a preview of the coming night's dinner—was a frequent after-school treat.

Today, Mom is more likely to be in the office than the kitchen in the afternoon, and even if you grew up in a Jewish household, you may not be familiar with all of the foodstuffs used in traditional Jewish cooking. This little glossary comprises our cookbook's Cliffs Notes; in addition to momma foods, it includes some Israeli dishes and restaurant kitchen staples.

CHICKEN SOUP OR STOCK: The penicillin of Jewish mothers, this golden elixir is also the basis of many other soups and stews. If you don't want to make your own stock, you can buy it canned in the supermarket.

DERMA STUFFING: Almost everyone we know who grew up in a Jewish home waxes nostalgic about stuffed derma, or *kishke*. If you're coming to it as an adult, you might be better off not knowing that the casings for stuffed derma are a cow's intestines. Not that you eat the casings—just the spicy stuffing, which is mostly bread crumbs, onions, and seasonings, plus some kind of fatty stuff you don't want to know about either. Derma stuffing adds zest to cholents.

EGG BARLEY: Egg barley (also called farfel) isn't a grain; it's barley-shaped egg noodle pasta.

GRIBENES: Gribenes, a by-product of making schmaltz (page xxii), are onion-flavored goose or chicken cracklings (crunchy fried morsels of skin or fat). They can be used to add zing to mashed potatoes, kasha varnishkes, chopped liver, and stuffings . . . or as a heavenly spread on fresh-baked rye, pumpernickel, or challah.

HELLMANN'S MAYONNAISE: You'll note that all our recipes calling for mayonnaise use Hellmann's; even though we didn't win their sandwich competition (page 129), we agree, it does "bring out the best."

JEWISH MUSTARD: On deli meats, only spicy Jewish mustard will do.

KASHA: The quintessential Jewish grain (via Russia), kasha is roasted buckwheat groats. It has a wonderfully nutty flavor.

KITCHEN BOUQUET: This brown sauce, available in supermarkets, is another restaurant kitchen staple. It adds flavorful oomph to gravies and sauces.

KOSHER SALT: Coarse-grained, additive-free kosher salt is used by observant Jews to leach the blood from meats (according to the rules of kashruth, "Thou shalt not eat the blood, for the soul resides in the blood"). Prior to the age of refrigeration, the practice may have also offered a health benefit; salting meat is a good way to preserve it. And religious or health reasons aside, even many non-Jewish chefs prefer kosher salt for its rich texture and flavor.

MATZO: matzo is the "bread of affliction" that Jews ate during the exodus from Egypt. It's flat and unleavened, because they didn't have time to let it rise as they hastened to freedom across the Sinai. Jews eat matzo on Passover to remember the suffering of their ancestors, who were slaves in Egypt. There are dozens of wonderful matzo recipes, including matzo brei (fried matzo), matzo balls (dumplings), matzo meal latkes, even matzo blintzes.

MATZO FARFEL: This is matzo broken up into very small pieces.

MATZO MEAL: Matzo meal is simply matzo ground up to the consistency of a coarse flour. It has no other ingredients. In Jewish cooking, it's used for breading fried foods, as the basis for latkes, and often in place of flour as a thickening agent.

ROUX: Roux is a mixture of flour and fat that is slow-cooked over low heat and used to thicken sauces, stews, and soups. In traditional non-Jewish cooking, the fat used is usually butter, but since the Deli uses roux mainly in dishes that contain chicken stock, we substitute corn oil for butter to keep things kosher.

SCHMALTZ: Along with chicken soup, schmaltz (rendered chicken or goose fat) is the key ingredient of Jewish cooking, standing in for the butter and olive oil of other European cuisines. When we were children, its alluring aroma permeated our mothers' kitchens. In Orthodox neighborhoods, you can buy schmaltz at the supermarket, and regular supermarkets often carry it around Jewish holidays. You can usually get schmaltz at a kosher butcher shop. If you want to make your own, follow this recipe:

Schmaltz and Gribenes

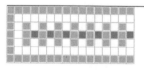

This recipe uses the fat and skin from about 4 chickens. You can save it up in your freezer over the course of time. For even more flavorful schmaltz, add a few cloves of garlic.

MAKES ABOUT 2 CUPS

4 cups chicken fat and skin, cut into ½-inch pieces or smaller
Kosher salt

Pinch of pepper
1 cup onion rings, about ⅛-inch thick

1. Wash fat and skin well in a colander, and pat dry. Place in a heavy skillet, and sprinkle lightly with salt and pepper.
2. Cook, uncovered, over low heat (you can turn it up a bit once the fat has begun melting). When the fat starts to melt and get slightly brown, add onions (and garlic cloves if you like), and continue cooking until onions and cracklings are golden brown and crunchy.
3. When partially cooled, strain over a bowl to remove onions and cracklings, and refrigerate them in a covered glass jar. Pour schmaltz into another jar, cover, and refrigerate.

VEGETABLE STOCK: Vegetable stock makes a tasty alternative to chicken or beef stock for soups and stews, and if you're kosher, it allows you to use butter instead of oil when preparing roux. Save cooked carrots and beets to serve as vegetable dishes.

Vegetable Stock

12 cups water
1 large onion, peeled and cut into eighths
1 medium beet, peeled and quartered
2 stalks celery, cut into 3-inch pieces
2 very large carrots, peeled and cut into 2-inch chunks
1 large parsnip, peeled and cut into 2-inch chunks
1 bunch of parsley (about the equivalent of 1 cup)
¼ pound fresh spinach leaves
¼ cup tomato paste
1 tablespoon salt
¼ teaspoon pepper
1 teaspoon sugar

MAKES A
LITTLE MORE
THAN
2 QUARTS

1. Place all ingredients in a large stockpot and bring to a boil. Reduce heat, and simmer for 1 hour. Strain out the broth.

Hon. Mayor Rudolph Giuliani batting 1.000 with a Second Avenue Deli salami at a Central Park softball game.

I am honored that you have asked me to contribute my thoughts to your cookbook. Though I'm glad the secrets of Abe's culinary genius are to be revealed, no written word can fully capture exactly how much he meant to his friends, his customers and his city, New York. Abe was a very special man. I know that any book written about his restaurant will also be very special.

In many ways, Abe was the embodiment of the immigrant experience in New York City. A Holocaust survivor who came here at the end of the Second World War seeking to build a new life, he gravitated to Second Avenue-once famous as the Yiddish Broadway-where he opened a 12-seat eatery in 1954. While the world of Yiddish theater was already fading away, Abe's business thrived, and he expanded his eatery into the East Village institution it is today.

He was a success story in every sense of the word. An astute businessman, he was also a man of integrity, joy and humanity. His family, friends, and customers remember with fondness his laughter and conversation. His employees recall his thoughtful acts of generosity during difficult times. And everyone remembers his determination to help the less fortunate with a bowl of soup or a sandwich, always offered with a kind word and a smile.

Abe's death was a terrible loss to our city, and he is missed by all who knew him. But his indomitable spirit - not unlike the spirit of his adopted city- lives on.

Sincerely,

Rudolph W. Giuliani
Mayor

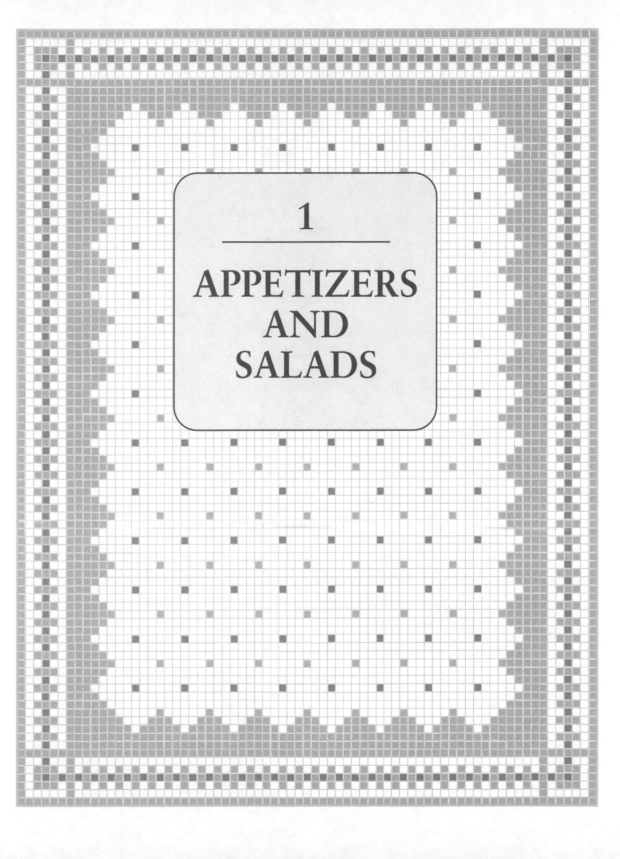

1

APPETIZERS
AND
SALADS

Chopped Liver
Mock Chopped Liver
Russ & Daughters' Chopped Herring
Coleslaw
Hawaiian Slaw
Health Salad
Macaroni Salad
Potato Salad
Potato Salad à la Russe
Antoinette D'Amato's Orzo Salad
Cucumber Salad
Creamy Cucumber Salad
Chicken Salad
Egg Salad with Onions and Mushrooms
Bow Tie and Broccoli Salad
Bow Tie Salad with Sun-Dried Tomatoes
Patrick Clark's Tomato and Black Olive Couscous
Lentil Salad
Pickles
P'tcha
Stuffed Mushrooms
Tahini Sauce
Hummus/Tahini
Baba Ganoush
Eggplant Salad
Falafel
Tabbouleh

As Jews dispersed throughout the world, they not only preserved their rich culinary heritage, but also expanded its parameters to include regional foods and recipes of their newly adopted nations. Ironically, the flight from persecution engendered an exotic and colorful Jewish cuisine. Its diversity is especially evident in this eclectic chapter, which runs the gamut from our inimitable Jewish deli classics—like chopped liver, potato and macaroni salads, and cole slaw—to Middle Eastern specialties like hummus/tahini, falafel, and eggplant salad.

Chopped Liver

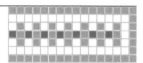

Chopped liver, like pâté de foie gras, dates from medieval Strasbourg, where both were originally created from goose livers raised by Jewish poultry breeders. The use of chicken and beef livers was an Eastern European innovation, but it took American ingenuity to bring chopped liver down to its lowest level: as a medium for sculptures of brides and bar mitzvah boys.

SERVES 8

1½ pounds beef liver
1 pound chicken liver
Corn oil for drizzling
1 tablespoon plus 2 teaspoons corn oil
1 tablespoon plus 2 teaspoons schmaltz

4 cups coarsely chopped onions
4 hard-boiled eggs, peeled
1 tablespoon schmaltz
2 teaspoons salt
¼ teaspoon pepper

1. Turn on broiler. Rinse beef and chicken livers thoroughly, and cut away membranes and extra fat. Cut beef liver into 1-inch pieces; chicken livers can remain whole. Place beef and chicken livers in a large baking pan, and drizzle with corn oil (pour oil into a flatware tablespoon and drizzle over livers; 2 tablespoons are ample). Broil 8 to 10 minutes (keep an eye on it to make sure it doesn't burn). Turn liver pieces, and broil for another 5 minutes. Liver should be fully cooked and lightly browned on both sides. Let chill in refrigerator.

2. In a large skillet, heat 1 tablespoon plus 2 teaspoons corn oil and the same amount of schmaltz, and sauté onions, stirring occasionally, until well browned. Let chill in refrigerator.

3. In food processor, combine liver, onions, hard-boiled eggs, schmaltz, salt, and pepper, and blend until smooth. You'll have to do it in batches. Chill before serving.

Note: Though the above is the official Deli version, some people prefer to use only chicken livers. They make a lighter, creamier chopped liver.

PROMOTIONS, PITCHES . . . AND PITCHING NO-HITTERS

Please Don't Eat the Art

IN 1976, ABE DONATED 350 pounds of chopped liver—not for the bar mitzvah of an indigent thirteen-year-old, but to *New York* magazine designer Milton Glaser's graphic-design studio, Pushpin. Working feverishly in their highly perishable medium (by its second day, the exhibit was deemed "ripe" for destruction), nineteen of the studio's artists put together a show at Manhattan's Greengrass Media Art Gallery called "Man and Liver." Works included Bill Sloan's *Barbra Streisand 1960—or Cry Me a Liver,* a sexy nude hen-woman by Robert Grossman, and an exquisitely sculpted rooster by Four Seasons chef Seppi Renggli. The winning entry was James Grashow's monumental six-and-a-half-foot-high rendering of King Kong straddling the World Trade Center's twin towers.

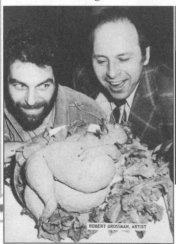

Abe with Pushpin founder and artist Seymour Chwast.

Abe and Pushpin artist Robert Grossman ogling a chopped liver nude hen-woman.

Chopped liver King Kong hovering over Abe and Pushpin artist James Grashow.

Mock Chopped Liver

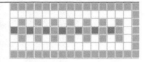

At the old Garden Cafeteria on East Broadway, which was the unofficial lunchroom of the neighboring Yiddish newspaper, *Forverts* (*The Forward*), this American creation was a favorite dish of writer Isaac Bashevis Singer.

1 pound string beans, trimmed
4 cups coarsely chopped onions
½ teaspoon paprika
2 tablespoons corn oil
1 tablespoon schmaltz

3 hard-boiled eggs
½ cup shelled walnuts
1½ teaspoons salt
¼ teaspoon pepper

SERVES 8

1. Cook string beans, drain, and place in refrigerator to cool.
2. Toss chopped onions with paprika. Heat corn oil and schmaltz in a large skillet (use 3 tablespoons of oil if you don't have schmaltz), and sauté onions until browned. Let cool in refrigerator, reserving frying oil with the onions.
3. Place string beans, onions, and reserved oil, along with all remaining ingredients, in a food processor. Blend, leaving some texture. Serve chilled with crackers or matzo.

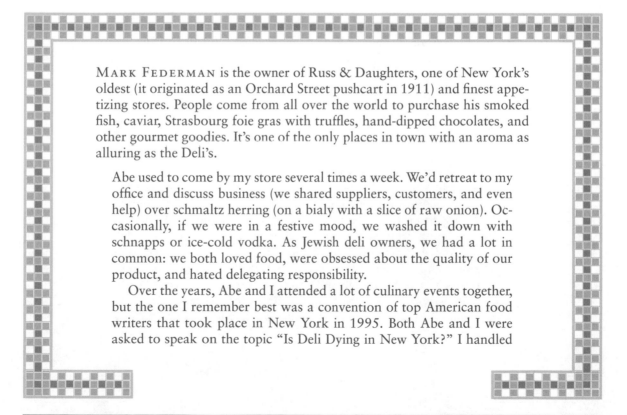

MARK FEDERMAN is the owner of Russ & Daughters, one of New York's oldest (it originated as an Orchard Street pushcart in 1911) and finest appetizing stores. People come from all over the world to purchase his smoked fish, caviar, Strasbourg foie gras with truffles, hand-dipped chocolates, and other gourmet goodies. It's one of the only places in town with an aroma as alluring as the Deli's.

Abe used to come by my store several times a week. We'd retreat to my office and discuss business (we shared suppliers, customers, and even help) over schmaltz herring (on a bialy with a slice of raw onion). Occasionally, if we were in a festive mood, we washed it down with schnapps or ice-cold vodka. As Jewish deli owners, we had a lot in common: we both loved food, were obsessed about the quality of our product, and hated delegating responsibility.

Over the years, Abe and I attended a lot of culinary events together, but the one I remember best was a convention of top American food writers that took place in New York in 1995. Both Abe and I were asked to speak on the topic "Is Deli Dying in New York?" I handled

Russ & Daughters

the fish aspect, he the meat, and together we supplied a massive buffet for the convention. I was a little nervous about speaking, so a few days before the event, I started making notes for my speech, which soon evolved into one hundred pages! I called Abie to see what he had prepared, and he said "Nothing."

When I got up to speak, I was so overprepared that I went on for about half an hour, until they were almost ready to pull me off the stage with a hook. Much of my speech mirrored a popular theme at the convention—the current trend toward lighter, less fatty foods. Fish, I maintained, was good for you.

Then Abie got up without any notes, looked at the audience for about a full minute in total silence, and exclaimed, "What am I gonna tell you? My food will kill you." He got a lot of laughs, and went on to speak comfortably, and at an appropriate length, about the deli business. After his speech, all the health-conscious speakers and food writers made a beeline to the buffet . . . where the very first things to go were Abe's fatty mountains of kishke, pastrami, and corned beef!

In keeping with my own speech, I'm supplying the recipe for Russ & Daughters' famous chopped herring salad, which contains only healthy ingredients.

Russ & Daughters' Chopped Herring

SERVES 6

1½ pounds pickled herring fillets, coarsely chopped
1¾ cups cored, peeled, and coarsely chopped Granny Smith apples

¾ cup coarsely chopped celery
½ cup coarsely chopped sweet onions (such as Vidalia or Maui)
Sugar (only if needed)

GARNISH
Lettuce leaves
1 Granny Smith apple

4 red potatoes, cooked in skins and chilled
Dill

1. Grind all ingredients (coarse chopping is for measurement purposes only) except garnish, in a grinder or food processor. Do not purée; chopped herring should have considerable texture. Since fillets vary in sweetness, add sugar (carefully) to taste if needed.
2. Create individual portions atop beds of large lettuce leaves, garnishing each mound of herring with a thin slice of Granny Smith apple, and surround it with slices of cold red potato and a few sprigs of dill.

Coleslaw

Our customers rave about our take on traditional deli slaw. We make and serve about 1,000 pounds daily.

2 pounds green cabbage
¼ cup very finely grated carrot
3 tablespoons white vinegar
3 tablespoons sugar

½ cup Hellmann's mayonnaise
1 teaspoon salt
¼ teaspoon white pepper
Chopped dried chives

MAKES ABOUT
2 QUARTS

1. Remove and discard loose outer cabbage leaves and core. Shred cabbage

(the easiest way to do this is to cut the cabbage in quarters, julienne each quarter into ⅛-inch or smaller strips with a sharp knife, then pulse chopped cabbage a few times in your food processor). Don't shred it too fine; you want texture and crunch. Place shredded cabbage in a large bowl, add carrots (these can be shredded very fine in the bowl of a food processor), and mix.

2. In a separate bowl, mix all other ingredients (except chives). Pour them over the cabbage and carrots, and toss to combine thoroughly. Chill for several hours, or even overnight. Garnish lightly with chives before serving.

Hawaiian Slaw

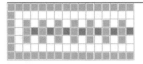

**MAKES ABOUT
2 QUARTS**

The addition of a few sweet ingredients gives prosaic coleslaw Hawaiian punch. When we serve this at parties, people always ask for the recipe.

2 pounds white cabbage
¾ cup finely grated carrot
¾ cup Hellmann's mayonnaise
*2 8¼-ounce cans crushed
    pineapple in syrup, completely
    drained of liquid (press extra
    liquid out in a strainer)*

½ cup golden raisins
3 tablespoons white vinegar
⅓ cup sugar
1 teaspoon salt
¼ teaspoon white pepper

1. Prepare cabbage and carrots as in the above coleslaw recipe.
2. In a separate bowl, mix all other ingredients. Pour them over the cabbage and carrots, and toss to combine thoroughly. Chill for several hours, or even overnight, before serving.

Health Salad

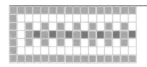

**MAKES ABOUT
1 ½ QUARTS**

As its name implies, this Deli staple is a healthier, though sweeter, version of coleslaw—one that contains no mayonnaise. It must be prepared at least a day in advance of serving.

1½ pounds white cabbage
*¼ cup paper-thin slices of celery
    (use a part of the stalk that's
    about ¾-inch wide)*
*15 ¾-inch paper-thin slices of
    green pepper (use a potato peeler
    to make slices sufficiently thin)*
*15 paper-thin shavings of carrot
    (flatten the top end of a very*

*large carrot, and shave them off
    with a potato peeler)*
¾ cup white vinegar
2 tablespoons olive oil
½ cup sugar
3 teaspoons salt
½ teaspoon white pepper
Chopped dried chives

1. Remove and discard loose outer cabbage leaves and core. Shred cabbage (the easiest way to do this is to cut the cabbage in quarters, julienne each quarter into ⅛-inch or smaller strips with a sharp knife, then pulse chopped cabbage just a few times in your food processor). Do not shred it very fine; you want texture and crunch. Place shredded cabbage in a large bowl; add celery, green pepper, and carrots; mix well.

2. In a separate bowl, thoroughly mix all other ingredients (except chives). Pour them over the cabbage and other vegetables, and toss to combine thoroughly. Chill overnight. Garnish lightly with chives before serving.

Macaroni Salad

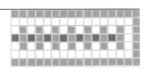

This macaroni salad, indigenous to Jewish delicatessens, goes best with a pastrami sandwich and a Coke. Prepare it a day in advance of serving if you can; it tastes better the second day.

SERVES 8

1 pound elbow macaroni
1 teaspoon olive oil
2 teaspoons salt
1½ cups Hellmann's mayonnaise
⅜ cup white vinegar
3 tablespoons sugar
4 tablespoons finely grated onion

¼ cup chopped green pepper, pieces about ¼ inch
⅓ cup grated carrot
1 teaspoon deli-style mustard
½ teaspoon white pepper
Dried chives

1. In a large stockpot, bring 5 quarts of water to a vigorous boil. Add macaroni, olive oil, and ½ teaspoon of the salt, and cook for 6 to 8 minutes (until tender). Rinse in cold water, drain well, and transfer to a large bowl.

2. In another bowl, mix mayonnaise, vinegar, and sugar thoroughly. Pour over macaroni, and mix well.

3. Add all other ingredients, except chives, and stir everything in thoroughly. Refrigerate, and serve well chilled, lightly sprinkled with chives.

Potato Salad

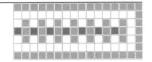

Like coleslaw and macaroni salad, this is a classic accompaniment to deli sandwiches.

SERVES 8

3 pounds red potatoes, peeled and chopped into 1-inch chunks
¾ cup very finely chopped onion
⅔ cup celery, chopped into ¼-inch pieces
⅜ cup white vinegar

2 tablespoons sugar
1½ teaspoons salt
¼ teaspoon pepper
1 cup Hellmann's mayonnaise
⅓ cup minced parsley
¼ cup grated carrot

1. Fill a large stockpot three-quarters full with water and bring to a vigorous boil. Add potatoes, lower heat, and simmer 25 to 30 minutes, until tender but firm. Rinse, drain, and set aside.

2. When potatoes are cooled a bit, but still warm, gently mix onion, celery, and warm potato chunks together in a large bowl.

3. In another bowl, make a vinaigrette using vinegar, sugar, salt, and pepper. Gently mix with warm potatoes, coating them thoroughly.

4. Gently stir in mayonnaise, parsley, and grated carrot. Serve chilled.

Potato Salad à la Russe

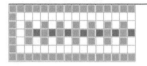

SERVES 8

Our Russian grandmothers were always throwing beets, peas, and carrots into the potato salad we ate at home, and we still love it that way.

2 medium dark red beets

3 pounds red potatoes, peeled and chopped into 1-inch chunks

1 cup carrots, diced into ¼-inch pieces

1 cup frozen peas

1 cup very finely chopped red onion (chop small pieces; then pulse them once or twice in a food processor)

½ cup sweet pickle relish

⅛ cup white vinegar

1 cup Hellmann's mayonnaise

⅓ cup very finely chopped fresh parsley

1½ teaspoons salt

½ teaspoon pepper

1. Cut greens, roots, and stems off beets. Wash beets, and cut in half vertically. Place in pot with water to cover, bring to a boil, lower heat, and simmer for 1 hour.

2. While beets are cooking, fill a large stockpot three-quarters full with water and bring to a vigorous boil. Add potatoes, lower heat, and simmer 25 to 30 minutes, until tender but firm. Rinse, drain, and set aside.

3. In a smaller pot, cook diced carrots for 25 minutes, add peas, and cook 2 minutes more. Rinse, drain, and set aside.

4. When beets are cooked, let them cool a bit; then peel, and chop into ⅜-inch pieces.

5. Place beets, potatoes, peas, carrots, and all other ingredients in a large bowl, and mix gently but thoroughly. Serve chilled.

THE FIRST UNITED STATES SENATOR from New York of Italian descent, Alfonse D'Amato was initially elected to the Senate in 1980 and served three consecutive terms. During his tenure, he was a staunch supporter of Israel (he flew to Tel Aviv during Operation Desert Storm while Iraqi Scud missiles rained down); of fostering Jewish emigration from the USSR; and of strong measures against terrorism (in 1997, Congress passed his bill that says to the nations of the world: "You can trade with the terrorist states of Iran and Libya, or you can trade with us. It's that simple"). D'Amato also relentlessly pursued Swiss banks, forcing them to acknowledge their obligation—and initiate procedures—to return stolen monies to Holocaust victims.

> I have to admit to being a bit biased. After all, Abe was a friend and supporter of mine. He was a great guy to have in your corner. You could easily forget that this guy—always helping people through his overwhelming generosity—had a business to run. I love the Second Avenue Deli, and I loved Abe dearly. I'm sure that Abe was also good to me because of my loyalty to the Jewish community and Israel. This was particularly important to him as a Holocaust survivor.
>
> You know, Washington is not New York—white bread and hoagies are more the staple down here. What a hit I was with all my colleagues when Abe would cater one of my events. They knew nothing of Abe's kishke, corned beef, knishes, pastrami, and goulash, but when they started to *fress* (Yiddish for pig out, though not on pig, of course), they did it with the gusto of any New Yorker.

Antoinette D'Amato's
Orzo Salad

SERVES 6
AS A SIDE DISH

Antoinette D'Amato, the senator's mother, is a whiz in the kitchen. On occasion, she caters Al's Senate lunches in Washington. This colorful salad takes only about 15 minutes to prepare. We loved it.

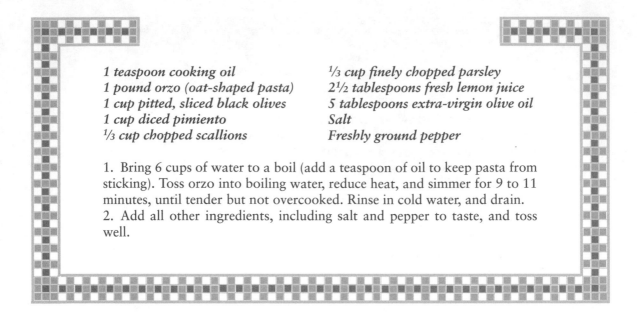

1 teaspoon cooking oil
1 pound orzo (oat-shaped pasta)
1 cup pitted, sliced black olives
1 cup diced pimiento
⅓ cup chopped scallions

⅓ cup finely chopped parsley
2½ tablespoons fresh lemon juice
5 tablespoons extra-virgin olive oil
Salt
Freshly ground pepper

1. Bring 6 cups of water to a boil (add a teaspoon of oil to keep pasta from sticking). Toss orzo into boiling water, reduce heat, and simmer for 9 to 11 minutes, until tender but not overcooked. Rinse in cold water, and drain.
2. Add all other ingredients, including salt and pepper to taste, and toss well.

Cucumber Salad

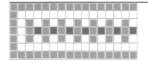

SERVES 6

The Deli's cucumber salad needs to marinate overnight, so plan to prepare it a day in advance.

2½ long, straight, thin cucumbers
4 paper-thin slices cut from the center of a large onion (separate the rings, and cut them into thin strips)
½ cup white vinegar

¼ cup sugar
2 tablespoons finely chopped fresh dill
½ teaspoon salt
⅛ teaspoon white pepper

1. Wash cucumbers well. Using a potato peeler, stripe the exterior of each cucumber by peeling ½-inch lengthwise strips (they'll alternate aesthetically with ½-inch strips of dark green peel). Don't worry about making your strips perfect; they'll look fine when the cucumbers are sliced.
2. With a sharp knife, cut ¹⁄₁₆-inch slices, and place them in a large bowl. In another bowl, mix all other ingredients thoroughly. Pour this mixture over the cucumbers, and toss very well, making sure all of the cucumbers thoroughly absorb the liquid. Cover bowl, and refrigerate overnight. Serve chilled.

Creamy Cucumber Salad

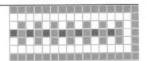

Like the salad above, this version needs to marinate overnight. So plan to prepare it a day in advance.

3 large cucumbers
½ cup grated onion
½ cup white vinegar
1 teaspoon sugar
1 cup sour cream

4 teaspoons (1 tablespoon plus
  1 teaspoon) chopped fresh dill
½ teaspoon salt
¼ teaspoon white pepper

SERVES 6

1. Peel and halve the cucumbers (if you like, stripe them first, as in the above recipe). Scoop out seeds with a spoon, cut into very thin slices (about ¹⁄₁₆ of an inch), and place in a large bowl. Mix in grated onion, vinegar, and sugar. Cover, and refrigerate overnight.
2. The following day, place cucumbers in a colander, drain the juice, and pat dry with paper toweling. Return to bowl. Add sour cream, dill, salt, and pepper, and mix well. Serve chilled.

Chicken Salad

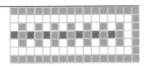

The Deli's classic chicken salad is simple but delicious.

4 cups chopped boiled chicken (see
  Note below)
½ cup very finely chopped celery

¾ cup Hellmann's mayonnaise
½ teaspoon salt
¼ teaspoon white pepper

SERVES 6

1. Toss all ingredients in a very large bowl, mixing thoroughly. Chill before serving.

Note: Boil chicken in water for 30 minutes with a few chunks of onion, carrot, and celery. One very large chicken will yield about 4 cups of meat. If you prefer only white meat in your chicken salad, use breasts only. When cooled, carefully remove chicken from the frame, chop it into pieces not bigger than ½ inch, and place pieces in a large bowl. Be sure not to toss any skin or bone in the bowl. For best results, pulse diced chicken a few times in your food processor to create a shredded texture.

Variation: For a variation on this salad, add 1 tablespoon dried tarragon, ½ cup golden raisins (sauté them very briefly in oil to bring out extra flavor; then let them cool to room temperature), and, just prior to serving, ½ cup peeled and cored McIntosh apple, diced into ½-inch pieces. Mix everything in thoroughly.

Egg Salad with Onions and Mushrooms

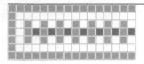

SERVES 6

Though you probably think of egg salad as archetypally American, Jews have been eating a mix of chopped egg, onion, and schmaltz for centuries.

1 tablespoon plus 1 teaspoon corn
   oil
2 tablespoons schmaltz
2 cups chopped onions

2 cups sliced mushrooms,
   thoroughly scrubbed and cut
   into ¾-inch slices, about
   ³/₁₆ inch thick
12 hard-boiled eggs
½ cup Hellmann's mayonnaise
¼ teaspoon white pepper

Note: If you don't have schmaltz, use corn oil throughout, skipping the added schmaltz in step 3.

1. Heat 1 tablespoon of the corn oil and 1 tablespoon of the schmaltz in a large skillet, and sauté the onions until nicely browned. Remove to a bowl with a slotted spoon.

2. Add 1 teaspoon each of corn oil and schmaltz to the skillet, and brown mushrooms well. Add to the bowl with the onions, and let cool.

3. Peel eggs, and mash them with a fork or potato masher in a large bowl. (If you like a smoother version, as we do, mash the eggs in a blender or food processor.) Add mayonnaise, 2 teaspoons of the schmaltz, and pepper, and mash in thoroughly (or blend in food processor). In a large bowl, use a fork to toss egg mixture with onions and mushrooms. Serve chilled.

Bow Tie and Broccoli Salad

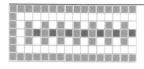

SERVES 6

1 tablespoon sesame oil
½ cup golden raisins
⅓ cup sunflower seeds
3 tablespoons sesame seeds

4 large stalks fresh broccoli,
   chopped into small florets,
   cooked, drained, and chilled
4 cups bow tie noodles, cooked,
   drained, and chilled
⅔ cup Hellmann's mayonnaise

1. In a skillet, heat sesame oil and sauté raisins, stirring frequently. Remove with a slotted spoon, and set aside in a small bowl. Quickly sauté sunflower and sesame seeds in remaining oil, stirring frequently, and remove to another small bowl.

2. In a large bowl, toss broccoli, bow ties, raisins, and mayonnaise, combining thoroughly. Just before serving, toss with sunflower and sesame seeds.

Bow Tie Salad with Sun-Dried Tomatoes

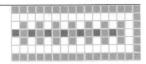

This salad comes from our catering menu, but people like it so much, we often offer it for take-out at the counter. It tastes best if you prepare it a day in advance and allow it to marinate overnight.

Note: To render onions, scallions, garlic, and parsley sufficiently fine, it's best to chop them first by hand, then pulse a few times in a food processor.

SERVES 6

1 pound bow tie noodles
1½ cups sun-dried tomatoes, chopped into ½-inch pieces (if not moist, soak in boiling water for 10 minutes. Then drain, chill, and chop)
¼ cup very finely chopped red onion
2 tablespoons finely chopped scallions
½ cup extra-virgin olive oil
1½ tablespoons red wine vinegar

1½ tablespoons balsamic vinegar
1 tablespoon fresh-squeezed lemon juice
1 teaspoon very finely chopped or crushed fresh garlic
3 tablespoons very finely chopped fresh parsley
1½ teaspoons sugar
½ teaspoon paprika
1 teaspoon salt
¼ teaspoon freshly ground pepper

1. Cook bow tie noodles, rinse in cold water, and drain. Set aside.
2. Place all ingredients in a large bowl, and toss thoroughly. Serve chilled.

PATRICK CLARK began his culinary career at age nine, visiting the kitchens of famous New York restaurants (such as The Four Seasons) with his father, also a chef. After formal training in the United States and Great Britain, and a stint in France with Michel Guérard, creator of *cuisine minceur,* he developed his own culinary style of French-nuanced contemporary-American cooking. Having garnered critical raves at New York celebrity haunts like The Odeon and Café Luxembourg, he went on to launch his own restaurant, the highly acclaimed Metro, in 1988. He was later lured to the plush and prestigious Hay-Adams Hotel in the nation's capital, where he attracted the notice of the Clintons, who asked him to move across the street and serve as White House chef. But the bright lights of Central Park's Tavern on the Green beckoned. Clark became the Tavern's executive chef in May 1995.*

*We were shocked and saddened to hear of Patrick Clark's untimely death in February 1998—just a few months after we had enjoyed a delightful lunch with him at Tavern on the Green to discuss his contribution to this book. Only forty-two, he succumbed to congestive heart failure.

I grew up in Brooklyn, in a Jewish neighborhood, where I regularly ate corned beef, pastrami, noodle kugel, kasha knishes, and, of course, countless Hebrew National franks. I even had a Jewish girlfriend whose mom made great matzo ball soup and invited me to Seders. But my passion was cheesecake. While other boys squandered their allowances on baseball cards, I saved mine to buy cream cheese, and I spent many hours in the kitchen trying to create a cheesecake beyond compare. By the time I was seventeen, I had perfected my recipe; it's one I still use today.

I've always loved the Second Avenue Deli, which is the only place I go when I crave pastrami on rye with mustard and sour pickles. (I might find plausible mustard and pickles elsewhere, but never the same quality of pastrami!) Years ago, Abe Lebewohl came to my restaurant, Metro, and introduced himself. After that, we frequently saw each other at the Deli and at food events and became friendly. He always took a lively interest in my career and showed a lot of enthusiasm about my coming to Tavern on the Green, stopping by often to sample my new menus.

Patrick Clark's Tomato and Black Olive Couscous

SERVES 10 AS A SIDE DISH

Extra-virgin olive oil
1 medium onion, finely diced
Salt
Freshly ground pepper
2 garlic cloves, finely chopped
2¼ cups tomato juice

1 10-ounce box Near East couscous
Sherry wine vinegar
¼ cup chopped kalamata olives
2 tablespoons chopped fresh
  oregano

1. Heat ¼ cup olive oil in a large stockpot. Add onion, and season lightly with salt and pepper. Cook until onion is translucent. Stir in garlic.
2. Add tomato juice, and bring to a boil. Stir in couscous. Remove pot from heat, cover, and let stand for 5 to 7 minutes.
3. Transfer to a bowl, and fluff couscous with a fork. Season with salt, pepper, sherry wine vinegar, and olive oil to taste (do a little at a time until you're pleased, but don't let it get soupy or soggy). Stir in olives and oregano. Serve at room temperature.

Lentil Salad

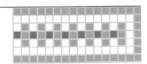

2 cups lentils
3/8 cup olive oil
1 tablespoon red wine vinegar
2 teaspoons balsamic vinegar
1/2 cup very finely chopped onion

1 teaspoon crushed fresh garlic
1 teaspoon salt
1/4 teaspoon fresh-ground pepper
1/2 teaspoon sugar

SERVES 6 TO 8

1. Rinse lentils under cold water in a colander, and pick through for stones and impurities.
2. In a stockpot, bring 9 cups of water to a vigorous boil. Add lentils, reduce heat, and simmer 35 minutes. Rinse in a strainer under cold water, drain, and place in a large bowl.
3. In another bowl, mix all remaining ingredients well. Pour over lentils and stir well. Serve chilled.

PROMOTIONS, PITCHES . . . AND PITCHING NO-HITTERS

Guardian of the Pickles

ON MAY 25, 1994, in celebration of National Pickle Week (yes, there is a National Pickle Week), fifteen strong-stomached and hungry hopefuls gathered at the Second Avenue Deli for a pickle-eating contest. Techniques varied: some contestants chopped the pickles into bite-sized pieces, while others chomped three or four whole ones at a time. The winner was Guardian Angels founder Curtis Sliwa, who once again proved himself a macho guy by downing close to five pounds of delectable dills in just fifteen minutes! "The secret," said Curtis, "is you belch after every second pickle to get rid of gas."

Pickles

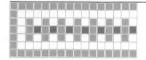

MAKES 20

You can pickle firm green tomatoes or beets the same way.

20 small Kirby cucumbers (choose firm, fresh, unwaxed, bumpy-textured cucumbers that are close to equal in size)
¾ cup kosher salt
15 whole garlic cloves, unpeeled
1 bunch of fresh dill

2 tablespoons pickling spices or:
1½ teaspoons mustard seeds
1½ teaspoons whole black peppercorns
1 teaspoon coriander seeds
1 teaspoon dill seeds
6 bay leaves
1 hot dried red pepper

1. Scrub the cucumbers with a brush in clear water.
2. Pour 1 gallon of water into a large stockpot, add salt, and bring to a boil. Turn off heat, and allow water to return to room temperature. While water is cooling, wrap unpeeled garlic cloves in a cloth napkin, and crush them lightly with the back of a large knife.
3. Pack the cucumbers tightly into wide-mouthed jars, add all other ingredients (distribute equally), and pour salted water over them. The cucumbers must be covered completely. Put the lid on, shake jar to distribute spices evenly, and store in a cool place (do not refrigerate). Open the jar once a day to skim off foam. In 4 days, the pickles will be half-sour, and can keep, refrigerated, for several weeks. For sour pickles, do not refrigerate until 6 days have passed.

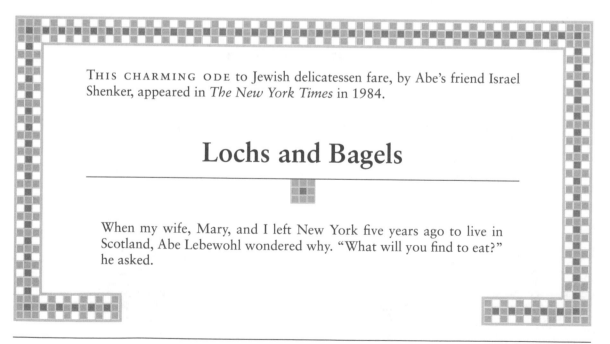

THIS CHARMING ODE to Jewish delicatessen fare, by Abe's friend Israel Shenker, appeared in *The New York Times* in 1984.

Lochs and Bagels

When my wife, Mary, and I left New York five years ago to live in Scotland, Abe Lebewohl wondered why. "What will you find to eat?" he asked.

Mr. Lebewohl owns the Second Ave. Kosher Delicatessen & Restaurant, at the corner of 10th Street, and austerity is not his line. He has pursued the good life throughout Western Europe and Israel, and once almost succeeded in catching a waiter's eye in Russia. Never having been to Scotland, he tried to visualize our setting. "It's like a shtetl?" he suggested. "Between one house and the next, it's a half a mile?" For him, our move to Scotland spelled ethnic starvation.

So he began shipping pastrami. The first parcel arrived like manna from heaven, and we ate as if our lives depended on it.

Our home is in the Trossachs, an area of rural splendor and deli deprivation. The closest Jewish restaurant is in Glasgow, 45 miles away. Last winter, we were snowed in for three weeks. At the height of a raging blizzard, the postman struggled to the door bearing a heavy parcel. Inside, we found a brief note from Mr. Lebewohl and a vast expanse of pastrami.

My wife, moved by the sight of lambs at the window, had renounced eating meat, her abstinence reinforced by the spectacle of pastrami on the hoof—lovely Highland cattle, unpickled, unspiced, unsmoked. Obedient to her master's choice, however, she prepared the pastrami, while the Saint Bernard went onto the ice floes with a rush order for mustard and sour pickles.

Day after day, I feasted on pastrami. Eventually, keen on the scent, local friends arrived to lend a few hands and hear wondrous accounts of this and other exotic delicacies. When I returned to New York for a visit in April, Mr. Lebewohl gave me a menu to nourish nostalgia on long winter evenings. Now, between pangs of heartburn and pastrami deliveries that continue to arrive by mail or occasional itinerant customer pressed into service by Mr. Lebewohl, rise visions of charms remote and inaccessible: boiled beef flanken, potato knishes, noodle pudding, gefilte fish, Yankee bean soup and the penitential half sandwich at half price after buying a whole one at full price.

As I nibble à la carte, my wife labors in the kitchen, indulgently permitting the lambs to trample our shrubs while she bakes shortbread and oatcakes to ship to the Second Ave. Deli, just to show Mr. Lebewohl that ethnicity bites both ways.

P'tcha

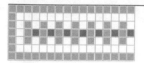

What with boiling calf's feet and embedding the meat in a glutinous jelly, this might be one of those dishes you have to grow up with to appreciate. It's also very garlicky. Abe once fed some p'tcha to an intrepid *New York Times* reporter with the caveat "Don't go on a heavy date after eating this."

2 calf's feet, cut into quarters
   (ask your butcher to do it)
2 cloves garlic, peeled
2 bay leaves
1 large onion, sliced
2 tablespoons white wine vinegar
1½ teaspoons salt

1 teaspoon whole peppercorns
2 cloves finely chopped or crushed
   fresh garlic
3 medium hard-boiled eggs, peeled
   and sliced
Lemon and red horseradish for
   garnish

1. Wash calf's feet thoroughly. Place them in a large stockpot, cover with water, and bring to a boil. Reduce heat, and simmer for 15 minutes. Discard cooking water.

2. Rinse the pot, and place calf's feet in it with fresh water to cover. Add 2 cloves garlic, bay leaves, onion, vinegar, salt, and peppercorns. Bring to a boil, cover, and simmer 3 to 4 hours, until the meat falls off the bones. Add a little water if necessary.

3. Remove meat from pot, and strain stock through a colander into a large bowl. Set bowl aside.

4. Chop the meat and cartilage (discard bones), mix with chopped garlic, and place in the bottom of a shallow pan or serving dish. Arrange egg slices on top, and pour strained cooking liquid over the meat and eggs. Refrigerate until completely jellied and firm (it should have the consistency of Jell-O). Serve cold, with lemon wedges and red horseradish.

Note: Sharon also likes to eat p'tcha hot, like a soup. Rena did not grow up with it and doesn't want to know anything about it.

Stuffed Mushrooms

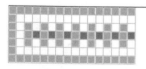

This specialty from our catering menu is a big hit at parties.

20 large mushrooms, thoroughly
   scrubbed (choose mushrooms
   about 1½ to 2 inches in
   diameter)

3 tablespoons corn oil

STUFFING INGREDIENTS

4 slices white bread
⁵⁄₈ pound very lean chopmeat
  (about 1 cup)
1 cup seasoned bread crumbs
¾ cup very finely chopped
  mushrooms (use the stalks)
1 cup very finely chopped onion
¼ cup very finely chopped sweet
  red pepper
1 tablespoon very finely chopped
  dill, or parsley, if you prefer

2 tablespoons very finely chopped
  scallions
1 tablespoon very finely chopped or
  crushed fresh garlic
3 eggs, beaten
½ teaspoon sugar
2 teaspoons soy sauce
1 teaspoon oregano
1 teaspoon thyme
1½ teaspoons salt
¼ teaspoon pepper

Note: Vegetables and herbs in the stuffing ingredients—mushroom stalks, onions, red pepper, dill or parsley, scallions, and garlic—should be chopped into ⅛-inch pieces. The best way to do this is to chop them first by hand, then toss them into a food processor and pulse a few times.

1. Remove mushroom stalks, wash thoroughly, and chop for stuffing. Set aside. Clean mushroom caps very thoroughly by scraping them with a knife under cold running water.
2. Pour corn oil into a large skillet, and, on high heat, quickly brown mushroom cap bottoms (place with hollow side up). Remove to a platter with a slotted spoon, and set aside.
3. Preheat oven to 375 degrees. Cut white bread into 1-inch cubes, place cubes in a colander, and soak in cold running water to soften. Squeeze out excess moisture, and, in a large bowl, work the bread and meat together with your hands.
4. Add all remaining stuffing ingredients, and combine very thoroughly. Stuff about 3 tablespoons of this mixture into each mushroom cap, forming it into a perfect mound.
5. Place stuffed mushrooms in a baking dish, and bake for 30 minutes or until they're crisp on top and the stuffing is thoroughly cooked. Serve hot or cold. Cold, they're especially good marinated in a vinaigrette.

VINAIGRETTE

1 tablespoon very finely chopped
  scallions
1 teaspoon Dijon mustard
¾ cup extra-virgin olive oil

2 tablespoons balsamic vinegar
1 tablespoon lemon juice
3 tablespoons red wine vinegar
Fresh-cracked pepper to taste

Combine all above ingredients and distribute evenly over mushrooms.

Variation: You can follow the identical procedure to stuff green peppers. Cut the peppers in half. Remove seeds, and cut away ribs, keeping the stems intact if possible (they look nice). Brown the bottoms in hot oil. Stuff each half level to the top instead of creating mounds, and bake for 40 minutes. Stuffed green peppers are also good cold, marinated in a vinaigrette. The amount of stuffing in the above recipe will be ample for 5 peppers (10 halves). To create a pretty platter, use a mix of green, red, and yellow peppers.

Mediterranean Medley

Abe's passionate commitment to Zionism included enthusiasm for Israeli cuisine, which Jewish settlers adapted from Middle Eastern neighbors and made their own. Israel's signature dishes utilize indigenous Mediterranean vegetables, enhanced by olive oil, garlic, and lemon juice. Chunks of warm, doughy, fresh-baked pita bread are their essential accompaniment.

Rectangles, another neighborhood favorite.

Tahini Sauce

Tahini sauce is a staple ingredient of Middle Eastern cuisines. It's also great on its own, as a dip served with raw vegetables and/or pita bread triangles.

1 cup tahini paste*
¼ cup fresh lemon juice
1 tablespoon chopped fresh garlic
¼ cup chopped parsley

1 teaspoon salt
¾ cup cold water
¼ teaspoon paprika

FOR GARNISH
Paprika

Finely chopped fresh parsley

1. Open tahini paste carefully to prevent oil from splashing. Pour contents into a bowl, and blend oil and paste thoroughly before measuring. If it's very thick, you may have to do this in a food processor or blender.
2. Put all ingredients, except garnish, in a food processor or blender to create a thin, smooth, and creamy sauce. Serve chilled. Sprinkle lightly with paprika, and garnish with parsley.

   *Tahini paste is a concentrate of puréed sesame seeds available in cans or jars at many supermarkets and fine food stores. Any store specializing in Middle Eastern groceries will have it. It's a thick paste, and, generally, the oil will have risen to the top.

Hummus/Tahini

SERVES 6 TO 8

We've prepared this recipe with both canned and fresh-cooked chickpeas, and the latter is much, much tastier. Since chickpeas are easy to cook, we suggest you make them fresh. Similarly, making your own tahini sauce, above, rather than buying a prepared product, significantly enhances this dip.

Advance planning is necessary here, because hummus/tahini dip is more flavorful if eaten a day after you've made it; you also need to soak the dried chickpeas overnight.

4 cups cooked chickpeas (to cook
    dried chickpeas, soak overnight,
    rinse, drain, and simmer in
    water with 1 teaspoon salt for
    1½ hours or until tender)
¾ cup tahini sauce (page 23)
2 tablespoons coarsely chopped
    fresh garlic

3 tablespoons extra-virgin olive oil
¼ cup water (if you cook the
    chickpeas, use cooking water)
⅓ cup lemon juice
½ teaspoon cumin
⅓ cup chopped fresh parsley
1 teaspoon salt
1 teaspoon paprika

ACCOMPANIMENTS
Toasted pita bread
Cucumbers
Tomato wedges

Black olives (dry-cured or Niçoise)
fresh parsley for garnish

1. Combine all ingredients—except paprika and 1 tablespoon olive oil—in a food processor or blender, and pulse to a smooth texture.
2. Serve well chilled, spread on a plate. Dissolve paprika in the remaining 1 tablespoon of olive oil, and drizzle a little on each serving from a spoon. Serve with warm pita bread, cucumber spears, tomato wedges, and olives. A little parsley also makes a nice garnish.

Baba Ganoush

SERVES 6

Eggplant, indigenous to India, traveled via Turkey to Arab countries and Eastern Europe. Today, it is an abundant Israeli crop and a staple ingredient in numerous recipes. Of all eggplant preparations, this is the most ubiquitous in Israeli homes and restaurants.

4 long eggplants *(they must be thin enough to fit whole into your broiler; about 1½ pounds each)*
2 tablespoons extra-virgin olive oil
½ cup tahini sauce *(see Note below and recipe on page 23)*
¼ cup fresh lemon juice
1 tablespoon very finely chopped or crushed fresh garlic
⅓ cup chopped fresh parsley
⅛ teaspoon cayenne pepper
1 teaspoon salt
Parsley for garnish
Pita bread

Note about tahini sauce: Tahini is a concentrate of puréed sesame seeds, which you can buy in a can or jar at many supermarkets. Any store specializing in Middle Eastern groceries will have it. To prepare the tahini sauce needed for this recipe, follow the recipe on page 23.

1. Wash eggplants, and prick skin in about twenty places with a fork. If you don't, they're liable to explode, creating a mess that is not to be believed.
2. Place whole eggplants in your broiler on a cookie sheet (or line the broiler with aluminum foil). Broil for 50 minutes, turning them about every 12 minutes. They will shrivel, get blackened and blistered, and generally collapse; this is what you want to happen.
3. Slit the eggplants on one side, and place them, slit side down, in a colander over a large bowl to cool and drain. When they've cooled sufficiently to handle comfortably, peel the eggplants, and scoop out the pulp into a bowl. Eggplants are a bit difficult to peel; try not to get any of the burned peel in the bowl. The 4 eggplants should yield about 4 cups of pulp. Return the eggplant to the colander, and drain a bit more liquid. Then put it in a food processor with all remaining ingredients (or mash by hand in a large bowl), and blend to a creamy texture. Chill for several hours before serving. Garnish with parsley, and serve as a dip with warm pita bread.

Eggplant Salad

SERVES 6

This Israeli salad is best made a day in advance, allowing the flavors to blend. We must confess, however, it's so good even when just cooked, we can barely resist scarfing it up hot from the skillet.

6 cups peeled eggplant, diced into
   3/4-inch pieces
Salt for sprinkling on eggplant
2 small cans tomato paste
   (12 ounces)
4 tablespoons wine vinegar
1/2 cup dry-cured black olives,
   pitted (these are very dark black
   and wrinkled)
1 teaspoon sugar
5 leaves fresh basil, chopped

1 teaspoon dried oregano
1 teaspoon salt
1/4 teaspoon pepper
2/3 cup olive oil
2/3 cup green pepper, diced into
   3/4-inch pieces
2 cups scrubbed mushrooms,
   chopped into *3/4*-inch slices,
   about *3/16*-inch thick
1 tablespoon finely chopped or
   crushed fresh garlic

1. Pat diced eggplant dry with paper towel and salt lightly.

2. In a large bowl, mix tomato paste, vinegar, olives, sugar, basil, oregano, salt, and pepper; set aside.

3. Heat olive oil in a large skillet. Add green peppers, onions, and mushrooms, and sauté on high heat for 4 minutes, stirring occasionally.

4. Lower heat, add eggplant, and continue cooking for about 7 minutes, until all the vegetables are nicely browned. At the last minute add garlic, and brown quickly.

5. Immediately add contents of bowl, stir the mixture in, cover, and simmer on very low heat for 20 minutes, stirring occasionally. Serve hot or cold.

Falafel

MAKES ABOUT 25

Abe, a frequent visitor to Israel, loved its most popular national dish. So we decided that, even though he never offered falafel at the Deli, we had to include it in this book. We tested recipe after recipe—with less-than-thrilling results—and were getting close to despair. Then it occurred to us that right across the street from the Deli was a very authentic Yemenite restaurant called Rectangles. Abe used to eat there occasionally and was a friend of owner Gili Tsabari. We stopped in and explained our plight, and chef Tzipora Said kindly shared her falafel expertise. Not only are these falafel delicious, but, of all the recipes we tried, they're also the easiest to prepare. But do plan in advance, since the chickpeas have to soak for at least 6 hours.

3/4 pound dried chickpeas
1 cup chopped onion
1 tablespoon chopped or crushed
    fresh garlic
3 teaspoons cumin
2/3 cup finely chopped fresh parsley
2/3 cup finely chopped fresh cilantro
1 1/2 teaspoons salt

1/4 teaspoon black pepper
3 tablespoons flour
1 1/2 teaspoons red pepper flakes
    (optional, for those who prefer
    spicier falafel)
Soybean oil for frying
2 lemons, halved

ACCOMPANIMENTS

Toasted pita breads, slit open on
    one side to form a pocket
Cucumber, diced into 1/2-inch
    pieces
Fresh tomatoes, diced into 1/2-inch
    pieces

Shredded lettuce
Coarsely chopped onions
Tahini sauce
Middle Eastern hot sauce
    (optional)

1. Soak chickpeas overnight (at least 6 hours). Rinse, drain thoroughly, and pat dry with a towel.

2. Combine raw chickpeas, onions, and garlic in a food processor or grinder, and pulse or grind. If you use a food processor, don't make your mixture perfectly smooth; it should have a slightly pebbly texture. Place mixture in a bowl and add the cumin, parsley, cilantro, salt, pepper, flour, and, if desired, cracked red pepper. Mix thoroughly, using your hands. Refrigerate for at least 1 hour.

3. Form mixture into firm cakes about 2 inches wide and 1/2 inch high. Refrigerate them for 1/2 hour or longer.

4. It's easiest to cook falafel in a deep fryer. Place as many falafel patties as fit in one layer in the bottom of your wire basket (do not stack), and set aside. Pour about 1 1/2 inches of soybean oil into your cooking pot, heat to sizzling, submerge wire basket in pot (oil must cover the patties completely), lower heat to medium, and cook for about 5 minutes, until falafel turns a light golden brown. Remove the wire basket, and carefully place falafel patties on a plate covered with paper toweling. Gently pat off excess oil with additional paper toweling. Squeeze some fresh lemon juice over each.

If you don't have a deep fryer, pour about 1 inch of soybean oil into a large skillet, and place patties carefully in the hot oil, using a spatula. Cook as above.

5. Place 3 falafel patties in the bottom of each pita and, layering salad ingredients with tahini sauce, continue filling pitas with a mixture of cucumber, tomato, lettuce, and onion. Serve hot sauce on the side.

Tabbouleh

MAKES ABOUT 2½ QUARTS

Bulgur wheat, a nutritious, nutty grain that figures largely in Middle Eastern cooking, makes a substantial basis for this tangy and refreshing salad. For a variation, substitute couscous (prepare according to directions on box) for bulgur.

1¾ cups bulgur wheat
¼ cup very finely chopped onion
¾ cup finely chopped parsley
2 tablespoons very finely chopped fresh mint (dried if unavailable)
¼ cup lemon juice
¾ cup extra-virgin olive oil
1½ teaspoons salt

¼ teaspoon pepper
2 cups tomatoes, seeded, and chopped into ¼-inch pieces
1 12-ounce jar sweet roasted red peppers, thoroughly drained of liquid and chopped into ¼-inch pieces
1 cup chickpeas

Note: Very fresh, seasonal tomatoes are best; off-season, toss your tomatoes into boiling water to cover for about 40 seconds, until skin peels off easily. Discard skins and seeds before chopping.

1. Boil 7 cups of water. Place bulgur wheat in a large bowl, and pour boiling water over it. Cover, and let stand for 3 hours. Drain in a strainer, press to thoroughly squeeze out excess water, and return to bowl. Set aside.
2. In another bowl, mix onions, parsley, mint, lemon juice, olive oil, salt, and pepper. Pour over bulgur wheat, and mix in. Place tomatoes and red peppers in a strainer to eliminate excess liquid. Add to bulgur wheat along with chickpeas, and toss to combine. Serve chilled or at room temperature.

Note: Serving each portion on a bed of lettuce in a domed mold (you can use a dessert cup or shallow wine goblet as a mold) makes for a nice presentation.

PROMOTIONS, PITCHES . . . AND PITCHING NO-HITTERS

ABE LEBEWOHL loved his restaurant, and he promoted it with pride, joy, and enthusiasm. When it came to the Deli, his any-excuse-for-a-party personality came to the fore; hence, such unlikely manifestations as green matzo balls on Saint Patrick's Day or an invitation to runners in the 1990 New York City Marathon to carbo-load on free kasha varnishkes. One way or another, his promotions were always expressions of his abundant generosity. For example, Abe not only invited the blind to free luncheon parties, he also hired major Borscht Belt comedians like Sam Levenson to entertain them and even printed up menus in Braille. Still other promotions were political in nature—like the eight-foot-high Robert Grossman statue of Mikhail Gorbachev he placed atop the Deli's canopy in 1992 to celebrate the collapse of the Soviet Union. "We owe him so much," Abe said at the time. "He brought freedom and democracy to the Soviet Union. It was unheard-of before he came to power. He started perestroika."

Baseball, Hot Dogs . . . and Kosher Salamis?

THE PARENTS OF Mets pitcher Frank Viola (Frank Sr. and Helen) were regular customers at the Deli. One day, in 1989, when they stopped by for a bite to eat, a *New York Post* photographer, who happened to be munching pastrami at another table, snapped their picture. This seemingly innocuous occurrence gave rise to one of Abe's wackiest schemes. He announced that he would give a free ten-inch-long salami to anyone presenting a ticket stub from a Mets game won by Viola throughout that season. In those days, Shea Stadium usually sold close to forty thousand seats for Mets games; that's a lotta salami!

Viola lost his first three games after the offer was made in early August.

Finally, he pitched a winning game, but it was at Dodger Stadium in Los Angeles, three thousand miles from the Deli. Nevertheless, a Manhattan man, who had sent away for a ticket to the L.A. game but did not attend, showed up at 9:00 A.M. the next day to claim his prize. Abe gave him two salamis for being the first to cash in.

But things really started hopping in early September, when Shea Stadium flashed the offer on the scoreboard during a Mets-Cardinals game. Dozens of ticket holders began showing up by the seventh inning; since the Mets were clearly going to demolish the Cardinals (Viola pitched a 13-to-1 victory), the Deli didn't hesitate to begin surrendering $7 salamis, more than four hundred of which were claimed in ninety minutes (seven hundred by day's end)! If anyone didn't like salami, they were given $7 worth of other items. One customer got so carried away, he urged Abe to run for mayor.

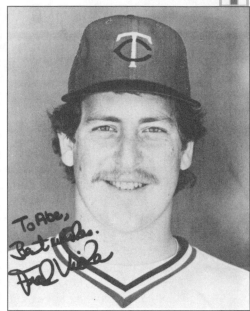

Frank Viola

"And everyone who votes for him gets a free salami," he yelled. Another man stunned Abe with 374 ticket stubs he'd collected from other fans or picked up off the ground! When he explained he was going to donate the salamis to City Harvest, a group that distributes food to the homeless, Abe upped the ante, rounding off the donation and contributing four hundred salamis.

2
_____

SOUPS

Mushroom Barley Soup
Lima Bean Soup
Chicken Soup
Chicken Soup with Chickpeas, Potatoes, and Spinach
Aunt Mary's Chicken Soup
Chicken Soup Live! With Regis & Kathie Lee
Antonio Pagán's Chicken Soup
Art D'Lugoff's Moroccan Chicken Soup
Split Pea Soup
Yankee Bean Soup
Cabbage Soup
Goulash Soup
Potato Soup
Turkey Gumbo
Vegetable Soup
Ima (Momma) Tihany's Cold Cherry Soup
Cold Fruit Soup
Borscht
Borscht, Ukrainian-Style
Red Lentil Soup
Croutons
Dumplings
Kreplach
Matzo Balls
Mimi Sheraton's Favorite Matzo Balls

As Esau, who sold his birthright for a bowl of red lentils (Genesis 25:30–34) could have told you, few things are more comforting than a steaming bowl of flavorful, full-bodied soup. Jewish soups—enhanced by noodles, kasha, garlicky croutons, kreplach, dumplings, and matzo balls (see recipes at the end of this chapter)—are especially hearty and nourishing. A generous serving of Second Avenue Deli split pea, mushroom barley, lima bean, or potato soup, sopped up with chunks of fresh challah, makes a richly satisfying meal in itself.

Note: Soups can all be stored, covered, in the refrigerator for up to 3 days. Their flavor is, generally, only enhanced by time.

Mushroom Barley Soup

"Flecked with carrots, celery, and onions, and fresh and dried mushrooms, it is a creamy, bracing antidote to midwinter snow and wind."
—Mimi Sheraton, *The New York Times*

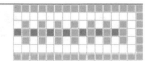

SERVES 6 TO 8

½ pound barley
10 cups clear chicken soup or stock
3 tablespoons corn oil
3 cups chopped onion
1 pound scrubbed, fresh mushrooms, sliced into pieces ⅛-inch thick
2 tablespoons finely chopped or crushed fresh garlic
5 large pieces dried mushroom (preferably shiitakes)

¾ cup carrot, chopped into ½-inch pieces
1 cup celery, chopped into ½-inch pieces
½ cup parsnip, chopped into ¼-inch pieces
Salt (the amount will depend on how much salt is in the chicken stock you use; if it's salty, you may not need any)
¼ teaspoon pepper

1. Place barley and chicken soup in a large stockpot. Bring to a boil, then reduce heat and simmer for 1 hour.
2. While the soup and barley are cooking, heat corn oil in a large skillet,

and sauté onions on high heat for 5 minutes, stirring occasionally. Add fresh mushrooms, and continue to sauté, stirring frequently, until everything is nicely browned. At the last minute, add garlic, and brown quickly. With a slotted spoon, remove contents of skillet to a bowl, and set aside. Meanwhile, soak dried mushrooms in hot water for 15 minutes to soften. Chop into ½-inch pieces, and set aside.

3. Add onion-mushroom mixture, dried mushrooms, carrots, celery, parsnips, salt (if needed), and pepper to the soup. Simmer for 1 hour and 15 minutes.

Lima Bean Soup

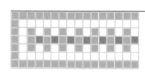

SERVES 8

3 cups uncooked lima beans
10 cups clear chicken soup or stock
1½ cups onion, chopped into
    ½-inch pieces
1½ cups carrot, chopped into
    ¼-inch pieces
¾ cup celery, chopped into ¼-inch
    pieces
1 cup parsnip, chopped into
    ¼-inch pieces

1 tablespoon finely chopped or
    crushed fresh garlic
Salt (the amount will depend on
    how much salt is in the chicken
    stock you use; if it's salty, you
    may not need any)
¼ teaspoon pepper
2 tablespoons cornstarch
2 tablespoons cold water

1. Boil dried lima beans in water to cover for 2 minutes, then turn off the heat, and leave beans soaking in the water for 1 hour. Alternatively, you can soak them overnight.

2. Place chicken soup and lima beans in a large stockpot. Bring to a rapid boil, then reduce heat and simmer for 30 minutes.

3. Add onions, carrots, celery, and parsnips to the pot; cover, and simmer for 20 minutes.

4. Add garlic, salt (only if needed), and pepper, and simmer for 15 minutes.

5. Place cornstarch in a bowl, and add 2 tablespoons cold water, one at a time, stirring until smooth and all cornstarch is dissolved. Add 1 cup soup liquid, a little at a time, and stir until smooth. Bring soup to a boil. Add cornstarch mixture to soup, and, stirring constantly, boil for 2 minutes.

A Chicken Soup in Every Pot

So many people contributed chicken soup recipes to our book that we created this special chicken soup section for them. Not all of these recipes are Jewish; they run the gamut from Moroccan to Puerto Rican versions.

CHICKEN SOUP WITH MATZO BALLS, AND THAT HEAVENLY PASTRAMI!

As hot dogs and apple pie typify American food, chicken soup is the glorious sine qua non of Jewish cuisine . . . both in itself and as the underpinning for many traditional recipes. Known as the "Jewish penicillin" (Moses Maimonides, Spanish philosopher and physician, touted its healing powers as far back as the twelfth century, even claiming it was "beneficial in leprosy"), a worthy chicken soup with matzo balls is said to cure colds and other respiratory ailments. At the very least, its inherent motherly comfort will cheer you up.

Chicken soup sets a warm gemütlich tone for holiday meals, and, for symbolic as well as culinary reasons, it has been the standard first course at Jewish weddings for centuries; its golden color suggests prosperity, and chickens (like their eggs) are fertility symbols. In the shtetls of Eastern Europe, weddings usually took place on Friday afternoons, out of doors, in front of the synagogue. The entire town would attend; there would be musicians, dancing, and platters piled high with food. After the ceremony, the groom would "say *drash*" (show off his knowledge of the Torah) at the Friday-night service. Then the bride and groom were taken to a private room and fed an especially nourishing chicken soup. Prepared by the bride's family, it was replete with the chicken's unlaid eggs, and rings of fat (like golden coins) floated on the surface.

Jewish storyteller Roz Perry told us a family tale about this Old World custom. The day before her parents' wedding, Roz's maternal grandfather, Mordecai, went to the market to purchase a chicken for the postnuptial ritual. A lifelong tightwad, he couldn't bring himself to spend a lot of money for a big, plump bird. When he returned home with a scrawny chicken—the kind on which the family habitually dined—Roz's grandmother, Rifka-Ruchel, rained curses on him for bringing home such an ill-fed fowl for the momentous occasion. Intense and relentless bickering ensued. Finally—for the sake of family peace and his daughter's future happiness—Mordecai returned to the market and exchanged the bony bird for a nice fat hen. Unfortunately, when Roz's parents were served the soup, her mother, unaccustomed to the luxury of rich food, found it revoltingly fatty and gagged on it. However, she forced it down, and it worked its magic; Roz's parents went on to have a fruitful and prosperous life in America.

Chicken Soup

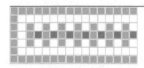

SERVES 8

1 pound chicken parts
2 stalks celery, including leafy tops, cut into 3-inch pieces
1 whole chicken, thoroughly rinsed
Salt to rub inside chicken
1 large whole onion, unpeeled (find one with a firm, golden-brown peel)

1 large whole carrot, peeled
1 medium whole parsnip, peeled
2 teaspoons salt
¼ teaspoon pepper
1 bunch of dill, cleaned and tied with a string

Note: The Deli's recipe calls for both a whole chicken plus 1 pound of chicken parts. You can, however, use just 1 large chicken and cut off both wings, the neck, and a leg to use as parts.

1. Pour 12 cups of cold water into a large stockpot, and throw in the chicken parts and celery. Bring to a boil. While water is heating, rub the inside of the whole chicken with salt.

2. Add the chicken to the pot, cover, reduce heat, and simmer for 30 minutes. Test chicken with a fork to see if it's tender and fully cooked; then remove it from the pot, and set aside on a large platter. Leave chicken parts in the pot.

3. Add onion, carrot, parsnip, salt, and pepper. Let soup simmer for 1 hour and 15 minutes.

4. When chicken cools, remove skin and bones and cut into bite-sized pieces. You can add it to the soup, just before serving, or save it for chicken salad.

5. Strain the soup, and discard everything solid except the carrot.

6. Drop in the dill for a minute before serving and remove. Add salt and pepper to taste. Slice carrot and toss into soup. Also add the chicken pieces if desired. Other options: Add cooked noodles, rice, kasha, or matzo balls (page 60).

CHICKEN SOUP is more than just a food; it's a defining Jewish-mother ritual. Herewith, a few examples of its arcane etiquette from humorist Myra Chanin, who has written an entire book on the subject.

Set out bowls and serve everyone soup. When they ask why you aren't joining them, tell them you'll eat after you finish cleaning the kitchen.

After everyone agrees that this is absolutely the best soup they have ever tasted, wait forty-three seconds and ask if they are *sure* the soup was all right.

. . . understand that your daughter is too busy with her important work to ever serve the child anything but canned.

From *Jewish Penicillin: Mother Wonderful's Chicken Soup* (101 Productions, © 1984).

Chicken Soup with Chickpeas, Potatoes, and Spinach

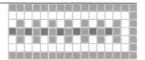

This is a variation on the Deli's famous chicken soup, directly above. The first nine ingredients (everything but the dill) are the same, so we haven't listed them here again. Prepare as the above recipe through steps 1 and 2.

Note: Consider the garlic toast recipe below to complement other soups

SERVES 8

and entrées. If you serve it with a dairy, pasta, fish, or other nonmeat meal, use butter instead of margarine; it tastes better.

ADDITIONAL INGREDIENTS

2 teaspoons cumin

1 pound red potatoes, peeled and cut into 1-inch chunks, ¾-inch thick

2 tablespoons olive oil

1 cup cooked chickpeas (preferably made fresh)

4 cups fresh spinach, very thoroughly washed

2 tablespoons fresh lemon juice

FOR THE GARLIC TOAST

French or Italian loaf, cut into ¾-inch slices

Fresh garlic cloves, crushed

Extra-virgin olive oil

Salt

Margarine

FOR THE ROUX

3 tablespoons corn oil

¼ cup flour

1 and 2. See chicken soup recipe above, steps 1 and 2.

3. Add onion, carrot, parsnip, salt, pepper, and cumin. Let soup simmer for 1 hour and 15 minutes. While the soup is simmering, boil potatoes in a separate pot until just cooked but firm. Drain potatoes, remove them to a bowl, and set aside. Also prepare the garlic toast for baking. Place bread slices on a double sheet of aluminum foil, and spread about ¾ teaspoon crushed garlic on each slice. Drizzle each slice well with olive oil, sprinkle lightly with salt, and top with thin slivers of margarine. Set aside.

4. When the chicken cools, remove skin and bones and cut into bite-sized pieces; set aside.

5. In a shallow baking dish, toss the potato chunks in olive oil, and broil for about 10 minutes, turning once so that they brown evenly. Keep an eye on them, so they don't burn. Remove potatoes to a covered dish, and set aside on an unlit burner. Adjust oven temperature to 375 degrees (the heat from the oven will keep the potatoes warm).

6. Strain the soup, and discard everything solid except the carrot. Dice carrot into ¾-inch pieces, and set aside.

7. Place aluminum foil with bread in oven, and bake for 15 minutes or until bread is nicely browned. Keep an eye on it, so it doesn't burn.

8. While the bread is browning, keeping your soup at a low simmer, spoon off 3 cups clear soup. Pour corn oil into a medium saucepan, and add flour, stirring well until it is completely dissolved. Put the roux pot on medium to high heat, and add the 3 cups of soup, a little bit at a time, stirring constantly to create a thick, totally smooth, pastelike roux. It will get a little less pastelike as you add more soup. Transfer the roux to the soup pot, and stir in well.

9. When soup is adequately thickened, add potatoes, chicken, carrot, chickpeas, spinach, and lemon juice. Cook for 1 minute more. Serve with garlic toast.

FORMER MAYOR DAVID DINKINS once said, "On a quiet dark street, on a subway late at night, or in a dangerous situation of any kind, to see a Guardian Angel is to feel that you are safe."

Curtis Sliwa founded New York's red-bereted volunteer crime-prevention patrols, the Guardian Angels, in 1979. Today his Angels combat crime, violence, and drugs in cities worldwide and provide inspirational speakers to educate youngsters about the organization's no-gang, no-gun, no-drug philosophy. Sliwa also hosts an evening radio show on WABC.

In the 1980s, when I moved to the East Village, I had a heavy public-speaking schedule promoting the Guardian Angels. All that public speaking frequently made me lose my voice, a problem I've been prone to all my life and for which I had only ever found one effective remedy—my aunt Mary's chicken soup. But Aunt Mary lives in Howard Beach, and I didn't usually have time to go out there. So I began buying chicken soup—to the amazement of countermen, three or four quarts at a time—from the Second Avenue Deli. One day, Abe Lebewohl saw me buying the soup and said, "You take care of the city, let me take care of you." He disappeared into the kitchen and was gone for such a long time I began to get nervous, so I ordered and ate a pastrami sandwich. He finally came back with what he called his "most potent" chicken soup—with carrots, celery, kasha, and even a little chicken fat! It worked like medicine. I had had a pounding headache and congestion when I came in. Within a half hour, my head had cleared, and I felt great. After that, he always fixed his special soup for me, and it always worked—a few ladles and Bingo!

In 1992, I was kidnapped in a stolen taxi, shot several times, and left for dead on a Lower Manhattan street. When I returned home from the hospital, my apartment was protected by a police guard unit as well as a crew of Guardian Angels. Every day for three months, while I recuperated, Abe (my own guardian angel) would send over daily care packages of food for the police and the Angels—and totally clear chicken soup (he strained it through a cloth) for me. It was practically the only thing I could digest, and I looked forward to it greatly each day.

In 1994, Abe told me he was planning a pickle-eating contest at the Deli and looking for someone who symbolized New York to compete. At the time, still recovering from gunshot wounds, I wasn't taking chances with my diet. I was eating only very bland food, and I was really sick of it. I decided to throw caution to the winds and enter his contest. I downed four and three-quarters pounds of garlic pickles in fifteen minutes, winning $500 for the Angels and a trophy. More important, winning the contest helped me focus mind over matter and stop worrying so much about my stomach, which has functioned perfectly ever since. I've gone on to compete in pizza-, hot dog–, and sushi-eating contests, and my stomach processes it all like it was manufactured by Roto-Rooter.

For *The Second Avenue Deli Cookbook,* I'd like to pass along the recipe for my Aunt Mary's very delicious and very elaborate chicken soup.

Aunt Mary's Chicken Soup

SERVES 8

This recipe makes a lot of soup. If you're not planning to serve it all at once, add snow peas, escarole, and pastina only to the part you're serving. Strained broth can be frozen to use as a base for future soups.

1 4- to 5-pound chicken, quartered
2 tablespoons kosher salt
1 large whole onion, peeled
3 cloves garlic, peeled, whole but crushed
2 medium carrots, chopped into ½-inch pieces
1 stalk celery, cut into ¾-inch pieces
½ small leek, well scrubbed and cut into ½-inch pieces
1 bay leaf

3 small plum tomatoes, cut into ¾-inch pieces (remove seeds)
1 whole small potato, peeled
½ bunch Italian parsley, tied
½ teaspoon black peppercorns
1 tablespoon salt
6 escarole leaves, coarsely chopped
½ cup snow peas
1 cup cooked Ronzoni egg pastina #155 (a very tiny star-shaped pasta)
Salt and pepper to taste

1. Place chicken and kosher salt in a large pot or bowl with very cold water to cover, and leave it to soak for 1 hour. Wash thoroughly, and set aside.
2. Pour 12 cups of cold water into a large stockpot, add onion and garlic cloves, and bring to a boil. Add carrots, celery, leek, and bay leaf; reduce heat, and simmer 30 minutes.

3. Add chicken, tomatoes, potato, parsley, black peppercorns, and salt to the stockpot. Continue to simmer for 2 hours and 20 minutes.

4. Place a strainer over a large bowl, and pour the soup into it. From the strainer, first remove all chicken pieces to a separate bowl, discarding fat, skin, and bones in the process. Also discard the onion, bay leaf, parsley, and as many peppercorns as you can find.

5. Pour liquid soup back into the stockpot, immediately replacing strainer atop the bowl. Separate out, as far as possible, the garlic cloves, carrots, and potato, and mash them in a different bowl. Skin and debone the chicken, cutting it into bite-sized pieces. Return all of these ingredients, along with the rest of the vegetables in the strainer, to the soup. Add escarole and snow peas, and simmer 5 minutes more. Add pastina, season to taste with salt and pepper, and serve.

ROZANNE GOLD is a prominent mover and shaker in the food world. She ran the kitchen at Gracie Mansion during the Koch administration, was instrumental in re-creating the Rainbow Room and Windows on the World, has been president of Les Dames d'Escoffier, and twice won the coveted James Beard Award for Best General Cookbook—in 1994 for *Little Meals: A Great New Way to Eat & Cook* and in 1997 for *Recipes 1-2-3: Fabulous Food Using Only 3 Ingredients*. She is also a frequent guest on national TV shows such as *Good Morning America, Live with Regis & Kathie Lee,* and *Today.*

Only a big-hearted soul, with a sense of humor, would create such an incongruity at his place of business—just to please a friend. Abe, dear Abe, who never ate a little meal in his life, bought fifty, count 'em, fifty, copies of my first cookbook, *Little Meals,* to display at the Second Avenue Deli of all places. Why? Each one of you who knew Abe knows the answer. It was love all around. Abe loved me because I was like him—a cook, a matchmaker, a chicken soup maven.

When I was Ed Koch's chef at Gracie Mansion, Abe was my hero. He made me look real good. I always suspected His Honor knew whose chopped liver he was eating. And at the Rainbow Room, when we did Seders for special guests, I suspect they also knew whose chopped liver they were eating.

I once went to a book party for Seymour Chwast's *Trylon and Perisphere: The 1939 New York World's Fair,* for which Abe had recreated the Trylon and Perisphere (official symbols of that fair) in chopped liver. Just to please a friend.

Just to please a friend. It seemed to be Abe's mantra. His raison d'être!

Almost nightly, for the past ten years, I have taxied down Second Avenue past the Deli to my home in Brooklyn. Whenever I needed that ineffable kind of nurturing—Abe's kind—I stopped in for a visit. It was the natural place to go.

I still taxi down that avenue past the Deli. And I think of Abe often. He was that kind of friend.

Chicken Soup Live! with Regis & Kathie Lee

SERVES 4

This soup has amazing restorative powers.

8 cups chicken broth
1 pound chicken backs and necks
1 red onion, finely diced
2 leeks, finely diced
3 carrots, peeled and finely diced
2 celery ribs, finely diced
1 turnip, peeled and finely diced
2 large cloves garlic, minced
1 tablespoon dried basil leaves
¼ cup chopped fresh parsley
Salt
Pepper

1. Put chicken broth in a pot, and bring to a boil. Add remaining ingredients. Lower heat, cover, and cook 1 hour.
2. Remove chicken pieces, using tongs. Continue to simmer ½ hour longer.
3. Skim fat. Adjust seasonings by adding salt and pepper and additional chopped parsley to taste.

Optional: Add 8 large matzo balls or add 2 cups cooked orzo, the juice of 1 lemon, and ¼ cup chopped fresh dill.

Adapted from *Little Meals: A Great New Way to Eat & Cook* (Villard Books, © 1993).

ANTONIO PAGÁN—former New York City councilman (whose district included the Second Avenue Deli) and candidate for Manahattan Borough president—is currently the commissioner of the New York City Department of Employment. He champions a "roll up your sleeves and get things done" approach to government. His leadership was instrumental in the conversion of Tompkins Square Park from an open-air drug market to a beautiful urban oasis.

I first met Abe Lebewohl in the mid-1980s at a Community Board meeting, where we were both involved in doing something about a neighborhood shelter that was bringing a lot of crime into the area. We became pals, and, over political chitchat at the Deli, he introduced me to Jewish food, overcoming any reluctance on my part—e.g., to kishke, which he informed me was the stuffed casing of a cow's intestine!—with his usual candor ("Try it. You eat more disgusting things"). I was soon converted; by 1994, when he celebrated the Deli's fortieth anniversary with a one-day return to 1954 prices, I arrived when the doors opened and stuffed myself to bursting, sampling almost every item on the menu (the one exception was gefilte fish; you have to be born Jewish for that).

Over the years, our political discussions focused on four areas only: New York, the Lower East Side/East Village, Russia, and Israel. The rest of the world didn't exist for him. When I ran for councilman, he was my biggest supporter, raising money (he threw my first fundraiser), drumming up support (as the unofficial "Mayor of Second Avenue" he had tremendous influence), and encouraging me to bring reporters, especially hostile ones, to the Deli. As I sweated through tough interviews in a Deli booth, Abe was stuffing knishes into reporters' mouths, bantering with them, and sending them off with big bags of food. No one was happier than Abe when I won the election . . . well, maybe my mother.

A great friend and a political ally, Abe was also a mentor. When I was invited to Israel along with other developing American political leaders, he spent several months prior to my trip briefing me about Israeli history, politics, and culture. More importantly, he served as a political role model, always evaluating issues individually rather than according to a party line, striving to understand everyone's point of view before adopting a position, and never looking at people's differences but emphasizing instead what they had in common.

Antonio Pagán's
Chicken Soup

SERVES 8

This is my own version of a traditional Puerto Rican chicken soup.

½ bunch fresh cilantro, coarsely
    chopped
3 cloves garlic
1 cup coarsely chopped onion
1 medium green pepper, coarsely
    chopped
½ cup cold water
8 cups plain chicken soup, stock, or
    broth (fresh or canned)
2 Idaho potatoes, peeled and cut
    into 1-inch cubes

2 cups cooked chicken meat
    (preferably from a roasted
    chicken), cut into bite-sized
    pieces
Salt (the amount will depend on
    how much salt is in the chicken
    stock you use; if it's salty, you
    may not need any)
¼ teaspoon fresh-ground pepper

OPTIONAL INGREDIENTS AND GARNISHES
½ cup cooked white rice
Finely chopped dried fresh mint or
    basil leaves

Fresh-squeezed lemon juice
Extra-virgin olive oil

1. In a food processor, chop cilantro, garlic, onions, and green pepper to a
fine consistency. Add ½ cup cold water, stir, and set aside.
2. In a large stockpot, bring chicken soup to a boil. Add cilantro-garlic-
onion-green pepper mix, reduce heat, and simmer for 10 minutes.
3. Add potatoes, chicken, salt, and pepper, and continue to simmer until
potatoes are fully cooked.
4. Add rice, and adjust salt and pepper to taste. Garnish each bowl with
mint or basil leaves, a squirt of lemon juice (to taste), and a drizzle of extra-
virgin olive oil.

Art D'Lugoff's Moroccan Chicken Soup

SERVES 8

Jazz impresario Art D'Lugoff (page 168) gave us this soup recipe. We love it, because though it looks and tastes very impressive, it's quick and easy to prepare.

8 cups clear chicken soup or stock
2 cups diced cooked chicken
1/3 cup red pepper, chopped into
    1/4-inch pieces
1/3 cup green pepper, chopped into
    1/4-inch pieces
3 tablespoons fresh chopped dill
3 cups cooked couscous (prepare
    according to package directions)

1 tablespoon unsweetened
    cinnamon
Salt (the amount will depend on
    how much salt is in the chicken
    stock you use; if it's salty, you
    may not need any)
1/4 teaspoon pepper
Fresh lemon or lime

1. Combine all ingredients (except lemon or lime) in a large stockpot, and stir well. Bring soup to a boil; then reduce heat, and simmer for 2 minutes. Squeeze 2 teaspoons of lemon or lime juice into each bowl before serving, and garnish each portion with a citrus slice.

Split Pea Soup

Note: Vegetables (except the peas) need to be very finely chopped to the size of 1/8-inch pebbles; this is best done in a food processor.

SERVES 8 TO 10

2 1/2 cups dried split peas
10 cups clear chicken soup or stock
2 cups very finely chopped onion
1 cup very finely chopped carrot
3/4 cup very finely chopped parsnip
3/4 cup very finely chopped celery
1 large bay leaf
1 tablespoon finely chopped or
    crushed fresh garlic

Salt (the amount will depend on
    how much salt is in the chicken
    stock you use; if it's salty, you
    may not need any)
1/4 teaspoon pepper
3 tablespoons cornstarch
1 15-ounce can sweet peas, drained
Croutons (page 57)

1. Pour split peas into a colander and, under running water, wash and pick through to remove all foreign particles. Cover with water, let soak for 1 hour, and rinse. Repeat.

2. Place chicken soup, split peas, and onions in a large stockpot. Bring to a rapid boil, remove some of the foam with a slotted spoon, then reduce heat, and simmer for 30 minutes.

3. Add carrots, parsnips, celery, and bay leaf, and simmer for another 30 minutes.

4. Add garlic, salt (only if needed), and pepper, and simmer for another 15 minutes. Remove bay leaf.

5. Place cornstarch in a bowl, and add 3 tablespoons cold water, one at a time, stirring until smooth and all cornstarch is dissolved. Add 1 cup soup liquid, a little at a time, and stir until smooth. Bring soup to a boil. Add cornstarch mixture to soup, and, stirring constantly, boil for 2 minutes. Add canned peas, and stir in. Add salt to taste. Serve with garlicky croutons.

Yankee Bean Soup

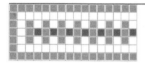

SERVES 10

A friend of ours once remarked that Yankee bean soup, a Deli menu staple, doesn't sound very Jewish. Perhaps we should rename it "Yankel" bean soup.

Note: Since you have to soak your beans overnight, plan advance preparation.

2½ cups Yankee beans (also known as navy beans)

10 cups plain chicken soup or stock

¾ cup celery, chopped into ¼-inch pieces

1 cup carrot, chopped into ¼-inch pieces

¾ cup parsnip, chopped into ¼-inch pieces

1½ cups onion, chopped into ¼-inch pieces

1 tablespoon finely chopped or crushed fresh garlic

Salt (the amount will depend on how much salt is in the chicken stock you use; if it's salty, you may not need any)

¼ teaspoon pepper

FOR THE ROUX
3 tablespoons corn oil

¼ cup flour

1. Soak beans overnight in cold water that covers them by a few inches.

2. Pour the chicken soup into a large stockpot, and bring to a boil. Add drained beans, reduce heat, and simmer for 1 hour.

3. Add 2 cups water, celery, carrots, parsnips, onions, garlic, salt, and pepper to the pot. Simmer for 30 minutes.

4. Keeping your soup at a low simmer, spoon off 2 or 3 cups of clear soup as best you can (don't worry if there's a bean or a piece of onion in it). Pour oil into a medium saucepan and add flour, stirring well until it is completely dissolved and smooth. Put the roux pot on medium to high heat, and add the soup, a little at a time, stirring constantly to create a thick, totally smooth, pastelike roux. It will get a little less pastelike as you add more soup. Transfer the roux to the soup pot, and stir in well. This is a fairly thick soup.

Cabbage Soup

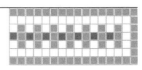

SERVES 8

4 to 5 soup bones (get them from your butcher)	2 teaspoons salt
	1/4 teaspoon pepper
2 cups canned tomatoes, drained and chopped into 3/4-inch pieces	1 small to medium cabbage, coarsely chopped (about 2 pounds when chopped)
2 cups chopped onion	3 tablespoons sugar
1 tablespoon chopped or crushed fresh garlic	3 tablespoons fresh-squeezed lemon juice

FOR THE ROUX
3 tablespoons corn oil   1/4 cup flour

1. Bring 10 cups of water to a boil in a large stockpot. Add soup bones, tomatoes, onions, garlic, salt, and pepper; reduce heat, and simmer 1½ hours.
2. Remove and discard soup bones. Add cabbage, sugar, and lemon juice. Simmer for another 40 minutes. Skim off fat with a slotted spoon. If you prefer a brothlike cabbage soup, skip the next step; the roux is optional.
3. Keeping your soup at a low simmer, spoon off 3 cups clear broth. Pour corn oil into a medium saucepan, and add flour, stirring well until it is completely dissolved. Put the roux pot on medium to high heat, and add the soup, a little at a time, stirring constantly to create a thick, totally smooth, pastelike roux. It will get a little less pastelike as you add more soup. Transfer the roux to the soup pot, and stir in well.

Note: If your soup bones had fat attached to them, check each bowl of soup before serving to make sure no pieces fell off.

Goulash Soup

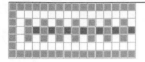

Hungarian soups are like stews, with large quantities of meat and vegetables in minimal broth. This goulash soup is best prepared a day in advance; it tastes much better on the second day.

SERVES 8

1 tablespoon onion powder
1 tablespoon garlic powder
4 teaspoons salt
¼ teaspoon pepper
¼ teaspoon cayenne pepper
2 pounds stew beef, trimmed of fat and cut into 1-inch cubes
2 tablespoons schmaltz (substitute olive oil if you don't have schmaltz)
3 cups chopped onions
2 tablespoons finely chopped or crushed fresh garlic

1 tablespoon schmaltz or olive oil
2 cups green pepper, chopped into ¾-inch pieces
2 tablespoons paprika
2 tablespoons tomato paste
2 bay leaves
½ cup water
2 pounds Idaho potatoes (about 4½ cups), peeled and chopped into ¾-inch chunks
3 cups drained and coarsely chopped canned tomatoes

FOR THE ROUX
3 tablespoons corn oil

¼ cup flour

1. Mix onion powder, garlic powder, 2 teaspoons salt, pepper, and cayenne thoroughly in a large bowl. Add the beef cubes, and toss to coat evenly. Marinate in refrigerator for at least 6 hours.

2. Heat 2 tablespoons schmaltz in a large skillet, and sauté onions until browned. Add garlic at the last minute, and brown quickly. Remove onions and garlic with a slotted spoon to a large bowl. Add 1 tablespoon schmaltz to skillet, sauté green peppers, and set them aside in a different bowl.

3. In remaining schmaltz (add a small amount if needed), brown the meat on all sides. Add to bowl with onions and garlic; add paprika, tomato paste, and 2 teaspoons salt. Mix everything together thoroughly.

4. Transfer contents of bowl with meat into a large stockpot or Dutch oven; add bay leaves and ½ cup water. Cover, and simmer 1 hour and 20 minutes.

5. Uncover pot, and add potatoes, tomatoes, and 6 cups of water. Bring to a boil, lower heat, and simmer for 45 minutes. Add green peppers, and simmer for 15 minutes longer.

6. Keeping your soup at a low simmer, spoon off 4 cups clear soup as best you can (don't worry if there's a piece of onion in it). Pour corn oil into a medium saucepan, and add flour, stirring well until it is completely dissolved. Put the roux pot on medium to high heat, and add the soup, a little at a time, stirring constantly to create a thick, totally smooth, pastelike roux. It will get a little less pastelike as you add more soup. Transfer the roux to the soup pot, and stir in well.

Potato Soup

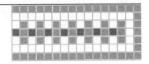

Someone once said, "Rich men eat vichyssoise, poor men eat potato soup." But money couldn't buy a better soup than this Russian peasant recipe.

SERVES 10

10 cups clear chicken soup or stock
3/4 cup celery, chopped into 1/4-inch pieces
1 cup carrot, chopped into 1/2-inch pieces
1 cup parsnip, chopped into 1/4-inch pieces
2 cups onion, chopped into 1/2-inch pieces
1 1/2 pounds Idaho potatoes, peeled and chopped into 3/4-inch pieces
1 pound round red potatoes, peeled and chopped into 3/4-inch pieces

2 tablespoons finely chopped or crushed fresh garlic
Salt (the amount will depend on how much salt is in the chicken stock you use; if it's salty, you may not need any)
1/4 teaspoon pepper
2 cups cooked spinach (optional)
2 tablespoons finely chopped dill (or a bit more to taste)

FOR THE ROUX
3/8 cup corn oil

6 tablespoons flour

Note: Spinach is not actually part of this recipe as served in the Deli. However, we were once having lunch on a day that spinach was the vegetable du jour, and we threw some into our potato soup and liked it. If you'd like to add spinach, add it only to the amount you're serving. It will get limp if refrigerated in the soup.

1. Pour chicken soup into a large stockpot, and add celery, carrots, parsnips, and onions. Bring to a boil. Reduce heat, cover, and simmer for 20 minutes.
2. Add potatoes, garlic, salt (if needed), and pepper to pot. Cover, and simmer 30 minutes (or until potatoes are well cooked).
3. Keeping your soup at a low simmer, spoon off 3 cups clear soup as best you can. Pour corn oil into a medium saucepan, and add flour, stirring well until it is completely dissolved. Put the roux pot on medium to high heat, and add the soup, a little at a time, stirring constantly to create a thick, totally smooth, pastelike roux. It will get a little less pastelike as you add more soup. Transfer the roux to the soup pot, and stir in well. This is a fairly thick soup.
4. Stir in spinach and dill just prior to serving, and add salt to taste.

Turkey Gumbo

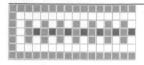

SERVES 8

10 cups plain chicken soup or stock
1 stalk celery, cut into sticks (approximately ¼ inch by 1 inch)
5-inch carrot, cut into sticks (approximately ¼ inch by 1 inch)
3 cups chopped onion
5-inch parsnip, cut into sticks (approximately ¼ inch by 1 inch)
¾ cup uncooked bow tie noodles
1 cup cooked white-meat turkey, chopped into ¾-inch pieces

½ cup fresh okra, cut into ¼-inch slices
½ cup frozen peas
1 tablespoon finely chopped or crushed fresh garlic
Salt (the amount will depend on how much salt is in the chicken stock you use; if it's salty, you may not need any)
¼ teaspoon pepper
1 cup cooked rice

FOR THE ROUX
3 tablespoons corn oil

¼ cup flour

1. In a large stockpot, place chicken soup, celery, carrots, onions, and parsnips. Bring to a boil, then reduce heat, and simmer for 20 minutes.
2. Add bow tie noodles and turkey, and simmer for 15 minutes.
3. Add okra, peas, garlic, salt (if needed), and pepper, and simmer for 5 minutes.
4. Add rice, and simmer for 3 minutes.
5. Keeping your soup at a low simmer, spoon off 3 cups clear soup as best you can. Pour corn oil into a medium saucepan, and add flour, stirring well until it is completely dissolved. Put the roux pot on medium to high heat, and add the soup, a little bit at a time, stirring constantly to create a thick, totally smooth, pastelike roux. It will get a little less pastelike as you add more soup. Transfer the roux to the soup pot, and stir in well.

Vegetable Soup

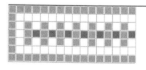

SERVES 9

This soup is thick, hearty, and satisfying . . . and everything in it is good for you.

10 cups plain chicken soup or stock
½ cup barley
¾ cup dried lima beans
1 cup water

1½ cups onion, chopped into ½-inch pieces
¾ cup celery, chopped into ¼-inch pieces

1 cup carrot, chopped into ½-inch
   pieces
⅔ cup parsnip, chopped into
   ¼-inch pieces
1 cup coarsely chopped cabbage
1 cup corkscrew (fusilli or rotini)
   pasta; we use tricolor, which
   adds a festive touch
1½ cups canned plum tomatoes,
   chopped into ¾-inch pieces
1 tablespoon finely chopped or
   crushed fresh garlic

Salt (the amount will depend on
   how much salt is in the chicken
   stock you use; if it's salty, you
   may not need any)
¼ teaspoon pepper
¾ cup zucchini, chopped into
   ¼-inch pieces
¾ cup green pepper, chopped into
   ½-inch pieces
2 teaspoons cornstarch

1. Pour 7 cups chicken soup into a large stockpot, and bring to a boil. Add barley and lima beans, lower heat, and simmer for 1 hour. Check occasionally, and add a bit of water if it seems to be drying out.

2. Add 3 cups chicken soup, 1 cup water, onions, celery, carrots, parsnips, cabbage, pasta, tomatoes, garlic, salt, and pepper. Bring to a boil, then reduce heat, and simmer for 20 minutes.

3. Add zucchini and green pepper, and simmer for another 10 minutes.

4. Place cornstarch in a small bowl. Add 1 tablespoon cold water, stirring until smooth and all cornstarch is dissolved. Add 1 cup soup liquid, a little at a time, and stir until smooth. Bring soup to a boil. Add cornstarch mixture to soup, and, stirring constantly, boil for 2 minutes. Add salt to taste. This is a very thick soup, with little broth.

BORN IN TRANSYLVANIA IN 1948, Adam Tihany grew up in Israel, where, after serving in the army, he attended the Politecnico di Milano, School of Architecture and Urban Planning. Since 1978, he has directed his own design studio in New York and is considered one of the preeminent restaurant designers in the world today. His projects include, among many others, Baretto in Paris, Bice restaurants worldwide, Spago restaurants (in Las Vegas, Mexico City, and Chicago), Gundel in Budapest, Monte's in London, the Dan Eilat Hotel and Resort in Israel, and, in New York, Jean Georges and the spectacular Le Cirque 2000. We're especially proud to say that he also recently redesigned the Second Avenue Deli.

In addition, Tihany has created stunning lines of furniture and accessories, and Villeroy & Boch has produced many of his custom-designed china patterns. An accomplished chef, he is also the owner of Remi restaurants in New York and Santa Monica and the author (with Francesco Antonucci and Florence Fabricant) of *Venetian Taste,* which may be the world's most exquisitely designed cookbook.

Though I'd been introduced to him at social functions, and seen him bustling around the Deli, my first real meeting with Abe Lebewohl was in 1993 when he showed up at my office with a dream. At the height of the glasnost era, Abe passionately wanted to open the first kosher restaurant in Moscow . . . and he had chosen me to design it. Though I was flattered, I might have turned him down if this was a mere business proposition. It wasn't. Abe was on a mission, and he was very righteous—almost rabbinical—in his fervor. He felt like it was his duty to bring kosher food to the Russians, that it was something he owed to his native land and the continuing history of the Jewish people. It was about reestablishing culture via food and about challenging Russian Jews to openly display their Judaism by frequenting a kosher restaurant—a brave act in a country where religion had been underground for more than half a century.

He had already been to Moscow several times to check out the scene, which, his intense idealism notwithstanding, he viewed with a great depth of clarity. As soon as I agreed to accept the commission (there was no resisting his moral mandate), he arranged for us to fly there and view possible sites. It was my first trip to Moscow, and the mood in the streets was exhilarating; people were filled with a new hope for the future. We schlepped around town for several days with a rabbi, who was instrumental in putting the deal together, and a government-required Russian business partner. With his usual efficiency, Abe had everything under way; he'd even convinced McDonald's to supply him with kosher meats. He went back many times, always with abounding optimism and enthusiasm, trying to close the deal.

Sad to say, his efforts never came to fruition. In the end, corruption in the new Russia rendered his courageous and visionary project unfeasible. Abe retreated from Moscow, but our friendship flourished. And though we were never able to complete our project in Russia, I was, after Abe's death, able to fulfill another dream of his—the creation of the interior he had envisioned for the Second Avenue Deli.

Ima (Momma) Tihany's
Cold Cherry Soup

SERVES 8

2 pounds fresh cherries, including
   pits
2 cinnamon sticks
4 to 6 tablespoons sugar (adjust
   amount, depending on the
   sweetness of your cherries)

1 teaspoon fresh lemon juice
1½ cups cherry juice (available at
   health food and specialty food
   stores)
1 tablespoon white flour
Sour cream

1. In a stockpot, cover fresh cherries with water, add cinnamon sticks and sugar, and bring to a boil. Reduce heat, add lemon juice, and simmer for 10 minutes. Let cool to room temperature.

2. In a small saucepan, mix ½ cup of the cherry juice into the flour, stirring until completely smooth. Add the remaining cup of cherry juice, bit by bit, and stir in until smooth. Bring the mixture to a slow boil over low heat, stirring constantly. Remove from burner, and let cool to room temperature.

3. When both mixtures have cooled, combine them in a bowl, and refrigerate for at least 6 hours.

4. Place dollops of sour cream in deep soup dishes, then pour the soup over the top. Serve chilled.

Cold Fruit Soup

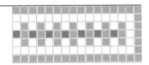

This is a great dish for dieting—unless, of course, you top it off with a dollop of vanilla ice cream or sour cream.

Note: Except for the cantaloupe, do not peel any of the fruits.

1½ pounds Red Delicious apples
   (core and remove seeds; quarter,
   and cut each apple quarter into
   3 pieces)
½ lemon, seeded and cut in
   quarters
6 peaches (remove pits; cut each
   peach into 8 pieces)

6 nectarines (remove pits; cut each
   nectarine into 8 pieces)
½ small cantaloupe (remove rind
   and seeds; chop into 1-inch
   pieces)
1 cup sugar
2 cups seedless grapes

MAKES ABOUT
3 QUARTS

1. In a large stockpot, bring 8 cups of water to a vigorous boil. Add apples and lemon, reduce heat, and simmer 15 minutes.
2. Add peaches, nectarines, cantaloupe, and sugar; simmer another 15 minutes.
3. Add grapes, and simmer 3 minutes longer. Chill before serving.

PROMOTIONS, PITCHES . . . AND PITCHING NO-HITTERS

The Anniversary Schmaltz

ONCE EVERY TEN YEARS, on the anniversary of the 1954 opening of the Second Avenue Deli, Abe celebrated with a one-day rollback to original prices. Each time, hundreds of customers lined up throughout the day and waited patiently in the cold weather (the Deli opened in March) to enjoy a corned beef or pastrami sandwich on rye for 50 cents. If folks in the fifties couldn't afford 50 cents, there were other options—35 cents would have been ample for a frankfurter with sauerkraut and a potato or kasha knish. And a hearty bowl of matzo ball soup was just 15 cents. On the other hand, big spenders could opt for a roast chicken dinner with potatoes and vegetable for a whopping $1.25! Mark March 11, 2004, on your calendar right now.

Borscht

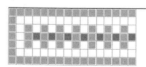

Borscht is best made a day ahead of time. It's much tastier on the second day. Also, because borscht is labor-intensive—and the cooking process tends to leave your kitchen looking as if you've committed a murder in it—we've made this recipe for a large amount. You'll work hard; you deserve leftovers.

SERVES 12

9 medium dark red beets, including
  tops
2 medium onions, peeled and
  halved
1 large whole clove garlic

1 bay leaf
4 tablespoons brown sugar
4 teaspoons salt
¼ cup fresh lemon juice

FOR GARNISH

Boiled potatoes, cut into ½-inch
  cubes
Hard-boiled eggs, sliced

Bunch of fresh dill
Sour cream

1. Cut greens and roots off beets, leaving about 3 inches of stems at the top. Scrub very, very thoroughly with a brush.

2. In a large stockpot, place beets, onions, garlic, bay leaf, and 10 cups of water, and bring to a boil. Cover, reduce heat, and simmer for 1 hour.

3. With a slotted spoon, remove beets to a large bowl and place it in the sink. Discard onion, garlic, and bay leaf.

4. Running cold water over the beets, remove skins and tops. In a food processor, or with a hand grater (a chore that is sure to send you racing to the appliance store for a Cuisinart), mince beets to a fine texture.

5. Because, no matter how thoroughly you washed them, there may be sand in the beets, strain the soup from the pot through a cheesecloth (or use a paper coffee filter), and set aside.

6. Rinse the stockpot, and pour the minced beets into it. Carefully (without splashing) pour the soup over the beets. Add brown sugar and salt, and simmer on low heat for 2 minutes. Add lemon juice, and stir.

7. Serve well chilled. Garnish each bowl with boiled potato, egg slices, ½ teaspoon dill, and a large dollop of sour cream.

Borscht, Ukrainian-Style

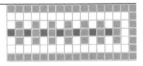

Like the cold borscht above, this recipe should also be prepared a day ahead of time. It's much better on the second day, after the ingredients have mingled.

SERVES 10

1 cup dried large lima beans
6 medium dark red beets
2 tablespoons corn oil
1 cup chopped onions
1 pound stew beef, trimmed of
  all fat and cut into 1-inch
  cubes
1 large bay leaf
1½ teaspoons finely chopped or
  crushed fresh garlic

½ cup plain tomato sauce
1 tablespoon salt
4 cups peeled potatoes, cut into ¾-
  inch cubes
4 cups coarsely chopped green
  cabbage
¼ cup fresh lemon juice
¼ cup brown sugar
2 tablespoons fresh chopped dill

1. Boil dried lima beans in water for 2 minutes, then turn off heat, and leave beans soaking in the water for 1 hour. Alternately, you can soak them overnight.

2. Trim beets of greens, roots, and stems. Peel and wash the beets.

3. Heat corn oil in a large skillet, and sauté onions on high heat for 4 minutes. Add beef cubes, and continue to sauté for about 5 minutes more, stirring occasionally, until meat and onions are nicely browned.

4. Drain lima beans, and place in a large stockpot with beets, beef and onions (with cooking juices), bay leaf, and 10 cups of water. Bring to a boil; then reduce heat, and simmer for 30 minutes. Turn off heat.

5. With a slotted spoon, remove beets from the pot, and let cool on a plate. Also use the slotted spoon to skim foam off the top of the soup (do this again later if necessary). When the beets are cool enough to handle, shred them in a food processor (or with a hand grater).

6. Return the beets to the stockpot, and add the garlic, tomato sauce, and salt. Simmer for 1 hour and 15 minutes.

7. Add potatoes, cabbage, lemon juice, and brown sugar. Stir, and simmer for 1 hour. Add chopped dill and stir. Remove bay leaf. Serve hot the next day.

Red Lentil Soup

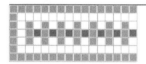

SERVES 10

This is the soup that Jacob prepared to tempt Esau into selling his birthright. See what you can get for it.

6 cups clear chicken soup or stock
3 cups water
4 cups red lentils (about 2 pounds)
2 teaspoons cumin
¹/₄ teaspoon cayenne pepper
2 tablespoons corn oil
2 cups finely chopped onions
1 tablespoon finely chopped or crushed fresh garlic

2 teaspoons coriander powder
Salt (the amount will depend on how much salt is in the chicken stock you use; if it's salty, you may not need any)
¹/₄ teaspoon pepper
Lemon slices and fresh chopped parsley for garnish

1. In a large stockpot, bring chicken soup and water to a boil. Add lentils, cumin, and cayenne. Stir, cover, reduce heat, and simmer 10 minutes.

2. Uncover, and simmer for another 25 minutes, stirring occasionally. Add a small amount of water only if necessary to keep from burning. While soup is cooking, heat corn oil in a skillet, and sauté onions, adding garlic to brown at the last minute. Remove with a slotted spoon, and set aside in a bowl.

3. Add coriander, salt (if needed), and pepper to stockpot. Cook on very low heat for 5 minutes.

THE SECOND AVENUE DELI COOKBOOK

4. Add onions and garlic to soup, and stir in. Garnish each bowl with very thin lemon slices and a bit of parsley.

Note: This is a very thick soup. You can thin it down with a little water if you like.

In the Soup

Soups should yield up all kinds of gustatory pleasures and treasures. In addition to the garlicky croutons, fluffy dumplings, savory kreplach, and feathery matzo balls described below, we often throw in kasha, noodles, or rice.

Croutons

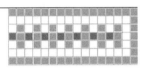

The Deli's croutons are fantastic, and very easy to prepare. Use them to enhance soups or salads.

Corn oil   *Garlic powder*
8 slices white bread, including
crusts, cut into ¾-inch cubes

MAKES ABOUT
4 CUPS

1. Heat corn oil (you'll need enough to cover the bread cubes) in a deep fryer. Deep-fry cubes in the wire basket for 8 to 10 minutes, tossing occasionally until all cubes are equally and fully browned. If you don't own a deep fryer, you can fry the croutons in a large skillet, removing them from the oil with a slotted spoon.
2. Drain in a bowl lined with paper towel, and remove excess oil carefully with additional paper toweling. Let cool for a few minutes, then toss in a large bowl with garlic powder to taste. Store in a covered container, the bottom of which is lined with paper toweling to absorb excess oil.

Some variations on the theme: In addition to garlic powder, toss the croutons with dill, thyme, oregano, or Italian seasoning.

Dumplings

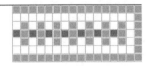

Everyone loves dumplings. Easy to prepare, they make a great alternative to matzo balls for your chicken soup.

2 eggs, beaten   *¼ teaspoon nutmeg*
4 tablespoons (½ stick) melted   *½ teaspoon salt*
margarine (let cool a bit after   *1 cup sifted flour*
melting, so it doesn't cook the   *½ teaspoon baking powder*
eggs)   *½ teaspoon salt for cooking water*

MAKES
ABOUT 35

1. Combine eggs, margarine, nutmeg, and salt in a large bowl, and mix thoroughly with a fork. Add flour and baking powder, mixing first with a fork, then with your hands until it forms a soft dough. Do not overknead.

2. On a well-floured board, using a floured rolling pin, roll out half of the dough at a time to ⅓-inch thickness. Using a 1-inch cookie cutter (or a bottle lid), cut out circles and place them, one at a time, on a wax-paper-covered plate.

3. Fill a large stockpot with water and ½ teaspoon salt, and bring to a boil. Use a knife to slide the dumplings from the plate into the boiling water. Cook for 6 minutes, and drain in a colander.

4. Toss into hot chicken soup, and serve.

Note: Before you add them to your soup, you can also sauté these dumplings in hot corn oil for a few minutes, until they turn a very light golden color. The idea is not to brown them, but to add a bit of crispiness. Drain on paper toweling before putting them in soup.

Another alternative: Cut your dough into small circles (⅛ inch high and ½ inch in diameter), or ½-inch squares, to create spaetzle; these need cook for only 2 minutes. They can also be sautéed as described above. Serve as a side dish with your entrée.

Finally, for a dairy meal, use butter instead of margarine in your dough, and sauté the dumplings or spaetzle in 1 tablespoon of butter. In another pan, sauté ½ cup of finely chopped onions in ⅓ cup of butter, and use as a sauce. Season the dumplings or spaetzle with salt and pepper to taste, and serve with sour cream.

Kreplach

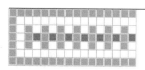

MAKES ABOUT 30

Called Jewish wontons or raviolis, kreplach are pasta dumplings, usually triangular in shape, filled with minced meat, onion-spiced potatoes, or cheese. Kreplach carries a lot of lofty symbolism; its triangular shape represents Judaism's three patriarchs: Abraham, Isaac, and Jacob. Equally lofty: the Jewish momma who can roll her kreplach dough to optimum thinness (so that, according to Sam Levenson, "a tempting bit of their buried treasure should show through"). If the wrappers are not paper-thin, your kreplach will taste like "craplach." However, though we've included wrappers in this recipe, there's really no reason to knock yourself out making them. Just purchase wonton wrappers in a Chinese food store or supermarket, and making kreplach becomes a cinch. There's even a kosher brand called Nasoya, available in many supermarkets; look for it near the tofu.

WRAPPERS

3 cups flour	*3 tablespoons cold water*
1 teaspoon salt	*1 egg, beaten, for binding kreplach*
3 eggs, beaten	*1 tablespoon salt*

1. Prepare a filling (see options below) and refrigerate before you begin preparing dough. Sift flour and 1 teaspoon salt into a large bowl, and create a well in the center.
2. Pour eggs into the well, and, wetting your hands, knead into a dough. Add water, and continue kneading until dough is smooth. Roll dough into a ball, place it in a bowl, cover the bowl with a damp cloth, and refrigerate for 30 minutes.
3. On a well-floured board, roll dough as close as possible to paper-thinness with a floured rolling pin. Cut into 2-inch squares. You can roll each individual square a bit thinner before you fill it. Have bowl with beaten egg, a teaspoon, and filling at hand.
4. Place a flatware teaspoon of filling in the center of the square and fold diagonally to create a triangle. Seal sides with egg mixture.
5. Bring a pot of water to a vigorous boil, add 1 tablespoon salt, drop in the kreplach, and cook for 20 minutes. Serve in chicken soup or, for dairy fillings, with sour cream and fried onions.

VARIOUS FILLINGS

MEAT FILLING

2 tablespoons corn oil	*2 tablespoons finely chopped fresh*
³/₄ cup finely chopped onion	*parsley*
½ pound chopmeat	*1 teaspoon salt*
1 egg yolk	*¼ teaspoon pepper*

1. Heat corn oil in a skillet, sauté onions until nicely browned, remove with a slotted spoon, and set aside. Add meat to the pan and sauté on high heat, stirring frequently until all meat is browned. Put the onions back in, and sauté with meat, stirring constantly for 1 minute. Let cool.
2. In a bowl, thoroughly mix meat-onion mixture with all remaining ingredients.

POTATO FILLING

2 tablespoons corn oil	*1 cup cooked, mashed potato*
³/₄ cup finely chopped onion	*2 tablespoons minced fresh parsley*
1 teaspoon finely chopped or	*1 tablespoon minced scallions*
crushed fresh garlic	*1 teaspoon salt*
1 egg yolk	*¼ teaspoon pepper*

1. Heat corn oil in a skillet, and sauté onions until nicely browned. At the last minute, add garlic, which browns quickly.

2. In a large bowl, combine onion-garlic mixture with all other ingredients, and blend thoroughly.

CHEESE FILLING
1 cup farmer cheese   *1 egg, beaten*
¼ cup sugar

1. Combine all ingredients in a bowl, and blend thoroughly.

Matzo Balls

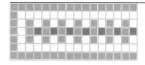

MAKES 12 TO 14

Abe experimented until he came up with the lightest, fluffiest, most Jewish-motherly matzo balls imaginable.

1 tablespoon plus ¼ teaspoon salt   *¼ teaspoon pepper*
4 large eggs   *1 tablespoon baking powder*
⅓ cup schmaltz   *1⅓ cups matzo meal*

1. Fill a large, wide stockpot three-quarters full of water, add 1 tablespoon of the salt, and bring to a rapid boil.
2. While water is boiling, crack eggs into a large bowl and beat thoroughly. Beat in schmaltz, ¼ teaspoon salt, pepper, and baking powder. Slowly fold in matzo meal, mixing vigorously until completely blended.
3. Wet hands and, folding the mixture in your palms, shape perfect balls about 1¼ inches in diameter (they will double in size when cooked). Gently place the matzo balls in the boiling water, and reduce heat to a simmer. Cook for 25 minutes. Remove with a slotted spoon and place 1 or 2 in each bowl of soup. Serve immediately.

AWARD-WINNING AUTHOR and food critic Mimi Sheraton began her career as a home furnishings writer for *Good Housekeeping*. However, it wasn't long before this child of a food-loving Brooklyn family (her mother was a great cook, her father in the wholesale fruit and produce business) found her true bent and became *Seventeen* magazine's food editor. Though best known as the restaurant critic for *The New York Times* (from 1975 to 1983), she also has written for many major magazines (*New York, Town & Country, Time, Condé Nast Traveler, Esquire, Harper's Bazaar, Vogue*, et al.), lectured widely, and authored a dozen books on food and travel, among them *From My Mother's Kitchen: Recipes and Reminiscences, The Whole World Loves Chicken Soup,* and *Food Markets of the World.*

Because as a restaurant critic I always tried to remain incognito, I never got to sit down and have a face-to-face schmooze with Abe, although we had several long telephone conversations—generally about the fine points of kashruth or New York's changing deli scene. But he never recognized me, and one day when I needed a chicken soup fix, I was seated within hearing distance of Abe explaining Jewish food to a young Japanese journalist. The idea of matzo balls stumped her, and to completely explain them, Abe had to go into matzos, Passover, the Exodus from Egypt, and, as far as I could tell, the entire Old Testament. Only when she tasted one did a glow of understanding come over her face.

Mimi Sheraton's Favorite Matzo Balls

MAKES ABOUT 12

3 extra-large eggs
6 tablespoons cold water
3 heaping tablespoons solidified
    schmaltz
1/2 to 1 teaspoon salt
Pinch of ground white pepper, to
    taste

2/3 to 3/4 cup matzo meal
2 tablespoons finely minced parsley
    leaves or 1 tablespoon finely
    minced dill
Handful of coarse kosher salt

1. Using a fork, beat eggs with cold water. Stir in schmaltz until it dissolves. Add salt and a pinch of pepper.
2. Gradually mix in matzo meal, 2 tablespoons at a time, until mix is the consistency of soft mashed potatoes and is a little spongy. Add salt and pepper as needed. Stir in parsley or dill. Cover bowl loosely, and chill for 5 to 7 hours.
3. About 30 minutes before serving time, remove matzo ball mix from refrigerator. Bring about 3 quarts of water to a boil, and add the handful of kosher salt. Wet the palms of both hands, and shape the mixture into balls about 1 inch in diameter. Drop gently into boiling water. Cover pot loosely, and boil at a moderately brisk pace for about 25 minutes, or until 1 ball tests done. Remove all carefully with a slotted spoon. Serve in chicken soup, allowing 2 matzo balls per serving.

3

MEATS:
BRISKETS,
STEWS,
AND BEEF
CHOLENT

THESE SUCCULENT STEWS, roasts, and piquantly spiced meat dishes are among our heartiest entrées. Slowly baked in casseroles or simmered in large stockpots, they'll suffuse your kitchen with wonderful aromas. Most of these well-stewed entrées were developed by Eastern European Jews, because the tough and sinewy cheaper cuts of meat they could afford required hours of cooking to become tender. But that's not the whole story; other meat recipes hail from the abundant sheep-producing regions of the Middle East, where lamb is traditional spring fare and the featured entrée at Sephardic Seders. Some entrées in this chapter are suitable for an elegant dinner party, while others consist of everyday dishes like meat loaf, corned beef hash, and potted meatballs.

Brisket

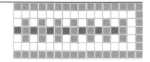

"If you buy 15 briskets, each one will be different. The man who slices it, he can't be a robot. When it's a little softer, he cuts it thicker; when it's a little harder, he cuts it thinner. When a person cuts a piece of meat, it's got to be in him. It's instinctive."

—*Abe Lebewohl*

SERVES 6

This cut of beef, taken from the front breast section, is a traditional holiday meat. It requires long, slow cooking to become a richly flavored, tender dish. The Deli's brisket needs to be marinated in spices for at least a day in advance of cooking, so plan ahead. Spice it in the morning and let it marinate overnight before cooking.

3 tablespoons onion powder
3 tablespoons garlic powder
3 tablespoons paprika
1 tablespoon salt
3/4 teaspoon pepper
1 teaspoon celery salt

1 4-pound brisket
4 tablespoons corn oil
1/2 cup water
3 cups chopped onion
2 tablespoons finely chopped or
    crushed fresh garlic

1. In a bowl, combine onion powder, garlic powder, paprika, salt, pepper, and celery salt; mix thoroughly. Dredge the brisket in this spice mixture, making sure every part of it is well covered. Place in a deep dish covered with aluminum foil, and refrigerate for 1 or 2 days.

2. Heat 2 tablespoons of the corn oil in a large skillet, and brown the meat on both sides.

3. Transfer brisket to a Dutch oven, add ½ cup water, cover, and simmer for 1 hour.

4. While meat is simmering, heat remaining 2 tablespoons corn oil in a large skillet, and sauté onions, stirring occasionally. When the onions are nicely browned, add garlic, which browns quickly.

5. Add onions and garlic to brisket pot. Cover, and continue simmering for 2½ hours, or until meat is fully cooked. To test for doneness, stick a fork in the leaner end of the brisket; when there is a slight pull on the fork as it is removed from the meat, it is done. Cook longer if necessary.

6. Remove brisket to a plate, and trim all visible fat. Then place the brisket (with what was the fat side down) on a cutting board, and carve thin slices across the grain (the muscle lines of the brisket) with a sharp, thin-bladed knife. Serve hot with gravy from the pot or cold in sandwiches.

Brisket with Potatoes, Carrots, and Prunes

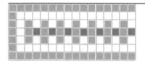

SERVES 6

This variation on the Deli's basic brisket recipe (directly above) is the kind of dish that becomes a staple when you're cooking for company; it's richly satisfying and impressive. It, too, needs to be marinated in spices for at least a day in advance of cooking, so plan ahead. Prepare as the above recipe through step 3; use the same ingredients, but omit the celery salt.

2 tablespoons corn oil
3 cups chopped onion
2 tablespoons chopped fresh or
 crushed garlic
½ cup honey
4 pounds red potatoes, peeled and
 chopped into ¾-inch chunks

2 cups carrots, diced into ½-inch
 pieces
1½ teaspoons fresh or dried basil
½ cup brown sugar
½ pound pitted prunes

1 to 3. Follow steps of brisket recipe above, using the same ingredients except for the celery salt.

4. While meat is simmering, heat 2 tablespoons of corn oil in skillet, and sauté onions, stirring occasionally. When the onions are nicely browned, add garlic, which browns quickly. Remove onions and garlic to a bowl, and set aside.

5. Add honey to the brisket pot, and stir it into the juices. Cover, and continue simmering for 30 minutes. (If you rub your measuring cup with vegetable oil, the honey will slide right out of it.)

6. In a large bowl, mix raw potatoes and carrots, basil, and onion-garlic mixture. Add to the pot, cover, and continue simmering for 1 hour.

7. Remove vegetables to a large bowl, and place brisket on a plate, leaving the meat juices in the pot. Add brown sugar, and stir in. Add prunes. Return half of the vegetables to the pot (it's best to put the ones that were previously on top, and are less cooked, on the bottom), place brisket on top of them, and pile the remaining vegetables on it. Cover, and simmer 1 hour longer, or until everything is fully cooked. To test for doneness, stick a fork in the leaner end of the brisket; when there is a slight pull on the fork as it is removed from the meat, it is done.

8. Remove brisket to a plate, and trim all visible fat. Then place the brisket (with what was the fat side down) on a cutting board, and carve thin slices across the grain (the muscle lines of the brisket) with a sharp, thin-bladed knife. Stir vegetable-prune mixture in pot to thoroughly combine flavors. If you'd like the brisket a bit hotter, place the slices on top of the vegetables, cover, and reheat.

CBS NEWS CORRESPONDENT MORLEY SAFER joined the network (at its London Bureau) in 1964 and has been a co-editor of *60 Minutes* since 1970. His experiences as head of the CBS Saigon Bureau during the Vietnam War years are described in his best-selling book *Flashbacks: On Returning to Vietnam*. Winner of numerous journalism awards, Safer is the recipient of nine Emmys and three Overseas Press Club Awards. In 1995, he was named a Chevalier dans l'Ordre des Arts et des Lettres by the French government for his outstanding contribution to the world of art and letters.

My mother, Anne Safer, was a remarkably inventive chef. Our house was a kosher one, but Mother never felt restricted in any way. Beyond traditional dishes, she loved to experiment. And even with traditional dishes, she added a flair that made our home a sought-after haven for all of our school friends whose own kitchens were a little less inviting. The Safer house was a spice island of delight in a sea of starchy blandness.

My sister, Esther Fisher, inherited Mother's gourmet gene. Like all great cooks, the real pleasure she gets comes from witnessing the delight others take in digging into her creations. This pleasure was also the essence of Abe. Of course, he witnessed it every day, with not dozens, but thousands—hundreds of thousands—of people, who felt more like dinner guests than mere customers. A truly great man, a great gourmet, and a great and generous person.

The recipe I've chosen is a family favorite. I know it is one that Abe would heartily endorse.

Anne Safer's Brisket

SERVES 8

4 large onions, unpeeled and sliced
   (the skins give a lovely golden-
   brown color to the gravy)
5-pound brisket

Salt
Pepper
3 cloves garlic, peeled and crushed
2 tablespoons pickling spice

1. Preheat oven to 375 degrees. Place onion slices on the bottom of a Dutch oven or roasting pan.

2. Season brisket by rubbing salt, pepper, and crushed garlic into both sides of the meat. Place brisket on onions, distribute pickling spice under and around the meat, cover, place in oven, and roast for 30 minutes. Lower oven temperature to 325 degrees. Continue cooking for another 2½ to 3 hours, basting several times with pan juices. If juices diminish, add a small amount of water. (*Note:* To test for doneness, stick a fork in the leaner end of the brisket; when there is a slight pull on the fork as it is removed from the meat, it is done.)

3. When done, remove meat, and refrigerate separately from gravy until both are cold. Skim fat from gravy, return sliced brisket to gravy in pan, and heat on top of the stove before serving.

Meat Loaf

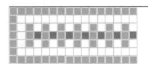

This is a terrific meat loaf, with sophisticated spicing raising it a bit above its prosaic hash house roots. Consider baking hard-boiled eggs into it, as in Raoul Felder's recipe, just below.

SERVES 8

2 tablespoons corn oil
2 cups finely chopped onion
1 tablespoon finely chopped or
   crushed fresh garlic
½ cup green pepper, chopped into
   ¼-inch pieces
7 slices white bread
1½ pounds chopmeat
½ pound chopped veal

2 eggs, beaten
⅓ cup fresh chopped parsley
½ teaspoon fresh or dried crushed
   rosemary
½ teaspoon fresh or dried thyme
1 tablespoon ketchup
1½ teaspoons salt
⅜ teaspoon pepper

1. Heat corn oil in a large skillet, and sauté onions until light golden brown. Add garlic at the last minute, and brown quickly. Remove to a bowl with a slotted spoon, and sauté green peppers in remaining oil. Add to bowl, and refrigerate.

2. Cut crusts off bread, cube, and soften with water in a strainer. Squeeze out excess liquid.

3. Preheat oven to 350 degrees. In a large bowl, thoroughly blend meats and bread, working them together with your hands. Add onion-garlic-green pepper mixture and all other ingredients. Blend thoroughly.

4. Place meat mixture in a loaf pan, and score a crisscross design along the top with a knife. Bake 50 minutes, pour off accumulated fat, and continue baking for 20 minutes more. Serve with mashed potatoes (page 172) or garlic-rosemary roast potatoes (page 170) and a green vegetable.

RAOUL FELDER, perhaps America's best-known divorce attorney, is the author of several books on subjects ranging eclectically from matrimonial and divorce laws to *A Guide to New York and Los Angeles Restaurants*. The *National Law Journal* has called him one of "America's 100 Most Powerful Lawyers."

Abe had a love/hate relationship with food. His preoccupation made for some strange culinary bedfellows, such as Al Goldstein (a frequent dining partner), whose usual field of endeavor is investigating the stuffing of body openings somewhat south of the mouth and with somewhat less gastronomic items. At the mere mention of food—or of a particular dish—Abe's eyes would light up with delight, and he would talk about it with the passion another person might bring to a discussion of a great painting or orchestral work.

He also had a constant weight battle and knew the caloric content of most foods. Once, observing me eating a plain bagel—which I thought was devoid of everything except the capacity to fill one's stomach—he explained to me that a "New York bagel" (he differentiated between an ordinary bagel and the New York variety) was possessed of some hundreds of calories. This destroyed for me what little self-righteous pleasure I might have taken in my virtuous dry bagel.

Abe was ever enthusiastic about food. One day, I was in the Deli with my daughter, Rachel, and she asked him something about pastrami, whereupon he gave us a guided tour of the kitchen, and we both learned more than we ever wanted to know about pastrami, its fat content, et cetera.

Abe was the most generous person imaginable; before a sentence requesting some assistance was finished, it was accomplished. Around Christmas one year, Jackie Mason and I distributed warm clothes and food to homeless people in Tompkins Square Park. Abe showed up with a truck, gave away mountains of food, and was prepared to keep the food flowing until the last unfortunate left. Another time, we were asked by some strikers to supply food for their picket line. Within two hours, Abe was there with his truck handing out food. Personally, I avoided asking Abe to cater office parties, because he absolutely refused to accept payment. His generosity, given so easily and graciously to most anyone who asked, made the manner of his death all the more reprehensible.

The following is a recipe that has long been in my family.

The Felder Family Meat Loaf

SERVES 6

2 pounds ground chuck or top
  round
2 tablespoons matzo meal
¼ cup grated onion
1 teaspoon finely chopped garlic

1 teaspoon salt
Freshly ground pepper to taste
1 raw egg
4 hard-boiled eggs, peeled
4 tablespoons coarse bread crumbs

1. Preheat oven to 375 degrees. With your hands, or a wooden spoon, mix together the beef, matzo meal, onion, garlic, salt, pepper, and raw egg.
2. Pack half the mixture along the bottom of a 5- by 9-inch loaf pan. Arrange the hard-boiled eggs down the center, end to end, pushing them gently into the meat. Pack the remaining mixture into the pan, over the eggs. Sprinkle the bread crumbs evenly on top.
3. Bake the loaf until cooked through, about 1 hour. After 30 minutes, tilt the pan and spoon off the fat. Pour a little of the clear juice over the top of the loaf. Near the end of the cooking time, spoon off fat again. If you choose, briefly place the loaf under the broiler to further brown the bread crumbs.
4. Let the loaf rest in its pan for about 20 minutes to settle before serving.

Potted Meatballs

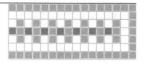

Okay, we admit it. Our menu's potted meatballs are baked in the oven, not cooked in a pot. We have no idea why Abe listed them as potted on the menu.

8 slices white bread, including crusts
2½ pounds chopmeat
2 cups grated onion (chop them to a grated texture in your food processor or put them through a meat grinder; then place them in a colander and press out extra moisture)
3 eggs, beaten
2 teaspoons garlic powder
1½ teaspoons salt
¼ teaspoon pepper

1. Cut bread slices in quarters, place them in a colander, and lightly moisten bread with water (don't drench it; just use enough water to make it doughy). Squeeze out excess moisture, and place bread in a large bowl with chopmeat. Knead bread and meat together thoroughly with your hands until there are no bready lumps. For best results, working in batches, combine bread and meat in a food processor.
2. Preheat oven to 350 degrees. Add all other ingredients, and mix well.
3. Roll out meatballs that are 2½ inches in diameter. Place them in a baking dish at least 2 inches deep, and bake them for 10 minutes. Add a cup of water to the baking dish, and bake them for another 30 minutes or until browned. Serve hot or cold, as an entrée or in sandwiches.

Abe with Joel Grey and Bob Hope

Meatballs and Cabbage

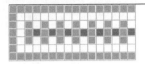

SERVES 6

We're not sure how it happened, but a lot of Jewish recipes use cranberry sauce for piquant sweetening. If the ingredients in this recipe sound like an odd combination, we assure you, once you've tried it, you'll want it again and again. Sharon's kids demand it on a regular basis.

2 cups (16 ounces) plain tomato sauce
1 16-ounce can Ocean Spray whole-berry cranberry sauce
3/4 cup golden raisins
2 tablespoons brown sugar
2 pounds chopmeat
8 slices white bread
2 eggs, beaten

1 cup very finely chopped onion
1/2 cup very finely chopped fresh parsley
1 1/2 teaspoons salt
1 cup flour for dredging meatballs
1 tablespoon corn oil for frying meatballs
1 small green cabbage (about 4 pounds), cut into 3-inch chunks

1. In a large bowl, mix tomato sauce, cranberry sauce, raisins, and brown sugar. Set aside.
2. Place chopmeat in a large bowl. Cut crusts off the bread, cube, soften with water in a strainer, and drain off excess liquid. Using your hands, work the bread thoroughly into the meat. Add eggs, onion, parsley, and salt; still using your hands, blend thoroughly.
3. Pour flour into a shallow pan or dish. Form meatballs about 2 inches in diameter, coat them thoroughly with flour, and place them (without stacking) on a large plate.
4. Heat corn oil in a large, deep skillet, and brown meatballs (reflour them if they're not sturdy enough) on medium heat. Don't crowd so many meatballs into the pan that you won't be able to turn them; use 2 pans, or work in batches.
5. Carefully transfer the browned meatballs to a large stockpot. Add chopped-up cabbage to the sauce and pour it over the meatballs. Cover, and simmer for 1 hour. Do not add water. Serve with broad noodles.

Meatballs in Homemade Tomato Sauce

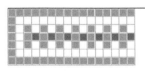

SERVES 6

FOR THE MEATBALLS (MAKES ABOUT 20)
1 pound ground beef
1 pound ground veal
1/4 cup matzo meal
2 teaspoons garlic powder
2 eggs, beaten

1/4 cup clear chicken soup or stock
2 tablespoons ketchup
1/4 teaspoon pepper
Flour for dredging
1 tablespoon corn oil

1. Using your hands, thoroughly mix beef, veal, and matzo meal in a large bowl. Add all other ingredients except flour and corn oil, and, still using your hands, mix in thoroughly. Pour about ¾ cup flour into a separate bowl. Form meatballs about 1½ inches in diameter, and dredge them well in flour. Heat corn oil in a large skillet, and sauté meatballs until brown and crispy, turning once with a fork (you'll probably have to do this in two batches). Refrigerate meatballs in a covered dish until needed.

FOR THE SAUCE

6 large ripe red tomatoes	*¼ cup finely chopped fresh basil*
¼ cup extra-virgin olive oil	*5 sun-dried tomatoes*
2 cups finely chopped onion	*1 16-ounce can tomato paste*
2 tablespoons finely chopped or crushed fresh garlic	*¼ teaspoon sugar*
2 teaspoons finely chopped fresh thyme	*1½ teaspoons salt*
	¼ teaspoon pepper
	1 bay leaf

1. Place tomatoes in vigorously boiling water (enough to cover) for about 40 seconds (until the skin begins to peel), and remove them to a plate. Remove tomato skins under cold running water. Let tomatoes cool. Remove and discard seeds (they add a bitter taste to your sauce).
2. Heat olive oil in a large skillet, and sauté onions until brown. At the last minute, add garlic, and brown quickly. Set onions and garlic aside in a large stockpot, including the cooking oil.
3. Blend tomatoes and all other remaining ingredients—except bay leaf, onion-garlic mixture, and meatballs—in a food processor.
4. Pour sauce into stockpot with onions and garlic, add ½ cup water and bay leaf, and simmer, stirring occasionally, for 30 minutes.
5. Add meatballs to pot, cover, and simmer 10 minutes. Remove bay leaf. Serve with spaghetti or other pasta.

Tzimmes with Meatballs

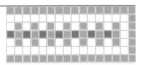

SERVES 7

Tzimmes (see also page 184) is traditionally served at Rosh Hashanah (Jewish New Year) to symbolize a sweet year ahead. There are infinite varieties, but the most common combine fruits with sweet and/or white potatoes, carrots (the coin-shaped pieces represent prosperity), cinnamon, and prunes. Some versions also feature chicken or beef. In Yiddish, to make a tzimmes means to make a big deal or a fuss over something . . . or over nothing. Someone complaining about a minor annoyance might be told "So, don't make such a big tzimmes out of it." Or you might make a big tzimmes over (meaning to honor) an esteemed guest. If you look at the recipe below, you'll see why a tzimmes has come to mean a fuss. It's a complex, multi-ingredient stew, the preparation of which involves a lot of peeling, dicing, and chopping. But the results more than justify the effort.

1 tablespoon corn oil
1 tablespoon schmaltz (use a
   second tablespoon of corn oil if
   you don't have schmaltz)
3 cups chopped onion
1 tablespoon finely chopped or
   crushed fresh garlic
2 cups peeled McIntosh apples, cut
   into ¾-inch slices, ¼-inch thick
1 cup carrots, diced into ½-inch
   pieces
2 cups peeled sweet potatoes, diced
   into ¾-inch pieces

2 cups peeled white potatoes, diced
   into ¾-inch pieces
1 cup dried, pitted prunes, halved
½ cup fresh pineapple, diced into
   ¾-inch pieces (if you use
   canned, make sure it's
   thoroughly drained)
¼ teaspoon cinnamon
2 cups plain chicken soup or stock
1 teaspoon salt
¼ teaspoon pepper

1. Prepare your meatballs first (see below). Heat corn oil and schmaltz in a skillet, and sauté onions until browned. Add garlic, and brown at the last minute. Remove with a slotted spoon to a large stockpot, and set aside. In remaining oil (add a little if necessary), sauté apples until they're soft and a light, golden hue. Remove to a small bowl, and set aside on counter.
2. Add all remaining ingredients—except meatballs and apples—to stockpot. Stir well, bring to a boil, cover, reduce heat, and simmer for 20 minutes, stirring halfway through.
3. Add meatballs, cover, and simmer another 10 minutes. Add apples and stir.

FOR THE MEATBALLS (MAKES ABOUT 20)
1 pound ground beef
1 pound ground veal
¼ cup matzo meal
2 teaspoons garlic powder
2 eggs, beaten

¼ cup clear chicken soup or stock
2 tablespoons ketchup
¼ teaspoon pepper
Flour for dredging
1 tablespoon corn oil

1. Using your hands, thoroughly mix beef, veal, and matzo meal in a large bowl. Add all other ingredients except flour and corn oil, and, still using your hands, mix in thoroughly. Pour about ¾ cup flour into a separate bowl. Form meatballs about 1½ inches in diameter, and dredge them well in flour. Heat corn oil in a large skillet, and sauté meatballs until brown and crispy, turning once with a fork (you'll probably have to do this in two batches). Place meatballs on a flat plate covered with aluminum foil, and refrigerate until needed.

Rozanne Gold's Coffee and Vinegar Pot Roast

Many of my favorite recipes come from community cooks who are never shy about displaying their naïveté. My adaptation of a dish originally known as "Lutheran Ladies Peking Beef Roast" says to "burn on both sides and douse with coffee." Improbable perhaps, but delicious. (See page 41 for another Rozanne Gold recipe.)

5 pounds chuck roast or bottom round
1 cup white wine vinegar

2 cups strong, hot black coffee

1. Put the meat in a large metal bowl, and pour the vinegar over it. Refrigerate it 24 to 48 hours, turning several times.

2. Remove the meat from the marinade, reserving the vinegar. Pat the meat dry with paper towels, and brown it in a heavy pot until nearly burned on both sides. The meat will generate its own fat.

3. Pour the coffee and 1 cup water over the roast, and scrape up the browned bits with a wooden spoon, incorporating them into the sauce. Add 2 tablespoons whole black peppercorns and ½ teaspoon salt. Cover, and cook slowly for 3½ hours, or until fork-tender. Turn several times during cooking. Remove the meat, and keep warm.

4. Add the reserved vinegar, and cook the liquid over high heat until you have about 3 cups. Add salt and freshly ground pepper to taste. Thinly slice meat, and simmer in the gravy for ½ hour longer.

Adapted from *Recipes 1-2-3: Fabulous Food Using Only 3 Ingredients* (Viking Penguin © 1996).

Roast Beef

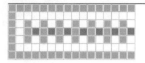

SERVES 8

You can follow this recipe for a roast beef of any size. We like to make a large one, so there are plenty of leftovers for cold sandwiches on rye slathered with mayo or mustard.

Note: The Deli's roast beef needs to be marinated in spices for at least 8 hours in advance of cooking, so plan ahead.

1 5-pound roast beef
2 tablespoons onion powder
2 tablespoons garlic powder
2 tablespoons paprika

1½ teaspoons celery salt
3 teaspoons salt
1 teaspoon freshly ground pepper

1. Pat roast dry with paper towels. Combine all remaining ingredients thoroughly, and rub well into the roast beef. Refrigerate for at least 8 hours to marinate before cooking.

2. Preheat oven to 350 degrees. Place roast, fat side up, in a large roasting pan. Roast meat for 1 hour and 40 minutes (if you use a different-sized roast, allow 20 minutes per pound). This will give you a medium-rare roast like we serve in the Deli. For a rare roast, 16 to 18 minutes per pound will suffice, 25 to 30 minutes for well done.

Boiled Beef in a Pot

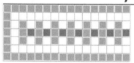

SERVES 6

4 pounds flanken
10 cups plain chicken soup
2 medium onions, peeled and
    quartered
3 stalks celery, chopped into 3-inch
    pieces
2 whole carrots

Salt (the amount will depend on
    how much salt is in the chicken
    stock you use; if it's salty, you
    may not need any)
¼ teaspoon pepper
½ pound egg noodles

1. Place all ingredients, except noodles, in a very large, wide-bottomed stockpot. Bring soup to a boil, reduce heat, cover, and simmer for 2 hours or longer, until the meat is fork-tender.

2. While flanken is simmering, cook noodles. Rinse, drain, and set aside.

3. Strain soup to remove the celery and onions. Return soup, meat, and carrots (cut into pieces) to the pot. Add noodles, and heat briefly. Divide the flanken into equal portions, and serve it in the soup.

Pepper Steak

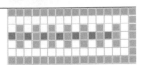

SERVES 6

6 tablespoons corn oil
2 pounds London broil, cut into ¼-inch slices (cut slices into pieces no larger than about 2 inches square; use sirloin for a more deluxe version)
3 cups coarsely chopped onions
1 tablespoon chopped or crushed fresh garlic

2 large green peppers, cut into approximately 1½-inch chunks (be sure to remove entire spine)
3 cups plain chicken soup or stock
2 tablespoons soy sauce
¼ teaspoon pepper
2 tablespoons cornstarch
3 tablespoons cold water

1. In a large skillet, heat 2 tablespoons of the oil, and brown the steak pieces evenly (you'll need to do this in batches). Remove with a slotted spoon, and set aside in a large bowl.
2. Clean skillet, or use another one. Heat 2 tablespoons oil, and sauté the onions until nicely browned. At the last minute, add garlic, and brown quickly. Remove with a slotted spoon to a separate large bowl. Add 2 tablespoons oil, and sauté green peppers in a covered skillet, stirring occasionally to brown them evenly. Remove with a slotted spoon, and add to bowl with onions and garlic. Set aside.
3. Return steak to the skillet, add chicken soup, and bring to a boil. Reduce heat, cover, and simmer on a low flame for 35 minutes, or until meat is tender. Add the onions, garlic, and green peppers, and continue simmering, uncovered, 5 minutes longer. Add soy sauce and pepper, and stir in.
4. In a bowl, dissolve cornstarch by mixing it thoroughly in cold water; set aside. Strain contents of skillet in a colander over a large bowl. Return all solids to skillet. Retain 1 cup pan juices (discard rest), and mix it, a little at a time, with cornstarch, stirring until smooth. Pour thickened juices back into the skillet, and boil for 1 minute. Serve with rice, egg barley, or kasha varnishkes.

Honey Beef

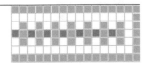

SERVES 6

½ teaspoon ginger
½ teaspoon cinnamon
1 teaspoon poultry seasoning
2 teaspoons onion powder
2 teaspoons garlic powder
2 teaspoons salt
¼ teaspoon pepper
2½ pounds stew beef, trimmed of fat and diced into 1-inch cubes

3 tablespoons olive oil
12 large cloves garlic, peeled
4½ cups chopped onion
1 tablespoon finely chopped or crushed fresh garlic
¼ teaspoon saffron
4 cloves
¾ cup honey
½ cup water

Note: You can also make this dish with lamb instead of beef.

1. In a large bowl, thoroughly combine ginger, cinnamon, poultry season-ing, onion powder, garlic powder, salt, and pepper. Toss beef cubes well in this spice mixture. Cover bowl, and refrigerate for at least 6 hours.

2. In a large skillet, heat 3 tablespoons olive oil and sauté whole garlic cloves until golden brown. Remove with a slotted spoon to a small bowl, and set aside. On high heat, sauté onions in remaining oil, stirring occa-sionally, until they're a light, golden brown. At the last minute, add chopped fresh garlic to brown. Set onion-garlic mixture aside in a separate bowl.

3. In remaining oil (add a bit if necessary), brown beef cubes on high heat, turning once. (Since the meat cubes won't brown evenly if they're piled up, you may have to do this in batches.)

4. Place beef and garlic cloves in a large stockpot or Dutch oven. Add saf-fron, cloves, and ¼ cup honey (if you rub the measuring cup with vegetable oil, it will slide right out), mixing everything well. Add ½ cup water, cover, and simmer 30 minutes. Preheat oven to 350 degrees, and continue to sim-mer 10 minutes longer.

5. Remove beef cubes with a slotted spoon, and place them on the bottom of a deep baking dish or a lidded casserole with a steam hole (if you don't have one, a cover of aluminum foil with two ½-inch holes poked in it will do). Cover beef with onion-garlic mixture, and pour sauce on top of every-thing. Bake 30 minutes. While you're baking, heat ½ cup of the honey in the top of a double boiler or in a saucepan on a very, very low heat.

6. Pour heated honey into baking dish, stir into other ingredients, re-cover with foil, and bake another 25 minutes or until beef is fork-tender. Remove beef, onions, and garlic cloves with a slotted spoon. Discard the juice, which is too sweet to make a good gravy. Serve with garlic-rosemary roast pota-toes (see recipe on page 170) or rice and a vegetable.

Hungarian Beef Goulash

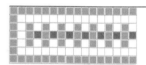

This famous dish dates to the ninth century, when nomadic shepherds (*gulyás*) cooked stews over open fires. Jews, who have lived in Hungary since Roman times, adapted it to their dietary laws, eliminating ingredients like sour cream.

SERVES 6

2 pounds (after fat is trimmed) stew beef, washed, trimmed of fat, and cut into 1-inch cubes
2 tablespoons Hungarian paprika
⅜ cup corn oil
2 cups chopped onion
4 teaspoons (1 tablespoon plus 1 teaspoon) crushed or chopped fresh garlic
½ cup celery, chopped into ½-inch pieces

2 cups green pepper, chopped into ¾-inch pieces
2 bay leaves
¾ cup carrots, chopped into ½-inch pieces, ¼-inch thick
3 pounds red potatoes, peeled and cut into 1-inch chunks
12 ounces tomato paste
1½ teaspoons salt
¼ teaspoon pepper

1. In a large bowl, toss beef cubes in paprika, covering them evenly.

2. Heat corn oil in a skillet, and sauté onions. Remove with a slotted spoon to a small bowl, and set aside. Brown garlic quickly in remaining oil, remove with slotted spoon, and set aside in a different small bowl. Sauté celery in remaining oil (it won't get very brown), remove with slotted spoon, and add to onions. Sauté green pepper in remaining oil (add a bit if necessary), remove with slotted spoon, and set aside in its own small bowl. Finally, sauté beef cubes in remaining oil (do it in batches so that they don't overlap and can brown evenly).

3. Place beef cubes, with pan juices, in a large stockpot (use a tall one, or you'll have a mess later from splattering sauce) with 6 cups water and bay leaves. Bring to a rapid boil. Add carrots, celery, and onions, and simmer for 1 hour.

4. In a separate pot, cook potatoes, drain, and set aside.

5. Add tomato paste, salt, pepper, and sautéed garlic to stockpot with beef cubes. Stir, and simmer for 30 minutes.

6. Add potatoes and green peppers, and stir. Simmer for ½ hour more, or until meat is fully tender and sauce is thick, not liquid.

"The best pastrami is made from beef plate, known as flanken, which is pickled, spiced, and smoked. It must be fat! To me, lean pastrami has no flavor. When fat-phobic customers order their sandwiches 'extra lean,' it annoys me. I satisfy them by placing a few lean slices of corned beef or pastrami on top of the regular fatty sandwich. Psychologically, it helps."

—Abe Lebewohl

Corned Beef Hash

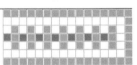

2 pounds very finely chopped corned beef (it's best to use a food processor or grinder)
6 cups peeled boiled red potatoes, chopped into ½-inch pieces
2 tablespoons corn oil
2 cups chopped onion

1 cup green pepper, chopped into ½-inch pieces
2 teaspoons finely chopped or crushed fresh garlic
¼ teaspoon pepper
Shortening for greasing pan

SERVES 6

1. In a large bowl, combine corned beef and diced cooked potatoes. Set aside.

2. Preheat oven to 400 degrees. Heat corn oil in a large skillet, and sauté onions until browned. Remove with a slotted spoon, and add to bowl with corned beef and potatoes. Sauté green peppers in remaining oil (add more if needed), tossing in garlic at the last minute to brown quickly. Remove with

a slotted spoon, and add to bowl with corned beef and other ingredients. Add pepper, and mix in well.

3. Grease a baking pan and spread corned beef mixture about an inch high. Bake for 20 to 25 minutes, until crust is browned (if it's not brown enough, stick it in the broiler briefly). Serve with scrambled, fried, or poached eggs.

BEFORE LARRY FLYNT, before Howard Stern, there was Al Goldstein— a man without equal in the pantheon of American iconoclasts. Best known as the publisher of *Screw* (which he launched in 1968 with an investment of $300), and for cable TV's *Midnight Blue*, Goldstein is also a "writer, photographer, gadget collector, film buff, lifelong atheist, cigar aficionado, and family man." As a journalist, Brooklyn's most irreverent son began his career making the rounds for *The New York Mirror* with famed reporter Walter Winchell. Since those days, his byline has appeared not only in *Screw, Playboy, and Penthouse,* but in *The New York Times, Business Traveler, Harper's,* and *Forbes.* Rampant sexual obsession notwithstanding, Goldstein has always maintained that he'd pass up a roll in the hay (not that he'd ever use such a euphemistic expression; his was more alliterative) for a pastrami sandwich any day. So it's not surprising that he first met Abe when he called the Deli to cater a party at Plato's Retreat.

Abe Lebewohl was the very definition of a man in love with his work, his friends, and his life. The greatest joy in being with Abe wasn't just eating his wonderful food, but in sharing his joy at the moment. He didn't want to be king, he didn't want to be Donald Trump, he only wanted to be Abe.

His Second Avenue Deli produced the most magnificent cholent, pastrami, and corned beef imaginable in a city known for first-class gourmet delis. But Abe wasn't just a deli owner. He was a man who wanted you to eat and be happy. Because to Abe, as to everyone who ate at his deli, eating was happiness!

He always reminded me of the main character in Terry Southern's classic novel *Candy*, a woman who only wanted to give great pleasure to the men in her life. But Abe was not fictional, he was real. He was like a beautiful, magnificent woman who only wanted you to have a wonderful orgasm. He was the nymphomaniac running rampant amidst the sensual delicacies at the Second Avenue Deli. He wanted you to have pleasure. It made him feel wonderful when you felt wonderful.

I was friends with Abe for many years, and he was the most generous man I've ever known. He had a wonderful heart, and he was a great storyteller, although sometimes while hearing the same story for the fifth time, I found myself concentrating less on his words and more on the fantastic food I was eating.

Years ago, after much kvetching about his weight, I told him about my secret place in North Carolina, a health spa called Structure House, which the actor James Coco introduced me to more than twenty years ago. For Abe to even think of losing weight seemed extraordinarily courageous. Away from the smells and the tastes of his palace of the palate, what chance would he have eating steamed fish and boiled spinach? But I saluted his desire to come with me to North Carolina and grab hold of his food excesses.

I went to Structure House the same day that Abe did, so I could introduce him to my friends. Since he was such a social animal, with such a great love for people, I wanted him to feel comfortable with my friends. Still, I knew that within days, if not hours or minutes, his circle of friends would be far bigger than mine.

For the three days I was at Structure House with Abe, I found it impossible to lose weight. He loved the diet program, which consisted of counting calories, writing everything you ate in a food diary, and taking therapy classes. My problem was that every time I saw him, I saw a counterman slicing corned beef and pastrami. It was Pavlovian for me, because Abe equaled great food. Ultimately, I was doomed to failure. Abe did lose weight, but I left.

In the same way that an obese person dreams about ten-thousand-calorie binges, Abe had a gargantuan appetite for life and for his friends. I've missed Abe so much since his death, and I hate the people who took him from me. This is selfish, because such a magnificent, kind man is no longer in the world. But let my words breathe life into him again. Let my memories of Abe vibrate with passion. He was truly one of the most unforgettable characters I have ever met.

Al Goldstein's Favorite Recipe

"Take chopped-up pastrami and corned beef. Add raw garlic, and start chewing."

Lamb Stew

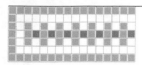

SERVES 6 TO 8

1 tablespoon paprika
2 tablespoons garlic powder
1 tablespoon onion powder
1 tablespoon plus 2 teaspoons salt
1¼ teaspoons pepper
3 pounds lamb shoulder or shank, trimmed of fat and cut into 1-inch cubes (retain bones; buy 4 pounds to end up with 3 pounds of actual meat)
3 tablespoons corn oil
3 cups chopped onion
2 tablespoons finely chopped or crushed fresh garlic
1 cup celery, chopped into ½-inch pieces

1 cup dry red wine (to be used ½ cup at a time)
1 28-ounce can plum tomatoes, including juice (chop tomatoes into chunks)
½ cup clear chicken soup or stock
3 bay leaves
3 pounds Idaho potatoes, peeled and chopped into ¾-inch chunks
2 cups carrots, diced into ½-inch pieces
1 10-ounce package frozen peas
3 tablespoons cornstarch
3 tablespoons cold water

1. In a large bowl, thoroughly mix paprika, garlic powder, onion powder, 1 tablespoon of the salt, and 1 teaspoon of the pepper. Toss lamb cubes in mixture, coating thoroughly, and marinate 6 hours or longer.

2. In a large skillet, heat 2 tablespoons of the corn oil, and sauté onions, stirring occasionally. When browned, add garlic, and sauté quickly. With a slotted spoon, remove onions and garlic to a large bowl. Sauté celery in remaining oil (add a bit more if needed), remove with a slotted spoon, and add to bowl with onions and garlic. Deglaze the pan by pouring ½ cup of the wine into the skillet, and, on low heat, scraping it clean. Pour wine and scrapings into the bowl with onions, garlic, and celery.

3. Heat the remaining tablespoon of corn oil in the same skillet, and brown the lamb cubes (it's best to do it in batches, so all pieces brown evenly). Remove the lamb to a large stockpot, and deglaze the pan once again, using the remaining ½ cup of wine. Pour wine and scrapings into the bowl with onions, garlic, and celery.

4. Add plum tomatoes, chicken soup, and bay leaves to the lamb in the stockpot, and bring to a boil.

5. Add potatoes and carrots. Cover, lower heat, and simmer for 10 minutes.

6. Add onions, garlic, celery, 2 teaspoons of the salt, and ¼ teaspoon of the pepper, and simmer, uncovered, for 15 minutes or until potatoes and carrots are fully cooked. Add peas, and cook for 3 minutes.

7. Place cornstarch in a bowl, and add 3 tablespoons cold water, one at a time, stirring until smooth and all cornstarch is dissolved. Add 1 cup stew juices, a little at a time, and stir until smooth. Bring stew to a boil. Add cornstarch mixture, and, stirring constantly, boil for 2 minutes. Pour lamb stew into a large serving bowl, and toss to mix ingredients thoroughly. Remove bay leaves and any loose bones before serving.

ACCLAIMED RESTAURATEUR Drew Nieporent is the owner (in some cases with celebrity partners like Robert De Niro, Sean Penn, Christopher Walken, Bill Murray, and Mikhail Baryshnikov) of some of New York's hottest restaurants: Montrachet, Tribeca Grill, Nobu, Layla, City Wine & Cigar Co., and TriBakery. His ever-expanding restaurant empire also includes Rubicon in San Francisco (with De Niro, Francis Ford Coppola, and Robin Williams), Nobu London, and FreeStyle, a wine-country restaurant in Sonoma, California. He's currently restoring Minton's Playhouse—an historic Harlem jazz club. And some time in the future, he'd even like to open a Jewish deli.

In June of 1992, I invited famous French *cuisinier* Paul Bocuse to present a formal multicourse wine-pairing dinner at Montrachet. The guests were New York food cognoscenti—major city chefs, reviewers, and restaurateurs. The afternoon of the dinner, I threw an elaborate "Welcome to New York" party for Bocuse in the lovely Urban Archaeology garden on Elizabeth Street (this is a grassy, tree-shaded Gotham oasis that nobody knows about, with a Corinthian colonnade and exquisite fountains and statuary). New York chefs—none of them French—were asked to prepare signature dishes for this afternoon event. Among those present were Mesa Grill's Bobby Flay, David Burke of Park Avenue Café, Shun Lee's Michael Tong, and Abe Lebewohl, who brought, as requested, vast quantities of pastrami. But Abe always went the distance. He surprised me as well with a magnificent chopped liver bust of Bocuse, complete with chef's hat and, around the neck, a ribbon comprised of red pepper strips hung with a lemon slice—for the Légion d'Honneur medal Bocuse wears at all times.

The party had a turn-of-the-century Folies Bergère theme, complete with an accordionist playing Edith Piaf music, a juggler in a striped shirt and beret adroitly tossing vast champagne bottles into the air, and a buxom leopard-bikini-clad fire eater whose act was on the salacious side. Bocuse walked through it all with an air of

French cuisinier *Paul Bocuse contemplating his chopped liver likeness at a party thrown by Drew Nieporent.*

blasé impassivity (he's not one to register great emotion). The only thing that really excited him was Abe's chopped liver sculpture. It was the undisputed hit of the day—though Bobby Flay said the best part of the event was listening to me try to explain to Bocuse in my high school French what the sculpture was made of.

Drew Nieporent's Braised Lamb Shanks with Dried Fruit

SERVES 6

This Passover dish has a dual inspiration: the wonderful garlicky leg of lamb my mother used to prepare for Seders when I was a child and my voyages of culinary discovery in the Middle East.

FOR THE MARINADE
2 cups dry white wine
5 tablespoons olive oil
4 shallots, chopped fine
4 carrots, cut into ¼-inch dice
4 garlic cloves, chopped fine
1 leek (white and pale green part only), halved lengthwise, washed well, and chopped fine

Bouquet garni (composed of 1 bay leaf, 1 fresh thyme sprig, and ¼ bunch fresh parsley sprigs—all tied together in a cheesecloth bag)
1 tablespoon cumin seeds
1 teaspoon coriander seeds

6 lamb shanks (about 6 pounds total)
Salt and pepper
3 tablespoons olive oil
2 tablespoons matzo meal (if you're not preparing this as a Passover dish, substitute flour)
3 medium vine-ripened tomatoes, chopped
2 cups water

4 tart apples, such as Jonathan or Granny Smith
⅓ cup orange juice
6 dried figs, chopped
6 dried pitted dates, chopped
6 dried apricots, chopped
2 tablespoons raisins
1 cup packed fresh mint leaves, washed well, spun dry, and shredded fine

1. Whisk together marinade ingredients, add shanks, and toss to coat. Cover, and marinate in refrigerator for at least 8 hours (or overnight).

2. Preheat oven to 325 degrees. Using tongs, transfer shanks to a plate, pat dry, and season with salt and pepper. Pour marinade through a sieve set over a bowl, and reserve vegetables, liquid, and bouquet garni separately.

3. In a 9- to 10-quart heavy roasting pan or Dutch oven, heat 2 tablespoons of the oil over moderate heat until hot but not smoking, and brown shanks on all sides in batches. Transfer to a plate. Add reserved vegetables, and cook in the oil remaining in pan for 5 minutes, stirring occasionally. Add vegetables to plate with shanks.

4. Add matzo meal to roasting pan, cook over moderately low heat, stirring, for 3 minutes or until smooth. Whisk in the reserved marinade liquid, and add reserved shanks and vegetables, bouquet garni, and tomatoes. Bring mixture to a boil, and simmer, uncovered, 20 minutes or until liquid is reduced by half. Add water. Braise, covered, in middle of oven for 3 hours, or until lamb is tender.

5. While shanks are braising, peel and core apples, and cut into ⅛-inch-thick slices. In a large, heavy skillet, heat remaining tablespoon of oil over moderate heat until hot but not smoking, and cook apples, stirring, for 2 minutes. Add orange juice, and simmer, covered, for 20 minutes. Keep apple mixture warm.

6. Arrange shanks around edge of a large platter, and spoon apple mixture into center. Keep shanks and apple mixture warm.

7. Bring braising liquid to a boil, skimming any fat that rises to surface. Discard bouquet garni. Add dried fruits and mint, and simmer sauce 5 minutes or until fruits are softened. Season sauce with salt and pepper, and spoon over shanks. Serve any remaining sauce separately.

COMEDIAN PAUL REISER'S MOTHER, Helen, and her husband, Sam, met the Lebewohls when their children all attended the same school, the East Side Hebrew Institute. Over the years, they became close friends. One night, the Reisers took Abe and his wife, Eleanor, to Le Petit Auberge, a favorite haunt near their home in Fort Lee, New Jersey. Since the Reisers knew Abe was always on the lookout for new dishes for the Deli, they especially wanted him to try the *spécialité de la maison,* a classic French cassoulet. Everyone watched as Abe took a bite, rolled it around his tongue, and declared, "It's nothing more than cholent."

Cholent

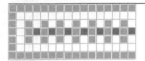

Cholent was probably conceived in Europe many centuries ago, though some Jewish historians claim it's even more ancient, dating back to the days of the Second Temple. A complete meal in a pot, it is traditionally made in advance and enjoyed on the Sabbath, when cooking is forbidden. In the Europe of our great-grandparents, every Friday afternoon, in cities as cosmopolitan as Cracow and Pinsk, to lowly shtetls like Debrecen and Pinchif, Jewish housewives would prepare their cholent *tup* (pot) with all its wonderful ingredients, and then off to the baker's oven it would go. There, the kettles would remain warming until the next day, when they were retrieved for a hearty lunch after morning synagogue services (the word *cholent* may be derived from the easily translatable German words *shule ende*). In modern times, observant Jews leave their Sabbath cholent to simmer all night on the stove or in the oven.

Though cholent is a traditional Sabbath meal, there's no reason not to enjoy this savory stew at any time. The Deli version is what Sharon's grandmother used to call *am g'naiden!*—a taste of Heaven.

Notes: If you are preparing cholent as a Sabbath dish, and plan to keep it warming on the stove or in a 225-degree oven (the optimum method for maximizing flavor, though a few hours will do as well for purely culinary reasons) overnight, you don't need to boil the potatoes in advance as this recipe does. You can prepare cholent several days in advance and keep it in the refrigerator.

See other cholent recipes on pages 111 and 168. Always consider adding eggs (as in Art D'Lugoff's recipe) to any slow oven-baked cholents.

1 tablespoon paprika	*3 cups chopped onions*
1 tablespoon garlic powder	*2 tablespoons finely chopped or*
1 tablespoon onion powder	*crushed fresh garlic*
1 tablespoon plus 2 teaspoons salt	*4 pounds large red potatoes,*
1¼ teaspoons pepper	*peeled, cut into ¾-inch pieces,*
2 pounds stew beef (after fat is	*cooked, and drained*
trimmed), cut into ¾-inch pieces	*1 teaspoon paprika*
6 tablespoons corn oil	*½ cup derma stuffing (optional),*
1 cup Yankee beans	*chopped into ½-inch pieces*
1 cup red beans	

1. In a large bowl, thoroughly mix paprika, garlic powder, onion powder, 1 tablespoon of the salt, and 1 teaspoon of the pepper. Toss beef cubes in mixture, coating thoroughly. Cover bowl, and refrigerate for 4 hours or longer.
2. In a large skillet, heat 2 tablespoons of the corn oil, and brown beef cubes (it's best to do it in batches, so all pieces brown evenly). Set aside.
3. Place Yankee beans and 11 cups of water in a large stockpot; bring to a boil. Add red beans and stew beef, and simmer, uncovered, for 75 minutes.

4. Preheat oven to 300 degrees. While beans and beef are cooking, heat 2 tablespoons of the corn oil in a large frying pan, and sauté onions until brown. At the last minute, add garlic and brown quickly. Set aside in a bowl.

5. Toss potatoes with the 2 remaining tablespoons corn oil and paprika, coating them thoroughly. Bake for 20 minutes. Set aside.

6. Add onions and garlic to the pot. Continue simmering for another 40 minutes.

7. Add derma, 2 teaspoons salt, ¼ teaspoon pepper, and potatoes. Simmer for 20 minutes more, or until everything is fully cooked and almost all the liquid is evaporated. Add a little water only if necessary to keep from burning. Cholent is a very thick stew.

Holishkes (Stuffed Cabbage)

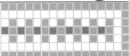

MAKES 7 PIECES

On Succoth, a joyous seven-day autumn harvest festival (a kind of Jewish Thanksgiving), stuffed foods—most notably holishkes, but also also kreplach, stuffed peppers, and strudels—are served to symbolize abundance. Stuffed cabbage has been a staple of Jewish cooking since the fourteenth century, when it was introduced in Russia by Tartars. There are an infinity of recipes for it, both Eastern European and Middle Eastern; ours, in a sweet-and-sour sauce, is of Polish derivation.

Note: When you're confronted with a bin of cabbages, you'll notice that some are quite light, whereas others have the heft of bowling balls. Choose the lightest ones for stuffing; their leaves peel off much more easily.

STUFFING
1½ pounds chopmeat
¾ cup uncooked white rice
1 cup finely chopped onion
2 eggs, beaten
½ cup water

1 tablespoon finely chopped or crushed fresh garlic
2 teaspoons salt
½ teaspoon pepper

SAUCE
2 cups plain tomato sauce
1½ cups finely chopped onion
½ orange, chopped with peel into ½-inch pieces; remove pits
⅔ lemon, chopped with peel into ½-inch pieces; remove pits
½ teaspoon cinnamon
1 cup white sugar
½ cup brown sugar
½ cup white vinegar

2 cups water
1½ teaspoons salt

1 large lightweight young green cabbage
1 medium green cabbage. You'll need 4 cups (if you don't have enough, supplement with leftovers from the large cabbage).

1. In a large bowl, combine all the stuffing ingredients. Stir them with a fork, then mix thoroughly with your hands. Cover and refrigerate.

2. In another bowl, thoroughly mix all sauce ingredients. Cover and refrigerate.

3. Fill a very large stockpot three-quarters full with water and bring to a rapid boil. While bringing the water to a boil, use a thin, sharp knife to make deep cuts around the core of the large cabbage (cut into the cabbage in a circle about ¼ inch out from the core). Lift out the core, making a hole about 2 inches wide and 2½ inches deep. This is a bit difficult—persevere.

4. Set out a baking tray near the stove. Stick a long cooking fork into the core hole of the large cabbage, and plunge it (carefully, so you don't splash yourself) into the pot of rapidly boiling water. The outer leaves will begin to fall off. Leave them in the boiling water for a few minutes until they're limp and flexible enough for stuffing; then take them out one at a time, and place them on the baking tray. Try not to tear the leaves. When all the leaves are on the tray, transfer it into the sink and pour the boiling water from the pot over them. Wash the leaves carefully in cold water. With a small, sharp knife, trim off the tough outer spines and discard them.

5. Find your largest leaves, and set them out on a plate. Set out all other leaves on another plate. One at a time, line each large leaf with another large leaf or two smaller leaves. (The idea is to strengthen your cabbage wrapping so that the stuffing stays securely inside during cooking. Be sure to align the spines of inner and outer leaves.) Stuff with ¾ cup of the meat-rice mixture, roll very tightly along the spine, and close both sides by tucking them in with your fingers. The spine should be vertical in the center of your roll.

6. Stir the 4 cups of chopped cabbage into the sauce. Pour ¾ inch of the sauce into a large, wide-bottomed stockpot. Arrange the cabbage rolls carefully on top of the sauce, and pour the remainder of the sauce over them to cover. Cover pot and simmer for 1 hour and 45 minutes. Serve with boiled potatoes and a vegetable.

Stuffed Baked Eggplant

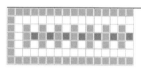

Eggplant, a favorite vegetable in the culinary repertoire of Middle Eastern Jews, is a common ingredient in ground-meat casseroles such as this Persian relative of moussaka.

SERVES 6

3 tablespoons olive oil
½ cup golden raisins
½ cup pine nuts
3 cups finely chopped onions
1 tablespoon finely chopped or
    crushed fresh garlic
1 pound ground meat (beef or
    lamb)
2 cups cooked long-grain rice
    (about ½ cup raw; cook for only
    15 minutes, as it will continue
    cooking in the oven)
3 cups plain tomato sauce

1 tablespoon cinnamon
1 teaspoon salt
¼ teaspoon pepper
4 medium eggplants
Olive oil for brushing eggplant
    slices
Salt
Pepper

1. In a large skillet, quickly sauté raisins in 1 tablespoon of the olive oil, stirring frequently until browned but not burned. Remove with a slotted spoon, and place in a large bowl. In the oil left in the pan, quickly brown the pine nuts and set aside separately from the raisins.

2. Add the remaining 2 tablespoons of olive oil to skillet, and sauté onions, stirring occasionally, until brown. At the last minute, add garlic and brown very quickly. Remove onion-garlic mixture to bowl with the raisins.

3. Add meat to skillet (add a small amount of oil only if needed), and sauté, stirring frequently, and breaking up lumps with a fork, until meat is fully browned and in loose pieces. Drain off oil in a strainer, and add meat to bowl of raisins, onions, and garlic. Add cooked rice, tomato sauce, cinnamon, salt, and pepper. Mix everything thoroughly, and refrigerate until needed.

4. Turn oven setting to broil. Peel the eggplants, and, using a sharp knife, remove stems and cut them into vertical slices about ¼ inch wide. (The easiest way to cut even slices is to cut off the bottom end of your eggplant to create a flat surface, and stand it on end.)

5. Brush both sides of each eggplant slice lightly with olive oil (don't add more if it soaks in), and season them lightly with salt and pepper. Place eggplant slices on a rack (if you have one) atop a cookie sheet; if you don't have a rack, you can place them directly on the cookie sheet. Broil for a few minutes until tops are brown, keeping an eye on them; there's only about a minute's difference between browning and burning. If some slices are browning faster than others, rotate the pan 180 degrees, and continue to broil. Turn slices, and brown the other sides. You'll probably need to do this in batches. Adjust oven temperature to 375 degrees.

6. Using a 10- by 12- by 3-inch (or similiar-sized) casserole dish, place a layer of eggplant slices along the bottom, overlapping them slightly. Continue with a layer of the meat-rice mixture, followed by eggplant slices, another meat-rice layer, and a topping of eggplant slices. Bake for 30 minutes.

7. Sprinkle each portion with toasted pine nuts just prior to serving.

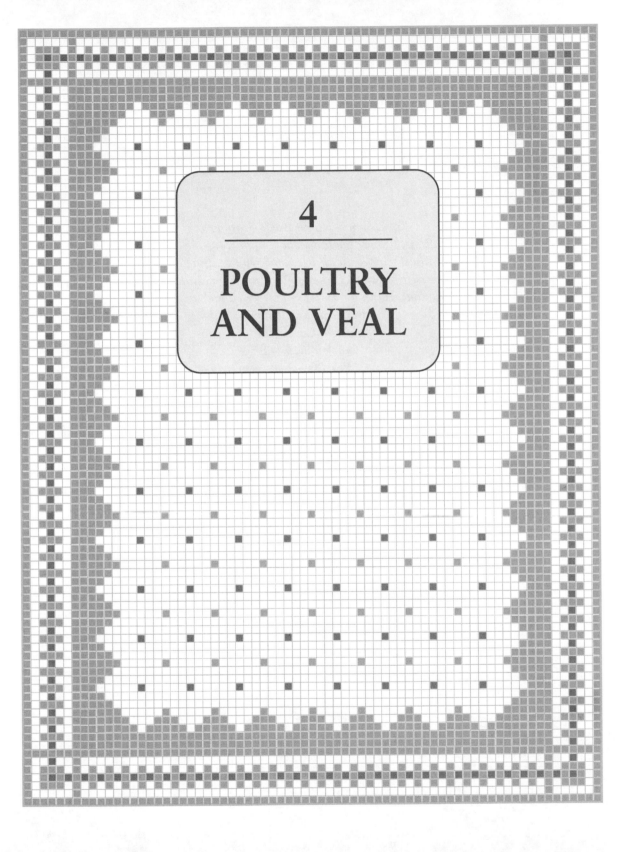

4

POULTRY AND VEAL

Roast Chicken with Bread Stuffing
Roast Chicken with Challah-Apple Stuffing
Roast Chicken with Rice and Fruit Stuffing
Boneless Breast of Chicken with Mushroom Stuffing
Ramona Torres's Arroz con Pollo y Habichuelas
Barbecued Chicken
Chicken Cacciatore
Chicken Paprika
Fried Chicken
Garlic Chicken
Chicken Cutlets
Chicken Fricassee
Cholent with Chicken
Braised Turkey Legs
Roast Turkey with Bread Stuffing
Turkey Meat Loaf
Broiled Chicken Livers
Stuffed Breast of Veal

Poultry is a mainstay of Jewish holiday meals—from golden-skinned roast chickens and turkeys filled with savory stuffings to spicy chicken cholent, a thick stew replete with lima beans, potatoes, and chickpeas. Stuffed breast of veal became a popular entrée at Seders and other festival dinners in nineteenth-century Eastern Europe, because, in those days, it was much cheaper than beef.

Roast Chicken with Bread Stuffing

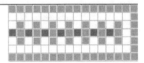

Among religious Jews, roast chicken has always been a frequent Friday-night entrée, because it can be left warming in the oven at a low temperature while Sabbath candles are lit, kiddush is recited, and the challah is blessed. Stuffing the chicken makes for a more festive meal.

Note: The chickens should be marinated in spices for a day in advance of cooking.

SERVES 6

2 roasting chickens

FOR MARINATING THE CHICKEN
4 tablespoons onion powder
4 tablespoons garlic powder
4 tablespoons paprika

2 teaspoons salt
1 teaspoon pepper

FOR BREAD STUFFING
4 tablespoons corn oil
2 cups chopped onion
3/4 cup celery, chopped into 1/2-inch pieces
3/4 cup carrots, chopped into 1/4-inch pieces
3 cups scrubbed mushrooms, chopped into 3/4-inch pieces, 1/4 inch thick

8 cups loosely packed, cubed French or Italian bread
1 tablespoon plus 1 teaspoon poultry seasoning
4 eggs, beaten
2 tablespoons schmaltz (optional)
1 1/2 teaspoons salt
1/4 teaspoon pepper

Action at the take-out counter.

1. Wash the chickens thoroughly in cold water, and clean out their cavities. In a bowl, combine onion powder, garlic powder, paprika, salt, and pepper. Mix thoroughly. Dredge the chickens (outside only) in this mixture, making sure all parts are well covered. Place in a dish covered with aluminum foil, and refrigerate overnight.

2. Preheat oven to 375 degrees. Heat 2 tablespoons of the corn oil in a large skillet, and sauté onions until brown. Remove with a slotted spoon to a large bowl. Add 1 tablespoon corn oil to skillet, and sauté celery and carrots until crisp and lightly browned. Remove with a slotted spoon to the bowl with the onions. Add the remaining 1 tablespoon corn oil to skillet, and brown mushrooms. Remove with a slotted spoon to the bowl with onions.

3. Place bread cubes in a colander, run cool water over them to soften (do not drench), and squeeze out excess liquid. Add bread and all other ingredients to bowl with sautéed vegetables, and mix thoroughly (use your hands).

4. Stuff the mixture into the cavities of the chickens, and tie their legs together with string. (You can further truss with skewers if you have them, but it isn't strictly necessary.) Place in a baking pan with 1 inch of water. Bake, breast up, for 1 hour and 20 minutes (or until the chickens are nicely browned and the legs move easily up and down). Baste every 20 minutes with pan juices. Place extra stuffing in a separate baking dish (see Note below), and bake it along with chickens (for 1 hour only), spooning pan

juices on it every 20 minutes (when you're basting the chickens) to keep it moist. Before serving, combine stuffing cooked outside the chickens with stuffing cooked inside them, add remainder of pan juices, adjust salt to taste, mix thoroughly, and warm briefly on stove if necessary.

Note: Use a deep dish—rather than a large, shallow one—to bake extra stuffing. The outside will form a delicious crust, but you don't want too much crust in relation to stuffing.

Variation: For Passover, make a matzo stuffing by substituting 10 cups of crumbled matzo for the bread cubes.

Roast Chicken with Challah-Apple Stuffing

This is an especially yummy stuffing. Here, too, the chickens need to be marinated in spices for at least a day in advance of cooking, so plan ahead. Follow step 1 of the above recipe, using the same spices.

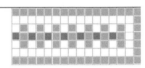

2 roasting chickens

SERVES 8

FOR THE STUFFING
4 tablespoons corn oil
2 cups chopped onion
1 cup celery, chopped into ½-inch pieces
2 McIntosh apples, peeled, cored, and cut into ¾-inch pieces, ¼ inch thick
¾ cup raisins
3 cups scrubbed mushrooms, chopped into ¾-inch pieces, ¼ inch thick

10 cups challah bread (when cubed)
1 tablespoon schmaltz (optional)
2 eggs, beaten
1 tablespoon plus 1 teaspoon poultry seasoning
¾ cup pecan halves
1 teaspoon salt

1. Follow step 1 from preceding recipe.
2. Preheat oven to 375 degrees. Heat 2 tablespoons of the corn oil in a large skillet, and sauté onions until brown. Remove with a slotted spoon to a large bowl. Sauté celery for a few minutes (it doesn't get very brown), and remove with a slotted spoon to the bowl with the onions. Add 1 tablespoon corn oil to the skillet, and sauté apples until lightly browned, adding the raisins when almost finished and browning for 1 more minute. Remove with a slotted spoon to the bowl with onions and celery. Finally, add remaining 1 tablespoon corn oil to skillet (or a bit more if needed), brown the mushrooms, and remove with a slotted spoon to the same bowl.
3. Cut the challah into ¾-inch cubes, place them in a colander, and moisten with water, by sprinkling a bit at a time and tossing. Do not soak. Press out

excess water, and transfer to the bowl with sautéed ingredients. Add schmaltz, eggs, poultry seasoning, pecans, and salt. Mix very thoroughly (use your hands).

4. Continue as per step 4 of the preceding recipe.

Roast Chicken with Rice and Fruit Stuffing

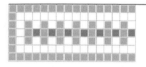

SERVES 8

This third stuffing is more of a Middle Eastern approach. Once again, marinate your chickens in the same spice mixture for at least a day in advance of cooking; follow step 1 of the roast chicken with bread stuffing recipe on page 93.

2 roasting chickens

FOR THE STUFFING
3 tablespoons corn oil
2 cups chopped onion
1 cup celery, chopped into ½-inch pieces
¾ cup raisins
1½ cups uncooked long-grain rice
2 cups plain chicken soup or stock, heated
¾ cup fresh-squeezed orange juice
1 teaspoon salt

¼ teaspoon pepper
2 McIntosh apples, peeled, cored, and cut into ¾-inch pieces, ¼ inch thick
4 teaspoons poultry seasoning
½ teaspoon cinnamon
3 eggs, beaten
¾ cup pecan halves
½ cup plain chicken soup or stock

1. Follow step 1 of roast chicken with bread stuffing on page 93.
2. Preheat oven to 375 degrees. Heat 2 tablespoons of the corn oil in a large skillet, and sauté onions until brown. Remove with a slotted spoon to a large bowl, and, in the remaining oil in the skillet (add some if necessary), sauté celery for a few minutes (it doesn't get very brown). Remove with a slotted spoon to the bowl with onions. Add a drop more oil if needed, quickly sauté raisins, and remove with a slotted spoon to the bowl with onions and celery.
3. Add 1 tablespoon corn oil to the skillet, and sauté the rice on medium to high heat for 2 minutes, stirring frequently.
4. Add 2 cups heated chicken soup, orange juice, salt, and pepper to the skillet of rice. Bring to a boil, cover, and simmer for 10 minutes. Remove rice mixture to a large bowl, and refrigerate for 10 minutes.
5. Combine rice with all other ingredients, except remaining chicken soup, and mix thoroughly.
6. Continue as per step 4 of the bread stuffing recipe, but add the ½ cup chicken soup to your extra stuffing.

Boneless Breast of Chicken with Mushroom Stuffing

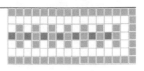

1 tablespoon salt
1 teaspoon pepper

3 tablespoons garlic powder
6 large boneless chicken breasts

SERVES 6

FOR THE STUFFING

5 tablespoons corn oil
2 cups onion, chopped into ¼-inch
   pieces
¾ cup celery, chopped into ¼-inch
   pieces
¾ cup carrots, chopped into
   ⅛-inch pieces (this is most
   easily done in a food processor)
3 cups scrubbed mushrooms,
   chopped into ½-inch pieces,
   ¼inch thick

8 cups loosely packed French or
   Italian bread, cubed into 1-inch
   pieces
1 tablespoon poultry seasoning
2 eggs, beaten
2 tablespoons schmaltz (optional)
1 teaspoon salt
¼ teaspoon pepper

FOR THE BASTING SAUCE

¾ cup fresh-squeezed orange juice
2 tablespoons soy sauce

3 tablespoons honey

FOR THE PAN JUICES

1 cup celery, chopped into ⅜-inch
   pieces
1 cup onion, chopped into ½-inch
   pieces

1 cup carrot, chopped into ¼-inch
   pieces
Clear chicken soup or stock

Note: Ask your butcher to remove the bones from the chicken while keeping the skin intact and the breast butterflied, not cut in half; also have him remove large pieces of fat.

1. Mix 1 tablespoon salt, 1 teaspoon pepper, and garlic powder in a bowl. Open the chicken breasts like the pages of a book, and rub insides well with this mixture. Refrigerate until needed.
2. Heat 2 tablespoons of the corn oil in a large skillet, and sauté onions until brown. Remove with a slotted spoon to a large bowl. Add 1 tablespoon corn oil to skillet, and sauté celery and carrots until crisp and lightly browned. Remove with a slotted spoon to bowl with the onions. Add remaining 2 tablespoons corn oil to skillet, and brown mushrooms. Remove with a slotted spoon to bowl with onions.
3. Place bread cubes in a colander, run cool water over them to soften, and squeeze out excess liquid, mushing the bread to a doughlike consistency.

Add bread and all remaining stuffing ingredients to the bowl with sautéed vegetables and mix thoroughly. Set aside.

4. In a separate bowl, mix orange juice, soy sauce, and honey to create a basting sauce. Set aside.

5. Preheat oven to 350 degrees. Spread chopped celery, onions, and carrots (1 cup each) evenly along the bottom of a large baking dish to flavor pan juices.

6. Cut about a dozen crosshatched slits in "open book pages" of each butterflied chicken breast by chopping rapidly with a knife (do not pierce through to the outer side or "book cover"; the slits should be no more than ⅛ inch deep). To further widen the breasts, cut a thin flap beginning about 1 inch from the center toward the edge of each side; fold the flaps out like ears. Fill each "book" with about ¾ cup stuffing. Fold bottom and top of each "book," roll "book covers" closed, and fasten with skewers. As you complete each stuffed breast, place it carefully over the vegetables in the baking dish, mounded skin side up.

7. When all the chicken breasts are arranged in the baking dish, brush the top of each with basting sauce, pour ¼ inch of chicken soup over the vegetables (not on top of the chicken), and bake for 45 minutes, brushing the chicken tops with basting sauce every 15 minutes.

8. Turn oven to broil. Brush tops of chicken with basting sauce once more, and place in broiler for 2 to 3 minutes, until nicely browned (be careful they don't burn). Serve each person a whole chicken breast, topped with a bit of the pan juice and its vegetables. Serve with a green vegetable and, if you like starchfests as we do, mashed potatoes.

Note: Bake extra stuffing in a separate dish, spooning pan juices into it every time you baste the chicken.

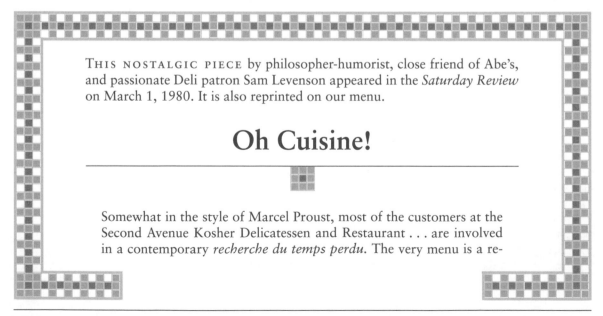

THIS NOSTALGIC PIECE by philosopher-humorist, close friend of Abe's, and passionate Deli patron Sam Levenson appeared in the *Saturday Review* on March 1, 1980. It is also reprinted on our menu.

Oh Cuisine!

Somewhat in the style of Marcel Proust, most of the customers at the Second Avenue Kosher Delicatessen and Restaurant . . . are involved in a contemporary *recherche du temps perdu*. The very menu is a re-

Abe gets a bear hug from his dear friend, the late comedian Sam Levenson.

membrance of things past, of a Jewish way of life all but destroyed by upward mobility.

Some of us grew up as part of that past. Others heard of it from their Italian, Greek, Ukrainian, Russian, Hungarian, Polish, Jewish, etc., parents or grandparents who came to America carrying a large bundle of hopes and a small bundle of pots, chopping bowls, rolling pins, mortars and pestles. After all, man does not live by freedom alone. They landed, along with their rich dreams and even richer appetites, on the Lower East Side—all at the same time.

There was not a cold tenement that did not smell of hot food. The aromas seeped through closed doors, dumbwaiters, halls, cellars, and the letter boxes. "Eating out" was unheard of. In the first place, you couldn't afford it. In the second place, "Poison they feed you." In the last, and most important place, to eat out was an insult to mama's cooking and to family tradition.

If you reached the point where you could eat out, or had to (a tragedy), you naturally sought out some place run by a mama and a papa, often by a whole family. The mama had to look like, dress like, talk like, and cook like "mama," and the food had to be kosher.

Eating out at the Second Avenue Delicatessen is like eating in. There is papa Lebewohl, mama Lebewohl, and two pretty daughters who "keep an eye."

The clue to Abe's success is culinary doubt—creative, inventive, positive doubt. He is privy to the highly inexact alchemy of traditional, instinctual Jewish cooking as handed down by word of mothers. The vital ingredient is "sense," not sense-organ sense, but common sense based on years of common scenting.

You have to feel what the food calls for and add that imprecise pinch, dab, smear, drop, or blip (an onomatopoeic word derived from the sound of one drop of oil falling into boiling water).

You can teach anyone, Jewish or not, how to make chicken soup, but you can't teach anyone (an ancient ethnic mystery) how to get it up to the temperature of molten lava. A good matzoh ball from such soup does melt in the mouth, but it also hardens again in the stomach. Cases of intestinal matzoh-ball blockage can be cleared by doses of 340-degree chicken soup.

The most popular main courses are chicken in the pot, boiled beef, Hungarian beef goulash, and Roumanian tenderloin steak. These are served with the Yiddish K rations: kasha (groats), kugel (noodle pudding), knaidle (billiard ball–size dough balls), kishka (stuffed cow's intestine). Interesting that linguistically there is no singular for certain Jewish delicacies. No one (except maybe an illegal alien) refers to a krep or a farf. It is kreplach, or farfel (confetti-size dough drops).

Among the fish specialties, gefuilte fish still leads the school. There are world-wide variations, but Abe Lebewohl has preserved the time-and-mama tested formula. Classical gefuilte fish experts started from the live fish in combinations of buffel (buffalo) carp, pike, or whitefish—depending upon the cost ("for the holidays they raise the price, the holdupnicks")—added egg, matzoh meal, and onions all chopped and molded into oval shapes. Onions were crucial. They made the mama cooks cry, releasing the salt tears (the secret ingredient?) which ran down their faces into the chopped fish, adding the flavor of four thousand years of Jewish suffering. The final product is eaten with horseradish strong enough to make the cooked fish tremble on the plate.

The East Side is now the home of new immigrants. The Second Avenue Delicatessen and Restaurant caters to some of these, but mostly to nostalgia-hungry exurbanites from every urb and suburb of America, who come a-searching in the old foods for some of the old values that made the crowded "co-op" living not only possible but stimulating; to value again fragrant human imperfection over deodorized, dehumanized perfection; to let the earthy horseradish, a real root, bring back bittersweet root-memories of a *temps perdu,* a time when dreams of a great tomorrow spiced many an unappetizing today.

Perhaps these customers are pilgrims in search of soul food for the soul, and Abe Lebewohl's menu proclaims: We deliver.

José Torres

PROFESSIONAL BOXER José Torres took up boxing in the Army at eighteen, and immediately became a middleweight champion, winning forty out of forty-one bouts, with thirty-four knockouts! At twenty, he represented the United States at the 1956 Olympic Games in Melbourne, Australia, garnering a silver medal; from 1965 to 1967, he was light-heavyweight champion of the world; and from 1993 to 1995, he served as president of the World Boxing Organization.

But his scope has always reached far beyond the ring, into politics, entertainment, writing (he authored the best-seller *Sting Like a Bee: The Story of Muhammad Ali*), acting (he's appeared in ten movies), and even choreography. He is presently a television boxing analyst for USA Networks' *Tuesday Night Fights en Español.*

Years ago, *New York Post* columnist Jack Newfield introduced me to his pal Abe Lebewohl at the Second Avenue Deli. Soon, Abe and I developed a friendship, and visiting his restaurant became like visiting family. He was a big boxing fan, but he never went to a single fight, because he was too damned busy at that restaurant. He always had time to go out to eat, though. My goodness, did he love to eat! He used to ask me how I stayed in such good shape, and, like most people, he thought I killed myself working out at the gym. Actually, though I do, of course, work out—especially after gorging on pastrami sandwiches at his place—my real trick for staying thin is simple: I don't eat a lot.

Abe could never really believe a big tough guy like me didn't eat that much. When he had his famous pickle-eating contest in 1994, he tried his damnedest to talk me into entering. I wanted to help out—not only for Abe but because my son, José, is a manager at United Pickles in the Bronx, which supplies the Deli and co-sponsored the contest. But I knew I could only get down two or three pickles tops; so, finally, I agreed to be a judge.

Abe was one of the sweetest men I ever knew. His philosophy was to be nice to everyone and to enjoy life, and all his friends enjoyed life a little more because he was around.

Ramona Torres's
Arroz con Pollo y Habichuelas

SERVES 6

José's wife, Ramona, taught us this traditional Puerto Rican chicken and rice dish, which is served with beans.

Note: Beans should be soaked 6 to 8 hours before cooking. Place them in a large bowl or pot, and cover with water by 2 inches.

FOR THE BEANS
1 pound dried pinto beans
1 large bay leaf
1/2 cup tomato sauce
1/2 teaspoon oregano

1 teaspoon salt
1/4 teaspoon freshly ground pepper
2 cups water

FOR THE RICE AND BEANS
4 tablespoons extra-virgin olive oil
2 cups green pepper, chopped into 1/2-inch pieces

2 cups onion, chopped into 1/2-inch pieces
3 tablespoons coarsely chopped fresh garlic

CHICKEN WITH RICE

Juice of 2 lemons
6 to 8 chicken pieces
2 teaspoons salt
¼ teaspoon freshly ground pepper
½ teaspoon oregano

2 tablespoons extra-virgin olive oil
½ cup Goya olive salad
¼ teaspoon Goya saffron
2 cups uncooked long-grain rice

1. Place beans and bay leaf in a large stockpot with water to cover. Bring to a boil, then reduce heat, and simmer for 1 hour, or until beans are tender but not mushy. Add extra water if needed during the cooking process. Drain, return beans to pot, cover, and set on an unlit back burner.

2. While beans are cooking, heat 2 tablespoons of the olive oil in a very large skillet, and sauté green peppers until browned. Remove with a slotted spoon, and set aside in a bowl. Heat 2 more tablespoons of oil in skillet, and sauté onions until browned. Remove with a slotted spoon, and set aside in a different bowl. At the last minute, add garlic, brown quickly, and set aside in a third bowl. Keep skillet on stove.

3. Squeeze lemon juice into 1 quart of water, and use it to wash chicken pieces well. Rinse with plain water. Place chicken parts on a large platter. Mix 2 teaspoons salt, ¼ teaspoon freshly ground pepper, and ½ teaspoon oregano in a small bowl, and rub chicken pieces evenly with this mixture. Set aside.

4. In a medium pot, place one-quarter of the sautéed green peppers, one-quarter of the sautéed onions, one-third of the sautéed garlic, tomato sauce, ½ teaspoon oregano, 1 teaspoon salt, ¼ teaspoon freshly ground pepper, and 2 cups water. Bring to a boil, then reduce heat, and simmer for 10 minutes. Add mixture to beans, and simmer, uncovered, on low heat for 30 minutes stirring occasionally.

5. Heat 2 tablespoons olive oil in skillet. Sauté chicken pieces on moderate heat in covered skillet for 20 minutes, moving pieces around occasionally to make sure they brown evenly.

6. Add remainder of the sautéed green peppers, onions, and garlic to chicken. Add olive salad and saffron, and stir everything in. Add rice, and stir in well. Add enough water to cover the rice by ½ inch and stir lightly. Bring to a boil, uncovered, for 2 minutes. Lower heat, cover, and simmer for 15 to 20 minutes, or until rice is tender and liquid almost completely absorbed. Serve with beans.

Barbecued Chicken

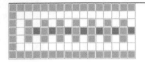

SERVES 6

Take a Polish immigrant restaurateur (Abe) who eats barbecued chicken somewhere and thinks it's the best thing since sliced challah. He brings some back to his Chinese chef, and the two of them spend night after night over a hot grill in the Deli kitchen trying to duplicate it. Hence, the Deli's unique Eastern European/Asian-style barbecued chicken, the recipe for which couldn't possibly replicate that of any barbecue joint in America. But it is good.

Though this recipe specifies baking and broiling the chicken, it is, of course, optimally prepared on a charcoal grill.

Note: This dish needs to marinate overnight, so begin preparations a day ahead of time. The basting sauce can also be prepared in advance.

1 14-ounce bottle Heinz ketchup
1 teaspoon Kitchen Bouquet (a browning sauce/gravy base available in supermarkets)
2 tablespoons soy sauce
2 tablespoons dry white wine
2 tablespoons very finely chopped or crushed fresh garlic
2 tablespoons sugar
1 teaspoon paprika

½ teaspoon cinnamon
1½ teaspoons salt
¼ teaspoon pepper
2 chickens, each chopped into about 6 pieces (or use 1 chicken plus preferred extra parts; use more or less, according to need, and taking into consideration that it's great cold the next day)

FOR THE BASTING SAUCE
½ cup fresh-squeezed orange juice, plus pulp and peel from ¼ orange
3 tablespoons lemon juice, plus pulp and peel from ½ lemon

¼ cup canned crushed pineapple
3 tablespoons honey
¾ cup Heinz ketchup
2 tablespoons Chinese duck sauce

1. In a large bowl, thoroughly mix everything except chicken and basting sauce ingredients. Add chicken, making sure all pieces are well coated. Cover bowl, and refrigerate overnight.

2. For the basting sauce, coarsely chop orange and lemon pulp and peel. Place them, along with citrus juices and crushed pineapple, in a food processor; pulse until smooth. Pour mixture into a saucepan, bring to a boil, then reduce heat, and simmer for 20 minutes. Add honey, ketchup, and duck sauce, and mix thoroughly. Set aside.

3. Preheat oven to 375 degrees. Remove chicken pieces from marinade, leaving only the amount of marinade that sticks to them. Discard the rest. Place in a baking dish, and bake 30 minutes.

4. Turn oven to broil. Brush chicken well with basting sauce, and broil for about 5 minutes (or until chicken browns on top; keep an eye on it). Turn chicken pieces, brush again with sauce, and brown other sides.

Chicken Cacciatore

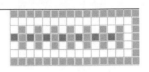

SERVES 6

1 tablespoon salt
¾ teaspoon pepper
1 tablespoon very finely chopped fresh garlic
2 chickens, each cut into about 6 pieces (or use 1 large chicken plus 2 breasts, also cut into pieces)
⅓ cup white wine
4 tablespoons corn oil
2 cups chopped onions
1 tablespoon finely chopped or crushed fresh garlic

¾ cup celery, chopped into ½-inch pieces
2 cups scrubbed fresh mushrooms, chopped into ¾-inch pieces
½ cup clear chicken soup or stock
¾ cup canned plum tomatoes, chopped into ¾-inch pieces
3 tablespoons tomato sauce
1½ tablespoons sugar
½ teaspoon oregano
1 teaspoon paprika
2 tablespoons cornstarch
3 tablespoons cold water

1. In a small bowl, mix 1 tablespoon salt, ½ teaspoon of the pepper, and 1 tablespoon garlic. Place chicken pieces in a shallow baking dish (or similar), and rub them with this mixture, covering thoroughly. Pour wine over chicken, cover the dish, and refrigerate for 4 hours or longer.

2. Pour 2 tablespoons of the corn oil into a large skillet, and sauté onions until nicely browned. At the last minute, add 1 tablespoon garlic, and brown quickly. Remove onions and garlic with a slotted spoon to a large bowl. Add 1 tablespoon corn oil to skillet, and sauté celery until very slightly brown (celery doesn't brown much) and crisp. Remove with a slotted spoon to bowl with onions and garlic. Add remaining 1 tablespoon corn oil to skillet, and brown mushrooms. Remove with a slotted spoon to the same bowl.

3. Add chicken soup, plum tomatoes, tomato sauce, sugar, oregano, paprika, and remaining ¼ teaspoon pepper to sautéed vegetables in bowl, and mix well. Place chicken in a skillet, and pour ingredients in bowl over the chicken and simmer 15 minutes. Turn chicken pieces and simmer 15 minutes longer or until chicken is thoroughly cooked and tender. (If you need 2 skillets to cook all your chicken, divide sauce equally between them.)

4. Remove chicken pieces to a platter. In a bowl, mix cornstarch with 3 tablespoons cold water until it is thoroughly dissolved. Spoon 1 cup sauce from skillet into bowl, about 2 tablespoons at a time, mixing thoroughly each time. Return cornstarch-thickened sauce to skillet, stir in, and boil for 1 minute.

5. Return chicken to pot. Serve with rice or egg barley.

Chicken Paprika

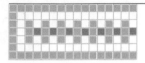

SERVES 6

Like goulash, chicken paprika evolved from recipes created by nomadic Magyar shepherds who cooked their meals alfresco in vast cauldrons hung over open campfires. Hungarian chefs refined and enhanced the dish, and Jewish cooks substituted schmaltz for bacon drippings and omitted sour cream from the sauce.

1 cup flour
1 teaspoon poultry seasoning
1 teaspoon rosemary
2 teaspoons salt
2 chickens, quartered
3 tablespoons schmaltz or olive oil
2 cups chopped onion
2 tablespoons finely chopped or
   crushed fresh garlic

2 cups green pepper, chopped into
   ³/₄-inch pieces
3 cups coarsely chopped canned
   plum tomatoes
1¹/₂ teaspoons sugar
4 teaspoons Hungarian paprika
¹/₄ teaspoon cayenne pepper
1 cup clear chicken soup or stock
Salt to taste

FOR THE ROUX
3 tablespoons corn oil

3 tablespoons flour

1. In a deep dish, mix flour, poultry seasoning, rosemary, and salt. Thoroughly dredge chicken pieces in this mixture, place them in a covered dish (do not overlap), and refrigerate until needed.

2. Heat schmaltz or olive oil in a large skillet, and sauté onions until nicely browned. At the last minute, add garlic, and brown quickly. Remove with a slotted spoon to a bowl, and set aside. Add green peppers to skillet, and sauté until lightly browned.

3. Transfer green peppers to a Dutch oven or wide-bottomed stockpot; add onions and garlic, tomatoes, sugar, paprika, cayenne, and 1 cup chicken soup. Mix well. Add the chicken pieces, and simmer, uncovered, for 30 minutes or until chicken is tender.

4. Keeping heat at a low simmer, spoon off a few cups of clear sauce as best you can (don't worry if there's a piece of onion in it). Pour corn oil into a medium saucepan and add flour, stirring well until it is completely dissolved. Put the roux pot on medium to high heat, and add the sauce, a little bit at a time, stirring constantly to create a thick, smooth, pastelike roux. It will get a little less pastelike as you add more sauce. Transfer the roux to the cooking pot, and stir in well. Add salt to taste. Place chicken and sauce in a large serving dish, and serve with noodles, dumplings, or spaetzle, and a side dish of cucumber salad.

Fried Chicken

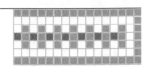

This dish is listed on our menu as chicken in the basket. We serve it with French fries and coleslaw (171 and 7).

SERVES 6

1 tablespoon salt
1/2 teaspoon pepper
3 tablespoons garlic powder
1 large chicken, plus 1 breast (or whatever other parts you favor), hacked into 3- to 4-inch pieces (ask your butcher to do it)

3/4 cup fine yellow cornmeal
3/4 cup flour
1 1/2 teaspoons garlic salt
4 eggs, beaten
1/2 cup water
Flour for dredging
Corn oil

1. In a bowl, mix salt, pepper, and garlic powder. Rub chicken pieces well on all sides with this mixture, and place in a covered dish. Refrigerate for 2 hours or longer.
2. In a large bowl, mix cornmeal, flour, garlic salt, eggs, and water. Stir vigorously to a smooth batter.
3. Dip each chicken piece in batter, coating it thoroughly, and place on a platter without stacking.
4. Dredge battered chicken pieces in flour, and place on a clean platter, once again without stacking. Refrigerate for 30 minutes.
5. Pour corn oil into a large, deep skillet (enough to cover chicken pieces), and heat to sizzling. Over medium to high heat, fry chicken for 20 minutes or until nicely browned.

Note: You can use the same batter and procedure to deep-fry small broccoli florets, carrot slices, and other vegetables. Ten minutes is ample for frying most vegetables.

Garlic Chicken

Once again, evidence of Chinese chefs in our kitchen.

SERVES 6

2 tablespoons crushed fresh garlic
1 teaspoon salt
1/4 teaspoon pepper
1 4-pound chicken, plus 1 breast (or whatever other parts you

favor), hacked into 4-inch pieces (ask your butcher to do it)
1/3 cup white wine

1. Thoroughly mix garlic, salt, and pepper. Wash chicken pieces, and rub them with the mixture. Place in a baking dish, add wine, and toss to cover thoroughly. Refrigerate for at least 3 hours.

2. Preheat oven to 350 degrees. Bake chicken in wine-garlic mixture for 30 minutes, basting with pan juices after 15 minutes.

3. Set oven to broil. Place baking dish in broiler, and broil for 5 minutes on each side or until chicken is nicely browned.

Chicken Cutlets

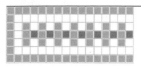

Nonkosher cooks soak chicken cutlets in milk or heavy cream to make them juicy and moist. We find nondairy creamer works just as well. Another alternative: Marinate cutlets in a commercial Italian salad dressing.

SERVES 6

3 large whole chicken breasts
1 pint nondairy creamer
   (preferably Rich's)
1½ cups flour
1 tablespoon garlic powder
1 tablespoon poultry seasoning

1½ teaspoons salt
¼ teaspoon pepper
3 eggs, beaten
½ cup water
2 cups seasoned bread crumbs
Corn oil for deep-frying

Note: Have your butcher split and debone the chicken breasts, remove all fat, and pound thin. Each whole breast yields two cutlets.

1. Place cutlets in a large bowl, one at a time, and pour nondairy creamer over each, making sure both sides of each cutlet are well soaked. Use the entire pint. Cover bowl, and refrigerate for 2 hours.

2. In a Pyrex baking pan (or similar shallow dish), place flour, garlic powder, poultry seasoning, salt, and pepper; mix well. Dredge cutlets in this seasoned flour, and set aside on platters (do not overlap). Mix eggs and water in a similar pan, and beat well. Place seasoned bread crumbs in a third pan. Dip each floured cutlet in the egg-water mixture, coating it completely; then dredge it thoroughly in bread crumbs.

3. Arrange breaded cutlets on platters (do not overlap), and place in freezer for 30 minutes.

4. Heat just enough corn oil to completely cover cutlets in a very large skillet (you'll need 2 skillets to accommodate all the cutlets in one batch). When oil is sizzling hot, deep-fry for 3 minutes. Turn cutlets, and fry 2½ minutes more. Drain on paper towels, and serve.

Chicken Fricassee

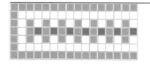

European housewives, strapped for cash, created meals using poultry leftovers and tiny marble-sized meatballs. This relatively inexpensive entrée would not only feed a large family, but the time consumed coaxing little pieces of chicken from the necks and wings would enhance everyone's feeling of repletion. Since people nostalgically crave the foods they ate growing up, one generation's economy dinner is the next generation's soul food.

SERVES 6

FOR MEATBALLS

¼ pound chopmeat
¼ cup finely chopped onion
2 slices stale white bread,
   moistened

1 egg, beaten
½ teaspoon salt
¼ teaspoon pepper

1 pound chicken gizzards
1 large bay leaf
10 chicken necks, thoroughly
   rinsed
1 cup celery, diced into ½-inch
   pieces
2 cups carrots, diced into ½-inch
   pieces
1 cup tomato purée

1½ cups chopped onion
1 teaspoon finely chopped or
   crushed fresh garlic
1 teaspoon salt
¼ teaspoon pepper
2 pounds chicken wings,
   thoroughly rinsed

1. Preheat oven to 350 degrees. Combine meatball ingredients in a bowl, and, using your hands, blend them thoroughly. Form them into ½-inch meatballs (you can use a melon baller to make them uniform), and place them in a baking dish. Bake for 20 minutes, and set aside.
2. In a large stockpot, place gizzards, 4 cups of water, and the bay leaf. Bring to a boil, then lower heat and simmer for 30 minutes.
3. Add chicken necks, celery, carrots, tomato purée, onions, garlic, salt, and pepper, and simmer for 15 minutes.
4. Add chicken wings and meatballs, and simmer for 15 minutes more. Remove bay leaf. Serve with kasha varnishkes or egg barley.

Annals of Jewish Waiters: Our Diane

AS INTRINSIC to an authentic Jewish deli as its state-of-the-art pastrami and corned beef is the fabled genre of the Jewish waiter. This so-called server (male or female) never heard the phrase "The customer is always right." He or she knows better. Some examples: A couple we know was dining at a Jewish deli in Queens. The husband ordered apple strudel for dessert, and his wife, confidently closing the menu with no fear of rebuff, said, "I'll have the same." The waiter sized up her chubby frame with a critical glance and quipped, "You, you don't need it."

And at our own beloved Second Avenue Deli, we once heard the following exchange:

Customer: "How is the stuffed breast of veal served?"

Waiter: "On a plate."

Many of our waitstaff are colorful characters, but Diane Kassner, a Deli fixture since 1987, is in a class by herself. As decorative as a doll, she's always dressed to the nines with massive jewelry and sequin- and pearl-studded frilly blouses under her bolero-style black jacket. Many customers come in just to catch her act, and some even send her flowers.

As she ladles out your chicken soup, Diane purrs, "I'll be the 'pourer,' you be richer." If time allows, she might even wax lyrical: "It's so delicious, it's nutritious. It's so edible, it's incredible." Ask for a straw and you'll hear "Haverstraw, that's upstate." Request ketchup, and as she's heading off to get it, she'll call back in her singsongy voice, "I'll ketchup to you in a minute." Russian dressing? She's "rushin' to get it." Mustard? "We supply, you apply." And when she needs you to rearrange dishes to create more space on a crowded table (Deli diners tend to order a lot of food), she urges gently, "Where there's a will, there's relatives."

Diane's fame extends beyond the Deli. Fox 5 TV's anchorwoman Rosanna Scotto captured Diane dancing in the Deli in celebration of the restaurant's fortieth anniversary in 1994 and featured her performance on *The Ten O'Clock News*. And Diane recited her above-mentioned ode to chicken soup on *Dateline NBC* in 1996. But her biggest coup was a May 1997 appearance on *Rosie O'-Donnell* in honor of National Pickle Week. Diane presented Rosie with a tray of our delicious pickles, and sang, to a national audience, a zany "pickle song" composed especially for the occasion and sung to the tune of "Hooray for Hollywood."

Diane Kassner posing with the Diane doll.

Famed waitress and Deli fixture Diane Kassner, promoting
National Pickle Week on Rosie O'Donnell.

Cholent with Chicken

On page 86, we talked about the history of cholent, the esteemed culinary centerpiece of midday Sabbath meals. In Europe, Jews were so sentimental about cholent that nineteenth-century German poet Heinrich Heine even wrote an ode to it: "Cholent, ray of light immortal! Cholent, daughter of Elysium. . . ." But as Jews assimilated in the New World, they adopted American quick-and-easy cooking methods (canned vegetables, frozen dinners, cake mixes), and labor-intensive dishes like cholent became a rarity at the dinner table. Happily, their baby-boomer offspring rebelled against American blandness, and authentic, complex dishes like cholent came back into fashion—both in cookbooks and in Jewish restaurants. Though not quite as eloquently as Heine, Second Avenue Deli trucks' license plates proudly proclaim, "Cholent"!

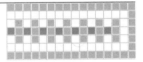

SERVES 8

Jack with the Deli's delivery truck.

1 tablespoon paprika
1 tablespoon garlic powder
1 tablespoon onion powder
1 tablespoon salt
1 teaspoon pepper
3 pounds chicken breast
1 cup dried lima beans
2 cups dried chickpeas
6 tablespoons corn oil
3 cups clear chicken soup or stock
3 cups chopped onions
2 tablespoons finely chopped or
    crushed fresh garlic

3 pounds large red potatoes,
    peeled, cut into ³/₄-inch pieces,
    cooked, and drained
1 teaspoon paprika
¹/₂ cup derma stuffing, chopped
    into ¹/₂-inch pieces (optional)
Salt (the amount will depend on
    how much salt is in the chicken
    stock you use; if it's salty, you
    may not need any)
¹/₄ teaspoon pepper
5 ounces raw fresh spinach,
    thoroughly washed, with stems
    removed

Note: Ask your butcher to cut the chicken breasts into 3-inch pieces and also to remove large pieces of fat. Do not remove skin.

1. In a large bowl, thoroughly mix paprika, garlic powder, onion powder, 1 tablespoon of salt, and 1 teaspoon of pepper. Toss chicken pieces in mixture, coating thoroughly. Cover, and refrigerate for 4 hours or longer.
2. Place lima beans and chickpeas in a large saucepan, and add enough water to cover by 2 inches. Bring to a boil for 2 minutes, remove from heat, cover pot, and let it stand for 1 hour. (Alternately, you can soak both overnight the night before.)
3. In a large skillet, heat 2 tablespoons of the corn oil, and brown chicken pieces (it's best to do it in batches, so all pieces brown evenly). Set aside.
4. Place chicken soup and 3 cups of water in a large stockpot, and bring to

a boil. Drain chickpeas and lima beans in a colander, add them to the stock-pot, and simmer uncovered for 40 minutes.

5. Preheat oven to 300 degrees. While beans are cooking, heat 2 table-spoons corn oil in a large clean skillet, and sauté onions until brown. At the last minute, add garlic and brown quickly. Set aside in a bowl.

6. Toss potatoes with the remaining 2 tablespoons corn oil and paprika, coating them thoroughly. Bake for 20 minutes. Set aside.

7. Add chicken, onions, and garlic to the pot. Continue simmering for another 30 minutes.

8. Add derma, salt (if needed), pepper, and potatoes. Simmer for 20 minutes more, or until everything is fully cooked and almost all the liquid is evaporated. Add a little water only if necessary to keep from burning. Cholent is a very thick stew.

9. Just before serving, add spinach leaves, and stir in until they just begin to wilt. (If you're saving some cholent for later, remove it from the pot before adding the spinach leaves; add fresh spinach leaves to the leftover cholent when you reheat it.)

Note: You can prepare cholent several days in advance and keep it in the refrigerator.

Braised Turkey Legs

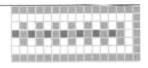

Note: If you make more than 6 legs at a time, add more onions and celery to the recipe in the proportion given below. You can also prepare braised turkey wings with this recipe.

SERVES 6

2 tablespoons garlic powder
2 teaspoons salt
$1/2$ teaspoon pepper
6 turkey legs (or as many as you
    need for the number of people
    you're serving)
2 cups chopped onion

$1/2$ cup chopped celery
1 teaspoon Kitchen Bouquet
    (a browning sauce/gravy base
    available in supermarkets)
$1/2$ teaspoon poultry seasoning
2 tablespoons cornstarch
Salt to taste

1. In a bowl, mix garlic powder, salt, and pepper. Rub turkey legs with the mixture, covering them thoroughly. Place legs on a platter and refrigerate for at least 4 hours.

2. Preheat oven to 400 degrees. Place chopped onion and celery in a baking dish at least 2 inches deep and large enough to hold all the legs (if you use more than 1 baking dish, put the same amount of onions and celery in each). Place turkey legs on top of vegetables, add 1 inch of water, and bake for 45 minutes, basting about every 20 minutes with pan juices.

3. Turn legs, reduce oven temperature to 375 degrees, and bake for another 45 minutes (still basting occasionally), or until legs are well browned and meat is cooked and tender. Remove from oven, and turn oven temperature

to warm. Remove turkey legs to a platter, and strain pan juices into a saucepan. Discard celery and onions, retaining 2 cups of pan juices in the saucepan. Return turkey legs to baking dish and keep them warm in the oven while you prepare the gravy.

4. Add Kitchen Bouquet and poultry seasoning to pan juices, and simmer on low heat.

5. In a small bowl, dissolve cornstarch by mixing it thoroughly in 3 tablespoons cold water. Add 1 cup gravy, a little at a time, and stir until smooth. Transfer cornstarch mixture back into gravy pot, and, stirring constantly, boil for 2 minutes. Add salt to taste. Serve over hot turkey legs. Or skip the gravy and serve the turkey legs cold.

Roast Turkey with Bread Stuffing

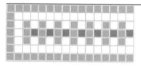

SERVES 8

At the Deli, we do a big Thanksgiving business every year, both in the restaurant and in take-out orders. This is how we prepare our holiday turkeys. As with our roast chickens, we first marinate turkeys overnight in a spice mixture.

Note: This recipe specifies a 14-pound turkey, but you can use it for a bird of any size. Allow about 20 minutes per pound for roasting.

1 14-pound turkey

FOR MARINATING THE TURKEY
5 tablespoons onion powder　　*2 teaspoons salt*
5 tablespoons garlic powder　　*1 teaspoon pepper*
5 tablespoons paprika

FOR THE BREAD STUFFING
5 tablespoons corn oil
3 cups chopped onion
1 cup celery, chopped into ½-inch pieces
1 cup carrots, chopped into ¼-inch pieces
4 cups scrubbed mushrooms, chopped into ¾-inch pieces, ¼ inch thick

10 cups loosely packed, cubed French or Italian bread
2 tablespoons poultry seasoning
2 tablespoons fresh dill
5 eggs, beaten
¼ cup schmaltz (optional)
1 teaspoon salt
¼ teaspoon pepper

Vegetable oil

1. Wash the turkey thoroughly in cold water, and clean out its cavity. In a bowl, combine onion powder, garlic powder, paprika, salt, and pepper; mix thoroughly. Dredge the turkey (outside only) in this mixture, making sure

all parts are well covered. Place in a dish covered with aluminum foil, and refrigerate overnight.

2. Preheat oven to 375 degrees. Heat 2 tablespoons of the corn oil in a large skillet, and sauté onions until brown. Remove with a slotted spoon to a large bowl. Add 1 tablespoon corn oil to skillet, and sauté celery and carrots until crisp and lightly browned. Remove with a slotted spoon to bowl with onions. Add remaining 2 tablespoons corn oil to skillet, and brown mushrooms. Remove with a slotted spoon to bowl with onions.

3. Place bread cubes in a colander, run cool water over them to soften, and squeeze out excess liquid. Add bread and all other stuffing ingredients to bowl with sautéed vegetables, and mix thoroughly.

4. Stuff the mixture into the cavity of the turkey. Don't pack it in too tightly, because it will expand a bit during the cooking process. Tie legs together with string, and skewer or sew the cavity skin closed. Place in a baking pan with 2 inches of water. Bake, breast up, for 4½ to 5 hours (or until the turkey is nicely browned and the legs move easily up and down). Baste every 20 minutes with pan juices (since there won't be much in the way of pan juices after the first 20 minutes, you can use vegetable oil instead for the first basting). Place extra stuffing in a separate baking dish (see Note below), and bake it along with turkey (for 75 minutes only; then refrigerate until needed), spooning pan juices on it every 20 minutes (when you're basting the turkey) to keep it moist. Before serving, combine stuffing cooked outside the turkey with stuffing cooked inside it, add pan juices, adjust salt to taste, mix thoroughly, and warm briefly on stove.

Note: Use a deep dish—rather than a large, shallow one—to bake extra stuffing. The outside will form a delicious crust, but you don't want too much crust in relation to stuffing.

Variation: For Passover, make a matzo stuffing by substituting 12 squares of crumbled matzo for the bread cubes.

Turkey Meat Loaf

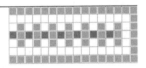

This lighter, healthier version of meat loaf can be enjoyed hot (perhaps with mashed potatoes and a vegetable), but we prefer to serve it chilled, along with cold cuts and potato salad. It's also a great sandwich filler.

SERVES 8

1 cup bread (French or Italian bread, or rolls, with crusts)
1½ pounds raw white-meat turkey
2 coarsely chopped medium onions (about ¾ of a pound)
⅓ cup chopped carrots
4 eggs, beaten

1½ teaspoons finely chopped or crushed fresh garlic
2 teaspoons sugar
1 teaspoon salt
¼ teaspoon pepper
Shortening for greasing pan

1. Preheat oven to 350 degrees. Cut bread into pieces so you can measure about a cup's worth. Sprinkle the bread with water to moisten (don't soak it), and squeeze extra moisture out.

2. In a food processor or meat grinder, fine-grind the turkey meat, onions, carrots, and bread together. Place the mixture in a large bowl.

3. Add eggs, garlic, sugar, salt, and pepper. Mix very thoroughly.

4. Grease a 5- by 9-inch loaf pan, at least 3 inches high. Put the turkey meat loaf mixture in the pan, and flatten the top with a spoon. (Alternately, you can form it into a mound, using your hands.) With a knife, score a crisscross design along the top of your loaf.

5. Place the meat-loaf-filled pan in a larger baking pan filled with about ½ inch of water (this will keep the bottom from burning during the lengthy baking process). Place the entirety in the oven and bake for 30 minutes. Wrap the top with aluminum foil, and bake 1 hour and 45 minutes more.

PROMOTIONS, PITCHES . . . AND PITCHING NO-HITTERS

Sardi's Downtown

Milton Berle at the Deli's opening-night party for Goodnight, Grandpa.

THE LOWER EAST SIDE'S thriving off-Broadway theater scene (La Mama, the Public Theater, et al.), inspired Abe to turn the Deli into "Sardi's downtown"—a venue for cast parties and theatrical celebrations. The first of these, in 1983, was for veteran comedian Milton Berle, then starring in *Goodnight, Grandpa* at a converted Yiddish theater two blocks from the Deli. *The New York Times* noted that Berle had had heartburn twice that week: from critics panning the play and from the cast party for three hundred on opening night at the Second Avenue Deli, where he consoled himself at a lavish buffet of chopped liver, kasha varnishkes, pastrami, corned beef, kreplach, potato knishes, and pigs in blankets. In spite of terrible notices, Berle remained dignified and even gallant: asked to pick his favorite dish, he pointed to his wife, Ruth.

Broiled Chicken Livers

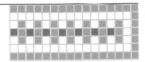

3 pounds chicken livers
1 tablespoon chopped or crushed
  fresh garlic
4 tablespoons corn oil

1 teaspoon salt
2 tablespoons soy sauce
Paprika
2 cups chopped onions

1. Set oven to broil. Wash livers well in cold water, and drain them in a strainer. Trim off all fat. Place in a baking dish large enough to accommodate them without stacking.
2. Add garlic, 2 tablespoons of the corn oil, salt, and soy sauce, and toss to cover the livers well. Sprinkle evenly with paprika.
3. Place baking dish in broiler, and broil for 8 minutes. Turn livers, and broil 5 minutes longer. While livers are cooking, heat remaining 2 tablespoons corn oil in a skillet, and sauté onions slowly, stirring occasionally, until well browned. Serve livers smothered with fried onions.

Stuffed Breast of Veal

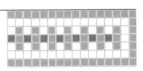

FOR THE STUFFING
5 tablespoons corn oil
2 cups chopped onion
3/4 cup celery, chopped into 1/4-inch
  pieces
3/4 cup carrots, chopped into
  1/8-inch pieces (it's easiest to get
  them to this pebbly size in a
  food processor)
3 cups scrubbed mushrooms,
  chopped into 1/2-inch pieces,
  1/4 inch thick

8 cups loosely packed, cubed
  French or Italian bread
1 tablespoon poultry seasoning
2 eggs, beaten
2 tablespoons schmaltz (optional)
1 1/2 teaspoons salt
1/4 teaspoon pepper

1 6- to 8-pound breast of veal (ask
  butcher to trim the breast and
  cut a pocket, approximately
  1/2 inch thick, to hold the
  stuffing)
Salt

Pepper
3 coarsely chopped onions
5 carrots, cut into 1-inch chunks
3 stalks celery, cut into 1-inch
  chunks
8 cloves garlic, whole

1. Begin by preparing the stuffing. Heat 2 tablespoons of the corn oil in a large skillet, and sauté onions until brown. Remove with a slotted spoon to a large bowl. Add 1 tablespoon corn oil to skillet, and sauté celery and carrots until crisp and lightly browned. Remove with a slotted spoon to bowl

with onions. Add remaining 2 tablespoons corn oil to skillet, and brown mushrooms. Remove with a slotted spoon to bowl with onions.

2. Preheat oven to 375 degrees. Place bread cubes in a colander, run cool water over them (don't drench), and squeeze out excess liquid, mushing the bread to a doughlike consistency. Add bread and all other stuffing ingredients to bowl with sautéed vegetables, and mix thoroughly (use your hands).

3. Rub the top of the veal with salt and pepper. Fill the veal pocket with stuffing (it will hold approximately 4 cups), and close tightly with skewers. Place extra stuffing in a separate baking dish (see Note below), and refrigerate until needed.

4. Place the coarsely chopped onions, carrot and celery chunks, and whole garlic cloves along the bottom of a large roasting pan. Cover vegetables with water. Place the stuffed breast of veal on top of the vegetables, pocket side up, and bake, covered with aluminum foil or a lid, for 2 hours.

5. After the veal has baked for 2 hours, place baking dish with extra stuffing in oven, spooning pan juices onto it. Uncover the veal, and bake 1 hour longer, or until it is dark brown and crisp. Every 20 minutes, spoon more pan juices into the extra stuffing.

6. Remove everything from the oven. Slice the veal along the ribs. Skim fat from the gravy, and serve it in a gravy boat, leaving the vegetables as they are or pulverizing them in a food processor. Combine stuffing cooked outside the veal with stuffing cooked in it, add some gravy, adjust salt to taste, mix thoroughly, and warm briefly on stove if necessary.

Note: Use a deep dish—rather than a large, shallow one—to bake extra stuffing. The outside will form a delicious crust, but you don't want too much crust in relation to stuffing.

5

FISH

Broiled Fillet of Sole à la Second Avenue
Filet of Sole in Onion-Butter Sauce
Fillet of Sole with Mustard-Horseradish Sauce
Fillet of Sole with Pine Nuts in Onion–White Wine Sauce
Alfred Portale's Whole Roast Red Snapper with Tomatoes, Lemon, and Thyme
Gefilte Fish
Poached Salmon with Herbed Mayonnaise
Salmon Cakes with Julienned Leeks
Baked Carp

ABE LOVED FISH. He loved developing new recipes for it, cooking it, and especially eating it. When he created his famous broiled fillet of sole à la Second Avenue, he not only wolfed down vast amounts of it ("It has no calories!" he enthused, with less than total accuracy), but made any friend or associate who stepped into the Deli sample a hefty portion while he stood by beaming like a proud papa. Though Abe prided himself on serving only the freshest and highest-quality fish available, he was too much the consummate New Yorker to actually go catch them himself. Instead, several mornings a week, he made predawn runs to the Fulton Fish Market, where he'd pore over the day's fresh catch. While the city slept, he relished the market's colorful bustle of activity—the pervasive aroma of saltwater and fish, cobblestoned streets slimy with fish guts, buckets of still-thrashing lobsters and eels, and rubber-aproned vendors (there are about 150) manning tiny stalls eerily lit by hanging bulbs and heated in winter by oil-drum fires.

Early one morning when it was still dark, Abe went out to get his truck (which he had absentmindedly forgotten to lock the night before) and found a bum sleeping in the back. Most people would have been angry. Abe didn't even disturb the guy but drove to the fish market as usual and made his purchases. He piled the fish next to his still-sleeping stowaway passenger and drove to Gertel's Bake Shop on Hester Street, where he purchased bread for the Deli, schmoozed with the bakers, and ate his ritual breakfast: a fresh-baked onion roll with cream cheese and lox and a cup of steaming hot coffee. Then he woke up the bewildered bum in the truck, handed him an identical breakfast, and chatted with him while he ate it on the way back to the Deli.

Broiled Fillet of Sole à la Second Avenue

Abe loved this preparation of fillet of sole and, because it was low in calories, made it the mainstay of his many diets. Unfortunately, those diets never worked for him, because in addition to the sole, he'd nibble corned beef, bits of salami, a rugalach or two, and perhaps just a smidge of halvah throughout the workday—just to assuage the pangs of hunger between meals.

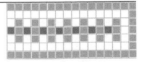

SERVES 6

Note: To make this into a more complete meal, cook potatoes (chopped into chunks) and string beans (or any other vegetable) on the stove in advance, then put them in to brown with the fish when you add the chopped vegetables.

*1 cup green pepper, chopped into
¼-inch pieces*
*1 cup scrubbed mushrooms,
chopped into ¾-inch pieces,
¼ inch thick*
*1 cup seeded fresh tomato, chopped
into ¼-inch pieces (for a more
piquant version, use sun-dried
tomatoes)*
*1 cup onion, chopped into ¼-inch
pieces*

½ teaspoon garlic powder
1 teaspoon salt
1 teaspoon pepper
*1 teaspoon very finely chopped
fresh dill*
2 tablespoons olive oil
*Softened unsalted butter or
margarine for greasing pan*
3 pounds fillet of sole
Lemon wedges

1. Set oven to broil. Place green pepper, mushrooms, tomato, and onion in a large bowl, and gently stir in the garlic powder, salt, pepper, dill, and olive oil. Set aside.

2. Grease a baking pan, and place fillets in the pan without overlapping (depending on the size of your baking pan, you may need to do this in two batches). Broil for about 5 minutes or until fillets are nicely browned. Spread the chopped vegetable mixture on top of the fillets (surround with potatoes and string beans or other vegetable if you wish), and broil for 4 minutes longer. Serve with lemon wedges.

*The greatest deli man
with "The Greatest."*

Fillet of Sole in Onion-Butter Sauce

Preparing clarified butter makes this recipe a little more time-consuming—okay, and caloric, but it's a poor soul that never rejoices. We think the extra time and calories are well spent.

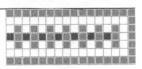

12 ounces (3 sticks) unsalted butter
3 large ripe tomatoes
2 cups coarsely chopped onions
1 tablespoon coarsely chopped fresh garlic
3 pounds fillet of sole
Salt

Pepper
Paprika
3 cups Brussels sprouts, cooked (optional)
5 medium potatoes, peeled, sliced, and cooked (optional)

GARNISH
Lemon wedges

Chopped parsley

Note: We like to prepare vegetables at the same time, and put them in the broiler to brown with the fish. Potatoes and Brussels sprouts are delicious with this dish, but you can use whatever appeals to you. Cook your vegetables on the stove while the onion-butter sauce is in the oven.

1. Preheat oven to 350 degrees. Melt the butter on low heat in a small saucepan, letting it bubble but not brown. Remove from stove, and let sit for several minutes. Skim off the milky foam at the top, and strain through a fine mesh or cheesecloth. Pour strained butter into another bowl, discarding the white foam at the bottom. You want only the clear, yellow part of the butter. Set aside.

2. Place tomatoes in vigorously boiling water (enough to cover) for about 40 seconds, or until skin begins to peel. Remove them to a plate. When tomatoes are cool enough to handle, peel off skins, remove and discard seeds, and chop coarsely.

3. Place butter in a baking pan (10 to 12 inches square or similar) with onions and tomatoes, and bake for 1 hour and 15 minutes, stirring at 30-minute intervals. Add garlic, and bake 30 minutes more. Remove from oven, and set temperature to broil.

4. Pour onion-butter mixture into a larger baking dish. Sprinkle fillets with salt, pepper, and paprika (they should be fully covered with paprika), and arrange them on top of the onions. If you've cooked Brussels sprouts and potatoes (or other vegetables), wedge them into the corners, and spoon some butter sauce over them; they'll brown nicely and taste fabulous. Broil for about 5 minutes or until fillets are browned and flake when tested with a fork. Serve with lemon wedges and parsley.

Fillet of Sole with Mustard-Horseradish Sauce

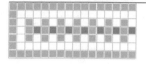

SERVES 6

This dish looks and tastes impressive, but it only takes about 10 minutes to prepare.

2 teaspoons Dijon mustard
2 tablespoons lemon juice
2 teaspoons white horseradish
6 tablespoons grated Parmesan cheese
12 ounces (1½ cups) sour cream

¾ teaspoon salt
¼ teaspoon pepper
½ cup finely chopped shallots
4 ounces (1 stick) unsalted butter
3 pounds fillet of sole
Paprika

1. Set oven to broil. In a bowl, thoroughly combine mustard, lemon juice, horseradish, Parmesan cheese, sour cream, salt, and pepper. Set aside.
2. In a small skillet, brown shallots in the butter. Add, including the melted butter, to the ingredients in the bowl.
3. Sprinkle the fillets evenly with paprika, and place them in a large baking pan (depending on the size of your broiler, you may need to do this in two batches). Do not overlap fillets. Spread sauce evenly on top, and broil for about 4 minutes (check after 3) or until fish flakes easily with a fork and sauce has browned. Serve with rice and a green vegetable.

Fillet of Sole with Pine Nuts in Onion–White Wine Sauce

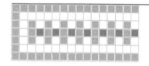

SERVES 6

½ cup pine nuts
2 tablespoons olive oil
3 cups chopped onions
1 teaspoon finely chopped or crushed fresh garlic
2 tablespoons lemon juice
1 cup dry white wine
1 cup drained and coarsely chopped canned plum tomatoes

1 tablespoon plus 1 teaspoon thyme
1½ teaspoons salt
1 cup flour
2 teaspoons garlic salt
½ teaspoon pepper
¼ cup sesame oil
3 pounds fillets of sole
1 teaspoon cornstarch
2 tablespoons cold water

1. In a large skillet, sauté pine nuts quickly in 2 tablespoons olive oil, stirring constantly. Remove to a small bowl with a slotted spoon, and set aside. Sauté onions in remaining oil (add a bit if necessary); when they're nicely browned, add garlic and sauté quickly. Add lemon juice, white wine, plum tomatoes, 1 teaspoon of the thyme, and ½ teaspoon of the salt. Simmer for 8 minutes. Transfer onion sauce to a small saucepan, and leave it on an unlit back burner.

2. In a shallow dish, thoroughly mix flour, garlic salt, 1 tablespoon thyme, 1 teaspoon salt, and pepper. Dredge fish fillets well in this seasoned flour, and set them aside on a large plate. Do not stack.

3. Pour sesame oil into a large skillet and, when oil is hot, fry fillets on medium to high heat until underside is golden brown. Turn with a spatula, and brown the other side. (Use 2 large skillets, each with ¼ cup of oil, to cook all your fillets at once.)

4. While fillets are frying, mix cornstarch thoroughly with 2 tablespoons cold water, and pour mixture into sauce. Bring to a boil, stirring, until sauce is moderately thickened.

5. Remove fish with a spatula to a platter covered with paper toweling and drain excess oil. Serve individual portions, topped with onion sauce and some of the pine nuts.

CULINARY WUNDERKIND AND OWNER of the elegant but comfortably simpatico Gotham Bar and Grill, Alfred Portale is famous for his exquisite vertical food presentations and his brilliantly innovative contributions to New American cuisine. After graduating first in his class from the Culinary Institute of America, he went on to work in the great kitchens of France with such luminaries as Michel Guérard, the Troisgros brothers, and Jacques Maximin. A few years ago, he received a James Beard Award naming him Best Chef in New York. Abe often said the Gotham was the only restaurant he knew where everything—food, presentation, and service—was always perfect.

Alfred Portale

Twelve years ago, I hosted a cooking class in the kitchen at the Gotham Bar and Grill. This subterranean room was brightened immeasurably that evening by an astonishingly enthusiastic "pupil," who was shocked at how much of our seasoning was accomplished with simple salt and pepper. He turned out to be a fan, and went on, in a thick Eastern European accent, to heap an embarrassing amount of praise on me.

The man, of course, was Abe Lebewohl, and we saw each other often in the years following that class.

Abe continued to prove himself a kind and wonderful man during his once-a-month visits to the Gotham dining room . . . and he made a special point of complimenting our food and service each time. When

I commented on his generous praise, he remarked—with a humility that defined him—that "It doesn't cost anything to be nice."

Over the years, Abe was a regular at my cooking demonstrations, and I suppose I was a regular at his "classes"—learning something about how to make people feel good from a real master. It may not cost anything, but it's an all too rare gift that he possessed in abundance.

Alfred Portale's Whole Roast Red Snapper with Tomatoes, Lemon, and Thyme

SERVES 4 TO 6

This fish dish—quick, delicious, and presented whole—makes an impact. And it actually makes its own colorful sauce, replete with Provençal flavors.

1 (6-pound) whole red snapper, cleaned and scaled
Coarse salt and freshly ground white pepper
3/4 cup thinly sliced shallots
6 garlic cloves, thinly sliced
1 cup peeled, seeded, and chopped ripe tomatoes (or use canned tomatoes if ripe are not available)

1 small lemon, thinly sliced, seeds removed
1 tablespoon coarsely cracked coriander seeds
4 sprigs fresh thyme
4 sprigs flat-leaf parsley, plus 2 tablespoons chopped, for garnish
1/2 cup extra-virgin olive oil

1. Preheat the oven to 400 degrees. Lightly oil the bottom of a roasting pan large enough to hold the whole fish. (If necessary, trim the fins with scissors to get a better fit.) Rinse the red snapper inside and out with cold running water, and pat it dry with paper towels. Slash 4 X's about 1/4 inch deep into the thickest parts on both sides of the fish to ensure even cooking. Season well with salt and pepper. Place the fish in the roasting pan, and scatter a few of the shallots and garlic in the cavity.

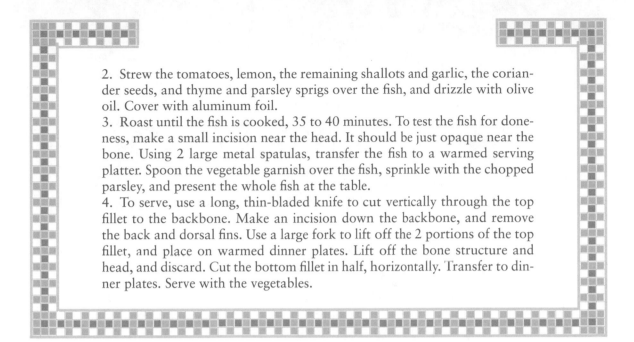

2. Strew the tomatoes, lemon, the remaining shallots and garlic, the coriander seeds, and thyme and parsley sprigs over the fish, and drizzle with olive oil. Cover with aluminum foil.

3. Roast until the fish is cooked, 35 to 40 minutes. To test the fish for doneness, make a small incision near the head. It should be just opaque near the bone. Using 2 large metal spatulas, transfer the fish to a warmed serving platter. Spoon the vegetable garnish over the fish, sprinkle with the chopped parsley, and present the whole fish at the table.

4. To serve, use a long, thin-bladed knife to cut vertically through the top fillet to the backbone. Make an incision down the backbone, and remove the back and dorsal fins. Use a large fork to lift off the 2 portions of the top fillet, and place on warmed dinner plates. Lift off the bone structure and head, and discard. Cut the bottom fillet in half, horizontally. Transfer to dinner plates. Serve with the vegetables.

Gefilte Fish

MAKES 12

Gefilte fish, today a prized delicacy, dates from the late Middle Ages in Germany, where it was conceived as a fish stretcher—an ancient relative of Hamburger Helper. Religious Jews embraced it as a highlight of Friday-night dinners, because it solved a spiritual dilemma: though the Talmud suggests eating fish on Friday nights, it is forbidden (because it's considered work) to separate fish from bones on the Sabbath. We've found that most people who say they don't like gefilte fish have only tasted the supermarket variety, sold in jars, which is like saying you don't like filet mignon when you've only tasted beef jerky. Happily, preparing authentic gefilte fish from scratch is not an arcane skill possessed only by Jewish great-grandmothers. With today's food processors, it's not even especially difficult. Our recipe is sweet, in the Polish tradition; Russian gefilte fish is more peppery.

FOR THE GEFILTE FISH BALLS

1 1½-pound fillet of whitefish and 1 ½-pound fillet of carp or pike (at fish store, ask for whole fish, filleted and skinned. Retain the heads and bones. Many stores will also grind the fish for you)
2 large onions (about 2 cups when grated; don't tamp it down)

1 stalk celery
½ medium carrot
6 eggs, beaten
4 teaspoons sugar
2½ teaspoons salt
⅜ teaspoon pepper
¾ cup corn oil
1 cup matzo meal

FOR THE COOKING

Heads and bones from fish

4 medium onions, peeled and
quartered

2 stalks celery, trimmed and
chopped into 3-inch pieces

2 medium carrots, peeled

1. In a food processor or grinder, grind fish (refrigerate heads and bones for later use), 2 onions, 1 stalk celery, and half a carrot. (If you use a food processor, make sure you leave no large pieces of fish or bones; you may want to transfer the mixture, bit by bit, into a wooden bowl, and go over it vigorously with a hand chopper.)

2. Place fish mixture in a large bowl, and add eggs, sugar, salt, pepper, and corn oil, mixing thoroughly with a wire whisk. Stir in matzo meal, and continue to mix until everything is thoroughly blended. Refrigerate for 1 hour or more (longer, even overnight, is better).

3. Fill 2 large stockpots three-quarters full of water, and bring to a vigorous boil. In each, throw in half the fish heads and bones, 2 onions, half the celery, and a carrot. Divide batter into 12 patties of equal size. (Don't worry that your batter is a little loose; it has to be that way to keep your gefilte fish light.) Transfer each patty to a large cooking spoon, shape into an oval, and very gently lower it into the boiling water. Put 6 in each pot. Lower heat and simmer for 1½ hours.

4. Remove fish balls and carrots from pots, and refrigerate on a covered plate. Discard everything else. Serve chilled with red and/or white horseradish. Slice carrots for garnish.

Abe's annual Israel Day Parade float celebrating "A Slice of Jewish Life."

PROMOTIONS, PITCHES . . . AND PITCHING NO-HITTERS

Bring out the Hellmann's, and Bring Out the Best

IN 1987, Best Foods, which manufactures Hellmann's mayonnaise, celebrated the seventy-fifth anniversary of its sandwich spread by challenging seven top New York delis to compete for the title of best sandwich (it had to be slathered with mayo, of course). In addition to the Deli, contestants included Katz's, the Stage, Sarge's, Lox Around the Clock, Wolf's, and the New York Delicatessen; Leo Steiner of the noted Carnegie refused to take part, stating, perhaps a tad churlishly, "I'm a solo, not a choir, act." And even Abe was a little doubtful, expressing his personal horror at *goyische* desecrations like mayo on pastrami. Judges were major media personalities, such as NBC weatherman Al Roker. The event culminated with the wheeling out of a vast birthday cake in the shape of a Hellmann's bottle. Actor Phillip Douglas, got up as an eight-foot jar of mayo, led everyone in singing "Happy Birthday."

Sad to say, we didn't win that competition. We were beat out by the New York Delicatessen's creation: smoked salmon and sable with cucumber, radish, and red onion on pumpernickel, smeared with herbed mayonnaise.

Poached Salmon with Herbed Mayonnaise

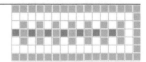

5 cups water
1 teaspoon sugar
4 bay leaves
2 medium onions, sliced thin
4 stalks celery, chopped into 3-inch
   pieces
³⁄4 cup thinly sliced carrots

1½ teaspoons salt
¼ teaspoon pepper
1 teaspoon thyme
2 teaspoons coarsely chopped fresh
   garlic
6 salmon steaks
Lemon slices for garnish

SERVES 6

Note: The herbed mayonnaise (green sauce) that accompanies this salmon needs to be prepared a day in advance.

1. Place water, sugar, bay leaves, onions, celery, and carrots in a large stockpot, and boil for 10 minutes. Add salt, pepper, thyme, and garlic, and stir in.
2. Place salmon steaks in large skillet, and pour above mixture over them (for 6 steaks, you'll probably need 2 skillets; divide broth ingredients equally). Simmer 6 minutes, or until fish flakes easily with a fork and center is pinkly juicy but not raw. Remove salmon from pan, discard all else, and trim off skin and fat. Serve chilled with herbed mayonnaise and cucumber salad (page 12). Garnish salmon steaks with lemon slices.

HERBED MAYONNAISE (GREEN SAUCE)

Keep this sauce in mind for other cold fish as well as poached salmon.

Note: The only reason to chop the cucumber and dill is to measure them, since they're going into the food processor.

1 cup peeled, chopped cucumber, with seeds removed
³⁄₈ cup chopped dill
3 tablespoons fresh-squeezed lemon juice

3 teaspoons Chinese mustard
³⁄₄ cup Hellmann's mayonnaise
¹⁄₈ teaspoon salt
¹⁄₈ teaspoon white pepper

1. Place the cucumber, dill, and lemon juice in a food processor, and combine very thoroughly.
2. Empty contents of food processor into a large bowl, add all other ingredients, and mix very well with a fork. Refrigerate overnight. Serve chilled, with salmon or any other cold fish.

Salmon Cakes with Julienned Leeks

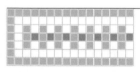

MAKES ABOUT 9

These salmon cakes are delicious hot, but they also make great cold sandwich fillings the next day with some lettuce and mayonnaise. The julienned leeks, an optional step, add crunchy appeal and make for a more elegant presentation.

¹⁄₄ cup olive oil
¹⁄₃ cup celery, diced into ¹⁄₄-inch pieces
³⁄₄ cup onion, diced into ¹⁄₄-inch pieces
¹⁄₃ cup red pepper, diced into ¹⁄₄-inch pieces

2 cups boiled potatoes, mashed a little coarsely
4 ounces whipped cream cheese
3 7¹⁄₂-ounce cans salmon, thoroughly drained
¹⁄₄ cup finely chopped fresh parsley

2 tablespoons finely chopped scallions	2 eggs, beaten
2 tablespoons fresh-squeezed lemon juice	¼ cup water
½ teaspoon marjoram	2 cups seasoned bread crumbs, placed in a shallow baking dish
1 egg, beaten	Paprika
1½ teaspoons salt	3 leeks
¼ teaspoon pepper	2 tablespoons butter
	Lemons

1. Pour olive oil into a large skillet, and sauté celery, onions, and red peppers, stirring occasionally, until nicely browned. Remove to a bowl with a slotted spoon, and set aside. Retain remainder of olive oil in skillet.

2. In a large bowl, mash potatoes, cream cheese, and salmon together. Add parsley, scallions, lemon juice, marjoram, 1 egg, salt, pepper, and sautéed vegetables, and integrate very thoroughly.

3. Cover a cookie sheet with wax paper. Form the fish-potato mixture into 3-inch patties (about ¾ inch high), and place them on wax paper. Place sheet in freezer for 1 hour.

4. Beat remaining 2 eggs with ¼ cup water. Dip fish patties, one at a time, in the egg-water mixture, coating them completely; then dredge well in bread crumbs. Sprinkle both sides of each patty fairly generously with paprika, place them back on wax-papered cookie sheet, and return to freezer for 15 minutes.

5. While patties are chilling, chop off the tops and roots of your leeks, retaining only the lighter green part that separates easily into layers. Wash all the layers thoroughly (they usually have soil deposits), and cut them (vertically) into thin sticks about 3 inches long and ⅛ inch wide. Set aside.

6. Add butter to olive oil in skillet, and heat. Carefully place the fish patties in the pan, lower heat a bit, and sauté until nicely browned on both sides, covering the skillet after you turn them to make sure they heat through. (You'll probably have to cook the patties in batches or use 2 skillets; in the latter case, you'll need double the amount of oil and butter.)

7. Remove patties from skillet, squeeze a lot of fresh lemon juice over them, and cover to keep warm. Toss the leeks into the remaining oil and butter and, stirring constantly, sauté until lightly browned and crispy. Serve salmon cakes immediately, topped with leeks.

Baked Carp

Carp was scarcely known in America before the latter part of the nineteenth century, when it was introduced by German immigrants. But it became even more widely available in the next few decades as millions of Jews arrived on these shores. Carp has always been a "Jewish fish"—a frequently enjoyed entrée and an essential ingredient of gefilte fish. After all, it was Jews (silk

SERVES 6

merchants trading in China) who brought carp to Europe in the first place, and it was Jews who farmed carp and popularized it in Poland.

½ cup tomato purée

2 cups onion, chopped into ¼-inch pieces

1 cup celery, diced into ¼-inch pieces

2 cups carrots, diced into ¼-inch pieces

2 large bay leaves

1 teaspoon sugar

3 pounds carp, sliced into 6 steaks

Salt

Pepper

Garlic powder

½ cup green pepper, chopped into ¼-inch pieces

Fresh lemon wedges

1. Preheat oven to 350 degrees. Place tomato purée, onions, celery, carrots, bay leaves, and sugar in a large skillet with 2 cups water. Bring to a boil; then reduce heat, and simmer for 10 minutes.

2. Sprinkle carp steaks lightly (*lightly* is the key word in this sentence) with salt, pepper, and garlic powder, and rub in well. Transfer contents of skillet and green peppers to a large baking dish. Arrange fish steaks over the vegetables, and bake, uncovered, for 25 minutes, turning them and basting with sauce midway (to test for doneness, slice open a large steak; the meat should be mostly white, with a little rosy pink around the edges).

3. Remove to a platter, discard bay leaves, and serve, hot or cold, with lemon wedges.

6

BLINTZES,
LATKES,
KUGELS,
AND MATZO
DISHES

Blintzes
Matzo Blintzes
Bobby Flay's Yellow Corn Pancakes with Smoked Salmon and Mango-Serrano Crème Fraîche
Potato Latkes
Matzo Meal Latkes
Drunken Matzo Meal Latkes
Nina Zagat's Omelette au Cointreau
Cheese Latkes
Vegetable Latkes
Wayne Harley Brachman's Matzo Farfel Pancakes
Noodle Kugel
Noodle-Apple Kugel
Potato Kugel
Broccoli Kugel
Matzo Kugel
Creamy Matzo-Apple Kugel
Matzo Kugel with Spicy Beef
Gleist Matzos
Veselka's Potato Pierogi
Matzo Brei

IF YOU GREW UP in a Jewish home, just reading the title of this chapter makes your mouth water. In addition to superb recipes for old standards—like cheese blintzes, potato latkes, pierogi, and potato kugel—we've come up with some innovative takes on old themes, such as drunken matzo meal latkes and a spicy matzo-beef kugel that is as much New Delhi as new deli.

Blintzes

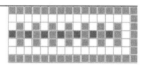

MAKES 10 TO 11

Blintzes, which evolved from Russian blini, are served on Shavuoth (the Feast of Weeks), a harvest festival that also commemorates the Lord's appearance before Moses on Mount Sinai. The reason: two blintzes placed side by side resemble, with a little imagination, the tablets Moses carried down the mountain. Cheese blintzes—along with other dairy fare—are also associated with Chanukah (see cheese latkes on page 146 for an explanation). In the Deli, of course, we make nondairy blintzes only, and their taste is just about indistinguishable from the dairy ones. To make pareve crêpes, substitute nondairy creamer for milk and margarine for butter in the recipe below.

CRÊPES
2 cups flour
⅛ teaspoon salt
4 eggs, beaten
1½ cups milk
2 tablespoons melted butter
1 tablespoon butter for frying
   crêpes
Corn oil for frying

1. Prepare filling (see details below), and refrigerate until ready to use. If you want to make more than one kind, simply reduce recipe amounts. It takes about 4½ cups of stuffing to fill 10 or 11 blintzes. Plan accordingly.
2. Sift flour and salt into a large bowl. Gradually add eggs and milk, beating with a wire whisk until perfectly smooth. Stir in melted butter. For best results, after whisking ingredients, mix batter in a blender until silky smooth. Refrigerate for 30 minutes.

3. Set out a dinner-size plate on your counter, and keep the batter bowl right by the stove. Heat 1 tablespoon butter in an 8- or 9-inch omelet pan. Keeping your heat medium-high, use a ladle to spoon batter into the pan. Tilt the pan so that batter covers evenly, creating a thin layer, and immediately pour all excess back into the batter bowl. When the crêpe is lightly browned on one side, loosen it around the edges with a fork and flip it, browned side up, onto the plate. Continue frying crêpes and piling them on the plate. Do not add extra butter to the pan. (The first wrapper, which absorbs too much butter, is not usable. Toss it. There's even a Russian proverb: "The first pancake is always a flop," which means the same as our "If at first you don't succeed, try, try again.")

4. To fill crêpes, place them, one at a time, on a plate, browned side up. Place a large dollop of filling (about a heaping ¼ cup, a little less if you're using fruit) about 1 inch from the "top" of the circle, leaving a margin of about 1½ inches on either side. Roll the top of the crêpe over the filling. Fold in side flaps, and continue to roll, top to bottom.

5. In a large skillet, heat about ½ inch corn oil on a high setting. Reduce heat to moderate, and fry the blintzes until brown and crispy (no more than 2½ minutes on each side). Serve with applesauce or, if you're preparing as a dairy dish, sour cream. You might also want to sprinkle a little confectioners' sugar on fruit or cheese blintzes. (You'll need 2 skillets to contain all the blintzes in one batch.)

POTATO FILLING

2 tablespoons corn oil or schmaltz	*4 cups mashed potatoes*
2 cups onion, chopped into ¼-inch pieces	*1 egg, beaten*
	½ teaspoon salt
2 teaspoons very finely chopped or crushed fresh garlic	*¼ teaspoon pepper*

1. Heat corn oil or schmaltz in a large skillet, and sauté onions until brown. At the last minute, add the garlic, and sauté until brown.

2. Place the onions and garlic in a large bowl with the mashed potatoes, egg, salt, and pepper, and combine thoroughly. Refrigerate until needed.

Variation: For a meat and potato filling, use only 3 cups of mashed potatoes and add a cup of finely minced brisket, pastrami, or corned beef.

KASHA FILLING

2 tablespoons corn oil or schmaltz	*2 eggs, beaten*
2 cups onion, chopped into ¼-inch pieces	*½ teaspoon salt*
	¼ teaspoon pepper
4 cups cooked kasha	

1. Heat corn oil or schmaltz in a large skillet, and sauté onions until brown.

2. Place the onions in a large bowl with the kasha, eggs, salt, and pepper, and combine thoroughly. Refrigerate until needed.

CHEESE FILLING

2 pounds farmer cheese
½ pound whipped cream cheese
1 egg, beaten

⅜ cup sugar
⅛ teaspoon cinnamon
⅛ teaspoon salt

1. Blend all ingredients thoroughly in a large bowl, and refrigerate until needed.

Note: In the Deli we make a delicious nondairy cheese filling by substituting Tofutti cream cheese for both the farmer cheese and the whipped cream cheese. We also add 3 tablespoons of matzo meal, ½ teaspoon cornstarch, and ½ teaspoon each of lemon and orange zest. The ingredients should be blended with an electric mixer.

SPINACH AND CHEESE FILLING

2 tablespoons corn oil
2 cups onion, chopped into ¼-inch
  pieces
2 cups cooked spinach
1 pound farmer cheese

1 pound whipped cream cheese
1 egg, beaten
½ teaspoon salt
¼ teaspoon pepper

1. Heat corn oil in a large skillet, and sauté onions until brown. Place in a large bowl.
2. Chop the cooked spinach very fine (it's best to pulse it a few times in a food processor). Add to bowl with onions.
3. Add all remaining ingredients, and combine thoroughly. Refrigerate until needed.

APPLE OR PEACH FILLING

Unsalted butter
5 cups apples or peaches, peeled,
  cored or pitted, and cut into
  ¾-inch slices, ¼ inch thick
  (choose somewhat hard, slightly
  unripe peaches)
1 cup raisins

1 cup sugar (adjust amount of
  sugar, depending on how sweet
  your fruits are; filling should be
  quite sweet)
1½ teaspoons cinnamon
Whipped cream cheese (optional)

1. Melt 1 teaspoon butter in your largest skillet, and, on high heat, sauté apple or peach slices until lightly browned on both sides. Do this in batches, so that you're browning only one layer of fruit slices at a time (don't pile them up); use ½ teaspoon extra butter for each batch. Don't overdo it. You want the fruit slices to keep their integrity, not turn into mush. Remove with a slotted spoon to a large bowl, and set aside. Add another ½ teaspoon butter to the pan, and quickly sauté the raisins. Add to bowl with apples or peaches.
2. Add sugar (use more or less than a cup, depending on the sweetness of your fruit) and cinnamon, and mix in well. Refrigerate until needed. When

you stuff the crêpes, you can add a dollop of whipped cream cheese along with the fruit if you wish.

BLUEBERRY FILLING
Unsalted butter
5 cups fresh blueberries
1 cup sugar (adjust amount of
  sugar, depending on how sweet
your fruits are; filling should be
  quite sweet)
Whipped cream cheese (optional)

1. Melt 1 teaspoon butter in your largest skillet, and, on high heat, stirring frequently, sauté blueberries very quickly—just until they turn dark and some juice comes out. Strain berries over a bowl, reserving liquid in a small saucepan.
2. Place berries in a large bowl, add sugar (use more or less than a cup, depending on the sweetness of your berries), and mix in. Refrigerate until needed. When you stuff the crêpes, you can add a dollop of whipped cream cheese along with the fruit if you wish. Also taste blueberry filling before stuffing; you may want to add a bit more sugar.

Note: The blueberry juice makes a delicious syrup. Mix 1½ teaspoons cornstarch with the same amount of water in a small bowl, until completely smooth. Bring juice to a boil, add cornstarch mixture, and heat for 1 minute, stirring constantly. Drizzle this blueberry sauce over cheese blintzes or use it to enhance pancakes, vanilla ice cream, or French toast.

Two handsome guys: Alec Baldwin and Deli manager Tony Sze.

THE SECOND AVENUE DELI COOKBOOK

Matzo Blintzes

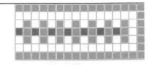

Your family will love this Passover treat. For us, these blintzes have become an annual holiday tradition.

MAKES
12 BLINTZES

WRAPPERS

6 squares Streit's matzo
2 eggs, beaten
⅓ cup water

½ cup corn oil for frying
Various fillings (see below)

1. Prepare one of the fillings described below, and refrigerate until ready to use.

2. Lay out a double layer of paper toweling on your counter large enough to hold all 6 matzo squares without piling them. Hold matzo squares under cold running water (do 1 square at a time) for about 10 seconds, until both sides are wet but not limp. Lay out the wet matzos on the paper toweling, and place a single layer of wet paper toweling on top. Leave them for 50 minutes, at which time you'll find that the matzos are pliable and can be rolled without breaking. You must have your fillings prepared at this time and be ready to fry the blintzes. (These moistened matzos are delicate; you might want to prepare a few extras in case some of them tear.)

3. In a bowl, beat eggs and water, and set aside. Using a sharp knife, cut a matzo square exactly in half along the grain. Place about ¼ cup of filling about 1 inch from one end (leave a ½-inch margin on both sides), and roll, vertically, against the grain. Work with care so as not to tear the matzo. Do not try to seal the sides. Dip each blintz in the egg-water mixture, and place it on a plate. Repeat until all matzo wrappers are filled and dipped.

4. You'll need 2 skillets to contain all 12 blintzes. Heat half the corn oil in each, carefully place blintzes in pans, and sauté, turning once, until nicely browned and crispy on both sides. Remove and serve.

POTATO FILLING

3 cups mashed potatoes
2 tablespoons olive oil
1 cup finely chopped onion
2 teaspoons finely chopped or
  crushed fresh garlic

1 egg, beaten
¾ teaspoon salt
¼ teaspoon pepper
Sour cream

1. Place mashed potatoes in a large bowl. Heat olive oil in a skillet, and sauté onions until brown. At the last minute, add garlic, and brown quickly. Remove with a slotted spoon to the bowl containing mashed potatoes.

2. Add egg, salt, and pepper, and combine thoroughly. Refrigerate until needed.

3. Stuff and cook matzos as indicated above. Serve with sour cream.

CHEESE FILLING

1¼ pounds farmer cheese	1 teaspoon vanilla
8 ounces whipped cream cheese	⅛ teaspoon salt
⅜ cup sugar	Sour cream
1 egg, beaten	Raspberry jam (optional)

1. Combine all ingredients (except sour cream and jam) in a large bowl, and blend thoroughly. Refrigerate until needed. Stuff and cook matzos as indicated above. Serve with sour cream and/or raspberry jam.

APPLE FILLING

Unsalted butter	½ cup raisins
3 cups peeled, cored McIntosh apples, cut into ¾-inch slices, ¼ inch thick	¾ cup sugar
	1 teaspoon cinnamon
	Confectioners' sugar
½ cup sliced blanched almonds	Sour cream

1. Melt 1 teaspoon butter in your largest skillet, and, on high heat, sauté apple slices until they're lightly browned on both sides. Do this in batches, so that you're browning only one layer of slices at a time (don't pile them up); use ½ teaspoon extra butter for each batch. Don't overdo it. You want the fruit to keep its integrity, not turn to mush. Remove with a slotted spoon to a large bowl. Add ½ teaspoon butter, and quickly brown almonds and raisins. Add to bowl with apples.

2. Add sugar and cinnamon to the bowl, and mix thoroughly. Refrigerate until needed.

3. Stuff and cook matzos as indicated above. When finished, remove to a serving dish, and sprinkle with confectioners' sugar. Serve with sour cream.

A MAJOR STAR in New York's culinary galaxy, the dynamic Bobby Flay has been garnering awards for Mesa Grill's sassy southwestern fare since 1991. In 1993, he opened Bolo, featuring innovative Spanish cuisine. The author of three cookbooks—*Bold American Food, From My Kitchen to Your Table,* and *Boy Meets Grill*—Flay also hosts a cooking show *(Hot off the Grill with Bobby Flay)* on the Food Network.

I think of the Second Avenue Deli as a comfort zone, especially during the cold winter months. When I'm very stressed—or feel the flu coming on—I jump into a taxi, race over to Tenth Street and Second Avenue, and make the driver wait outside with the meter running while I order matzo ball soup, a turkey sandwich on rye with Russian dressing, and chopped liver to go. I take it all home and eat it in bed watching TV. Then I'm ready to face the world again. It's better than Prozac and TheraFlu combined.

Note: Also check out Mesa Grill pastry chef Wayne Harley Brachman's matzo farfel pancake recipe on page 148.

Bobby Flay's Yellow Corn Pancakes with Smoked Salmon and Mango-Serrano Crème Fraîche

SERVES 4

½ cup yellow cornmeal
½ cup all-purpose flour
1 teaspoon baking powder
¼ teaspoon salt
2 tablespoons honey

1 large egg, beaten
½ cup plus 2 tablespoons milk
1 tablespoon unsalted butter, melted
16 paper-thin slices smoked salmon

MANGO-SERRANO CRÈME FRAÎCHE
½ cup crème fraîche or sour cream
1 roasted serrano pepper, finely diced
½ ripe mango, peeled, seeded, and finely diced

½ medium red onion, finely diced
Salt
Freshly ground pepper

1. In a mixing bowl, combine the cornmeal, flour, baking powder, salt, and honey. In a separate bowl, combine the egg, milk, and melted butter. Add the dry ingredients from the other bowl, and mix well.
2. Heat a griddle or cast-iron frying pan (use a nonstick pan if you don't have a cast-iron one) over high heat, and drop the batter by spoonfuls to

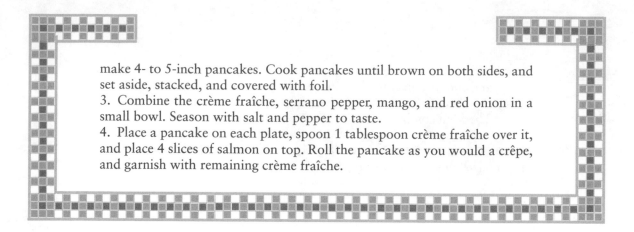

make 4- to 5-inch pancakes. Cook pancakes until brown on both sides, and set aside, stacked, and covered with foil.

3. Combine the crème fraîche, serrano pepper, mango, and red onion in a small bowl. Season with salt and pepper to taste.

4. Place a pancake on each plate, spoon 1 tablespoon crème fraîche over it, and place 4 slices of salmon on top. Roll the pancake as you would a crêpe, and garnish with remaining crème fraîche.

Potato Latkes

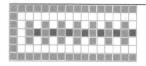

MAKES 20

Potato latkes are really just potato kugel (see below) in pancake form. For more about their Chanukah connection, see cheese latkes (page 146).

2½ pounds potatoes, peeled and
   quartered
2 large onions (use 1½ cups grated;
   don't tamp down)
3 eggs, beaten
1 teaspoon baking powder
¾ cup corn oil
1 cup flour
2½ teaspoons salt
¼ teaspoon pepper
2 cups matzo meal
½ cup corn oil for frying
Applesauce
Sour cream

1. Preheat oven to 400 degrees. In a food processor, fine-grate potatoes (don't liquefy; leave some texture), and strain to eliminate excess liquid. Don't overdo it; just let the water drain out. Fine-grate onions, and mix in a large bowl with potatoes. (If you don't have a food processor, you can grind the potatoes and onions in a meat grinder.)

2. Add eggs, baking powder, ¾ cup corn oil (most of it cooks out), flour, salt, and pepper; mix well. Fold in matzo meal, making sure that everything is very well blended.

3. Heat ½ cup corn oil in a deep skillet. Spoon batter (use a large kitchen spoon) into the pan to create pancakes about 3½ inches in diameter. Fry on low heat for 3 to 4 minutes until underside is a deep golden brown, turn, and fry for another minute or two. Drain on paper towel. Serve with applesauce and/or sour cream.

Matzo Meal Latkes

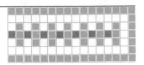

Without the grated onion, matzo meal latkes are a little on the bland side. However, you can always take a different, more Sephardic, approach: omit the onion; sprinkle the cooked latkes with a mixture of confectioners' sugar, cinnamon, and finely chopped nuts; and serve them with honey.

MAKES 20

1 cup matzo meal
2 teaspoons salt
2 tablespoons sugar
6 eggs
1½ cups water

¾ cup grated onion (optional)
¾ cup corn oil for frying
Applesauce
Sour cream

1. In a large bowl, combine matzo meal, salt, and sugar. Set aside.
2. Separate egg whites and yolks. Beat egg yolks, and combine with water. Add the yolk mixture to the matzo meal mixture, and let it stand for 30 minutes.
3. Beat egg whites with an electric mixer until they are stiff, and fold them into the matzo meal mixture. Add grated onion.
4. Heat corn oil until it sizzles in a deep skillet. Lower heat, and, using a cooking spoon, spoon batter into the pan, creating thin pancakes 3 to 4 inches in diameter. Fry for several minutes, turning when the pancake is firm and the bottom side is golden brown. Fry for another few minutes until the other side is done. Drain on paper towel. Serve with applesauce and/or sour cream.

Note: Occasionally stir mixture left in the bowl during the process of spooning latkes into the pan.

Drunken Matzo Meal Latkes

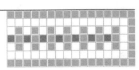

Our rum-soaked latkes add sophisticated splash to holiday meals.

3 cups fresh fruit
½ cup dark rum
1 cup matzo meal
1 teaspoon salt
6 tablespoons (³⁄₈ cup) white sugar
2 tablespoons brown sugar

6 eggs
½ cup water
¾ cup corn oil for frying
Confectioners' sugar
Cinnamon

MAKES ABOUT 20

Note: For the fresh fruit, you can use any *one* of the following: apples (peeled, pitted, cored, and finely chopped in a food processor or hand-grated), finely chopped pineapple, blueberries, peaches (peeled and very finely chopped but not grated), or bananas (chopped into ½-inch pieces). Or experiment with other fresh fruits and berries.

1. Place fruit in a bowl, pour rum over it, mix, and let stand for 50 minutes.
2. In a large bowl, combine matzo meal, salt, and white and brown sugars. Set aside.
3. In medium bowls, separate the egg whites and yolks. Beat the yolks, add water, and mix well. Add the yolk-water mixture to the matzo meal mixture, stir, and let stand for 30 minutes.
4. Beat the egg whites with an electric mixer until they are stiff and form peaks. Fold them into the matzo meal mixture. Add rum-soaked chopped fruit, and stir in.
5. Heat the corn oil in a deep skillet. Lower heat a little bit, and, using a cooking spoon, spoon batter into the pan, creating thin pancakes 3 to 4 inches in diameter. Fry for several minutes, turning carefully with a spatula when the pancake is firm and the bottom side is golden brown. Fry until the other side is done. Drain on paper towel. (Occasionally stir mixture left in the bowl during the process of spooning latkes into the pan.)
6. In a small bowl, mix confectioners' sugar with a bit of cinnamon and, using a sieve or sifter, sprinkle on top of latkes just before serving.

Another version of the above: Substitute Grand Marnier for rum, use blueberries or raspberries for the fruit, and add 1 tablespoon grated orange rind to your batter.

SINCE 1979, Yale Law School grads Tim and Nina Zagat have been rating the restaurants of America's major cities. Their books—with reviews based on thousands of visits—have become the bibles of culinary cognoscenti everywhere. Since 1988, the Zagat concept has been expanded to include ratings of hotels, resorts, spas, airlines, and car-rental companies, and their *NYC Restaurants Survey* has become the best-selling book in the Big Apple. We're very proud of the Second Avenue Deli's high Zagat rating. Says Tim Zagat:

I have so many memories of Abe—from our days working together on NY92 (a promotion in conjunction with the Democratic Convention, in which New York City restaurants offered prix-fixe lunches for $19.92) . . . to his tales of the tribulations involved in setting up a branch of the Second Avenue Deli in Moscow (a passionate plan of Abe's that, due to "red tape," even in the era of glasnost, never came to fruition). We shared political views and jokes, often simultaneously. Who couldn't love Abe's warm, bearish quality and generosity?

I will always particularly remember working on the $19.92 NYC lunches, in which most of the restaurants participating—places like the Gotham and Le Cirque—normally charged several times that much for a meal. A typical tab at the Second Avenue Deli, of course, was usually much less than $19.92. So how were we to make the Deli's participation look like a bargain? As always, Abe pulled an AYCE out of the hole. We invented the ALL-YOU-CAN-EAT lunch!

Nina Zagat's Omelette au Cointreau

SERVES 2

4 eggs
1 tablespoon granulated sugar
3 tablespoons Cointreau (to taste)

1½ teaspoons butter
Confectioners' sugar

1. In a bowl, beat the eggs, sugar, and Cointreau together until smooth.
2. In a 7- or 8-inch omelette pan, heat the butter over medium-high heat.
3. Pour the egg mixture into the pan, and stir, rapidly and constantly, with a fork (or, if you use a nonstick pan, with a wooden spoon). Try to gently shake the pan at the same time. When the eggs are nearly set, yet a little liquid still remains, stop stirring, and shake the pan for a couple of seconds, making sure that the bottom of the pan is completely covered by the egg mixture. At this point, the eggs should be set, yet still moist. Stop shaking the pan, and allow the bottom of the omelette to firm slightly (4 to 5 seconds).
4. Fold omelette into thirds by lifting the handle and tilting the pan at a 30-degree angle. With the back of a wooden spoon, fold the portion of the omelette nearest you toward the center of the pan. Using the spoon, fold this portion back into the pan, overlapping the first fold. Turn the omelette out onto a serving plate, so that it ends up folded side down. Dust with confectioners' sugar, and serve immediately.

Recipe inspired by Le Cordon Bleu and adapted by Richard Grausman.

Cheese Latkes

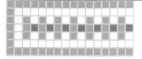

MAKES
12 TO 15

Chanukah—celebrating the rededication of the Temple after the Maccabees defeated Antiochus and the Syrian army in 165 B.C.E.—is a joyous occasion, a time for parties . . . and for latkes. But there's no reason to limit yourself to the traditional potato pancakes. Since Chanukah food is supposed to include dairy as well as fried foods, these cheese blintzlike latkes perfectly fill the bill.

Foods fried in oil (which realistically comprise about 90 percent of Jewish dishes) symbolize the flame that miraculously burned for eight days in the great Temple of Jerusalem with just one small vial of oil. Why dairy? It's kind of a grisly story. Holofernes, the leader of Nebuchadnezzar's Assyrian army, had become enamored of the beautiful widow Judith. She went to his tent and fed him salted cheese, after which he drank several cups of wine to quench his thirst. When he fell asleep, she cut off his head with his own sword, and brought it to Jerusalem to show his soldiers. Terrified, they fled the city. Dairy dishes eaten at Chanukah honor her heroic act.

Early morning at the Deli

6 eggs, beaten
15 ounces farmer cheese
1 cup matzo meal
6 tablespoons sugar
1½ teaspoons vanilla

3 tablespoons corn oil
½ teaspoon salt
¾ cup corn oil for frying
Applesauce
Sour cream

1. Place beaten eggs in a large bowl. Add farmer cheese and blend thoroughly. Add matzo meal, sugar, vanilla, 3 tablespoons corn oil, and salt, and mix well.

2. Heat ¾ cup corn oil in a deep skillet until it sizzles. Lower heat, and, using a cooking spoon, spoon batter into the pan, creating pancakes about 3 inches in diameter. Fry for several minutes, turning when the bottom side is golden brown. Turn and fry for another few minutes until the other side is done. Drain on paper towel. Serve with applesauce and/or sour cream.

Vegetable Latkes

1 cup matzo meal
2 teaspoons salt
2 tablespoons sugar
6 eggs
1½ cups water
¾ cup grated onion
1 cup peeled and very finely
    chopped zucchini

1 cup very finely chopped broccoli
¾ cup very finely chopped spinach
¾ cup peeled and very finely
    chopped carrot
3 finely chopped scallions (not
    including bulbs)
¾ cup corn oil for frying
Sour cream

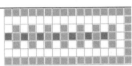

MAKES
ABOUT 20

Notes: Use your food processor to chop zucchini, broccoli, carrots, and scallions to correct size (⅛-inch pebbles), to grate onions, and to finely chop spinach.

For a little extra color and tang, throw in 5 or 6 finely chopped sun-dried tomatoes (drain them first thoroughly if they're in oil).

1. In a large bowl, combine matzo meal, salt, and sugar. Set aside.

2. Separate egg whites and yolks. Beat egg yolks, and combine with water. Add the yolk mixture to the matzo meal mixture, and let it stand for 30 minutes.

3. Beat egg whites with an electric mixer until they are stiff, and fold them into the matzo meal mixture. Add grated onion, zucchini, broccoli, spinach, carrots, scallions, and sun-dried tomatoes if you're using them.

4. Heat corn oil until it sizzles in a deep skillet. Lower heat, and, using a cooking spoon, spoon batter into the pan, creating thin pancakes 3 to 4 inches in diameter. Fry for several minutes, turning when the pancake is firm and the bottom side is golden brown. Turn and fry for another few minutes until the other side is done. Drain on paper towel. Serve with sour cream.

Note: Occasionally stir mixture left in the bowl during the process of spooning latkes into the pan.

WAYNE HARLEY BRACHMAN, executive pastry chef at Manhattan's Mesa Grill, Bolo, and Mesa City, started out as a member of a punk rock band and a performance artist. Then he fell in love with the art of pastry. "My idea," he says, "was to turn all our childhood dessert fantasies into sophisticated restaurant desserts." Hence, his haute versions of chocolate ice cream sandwiches and chocolate-peanut-graham cake with homemade roasted marshmallows! After stints at two famed New York restaurants—The Odeon and Arizona 206—Brachman joined Bobby Flay at Mesa Grill (see Bobby's yellow corn pancake recipe on page 141). He is the author of a southwestern-baking cookbook called *Cakes and Cowpokes*.

I grew up in New York, where, as a child, I enjoyed the dubious distinction of being able to eat more halvah at a sitting than any of my friends (I initiated and won contests). When I moved to the East Village in 1968, I began patronizing the Second Avenue Deli, but since my family never ate corned beef (I thought of it as watered-down pastrami and almost *goyische*), I never ordered it. It wasn't until a friend in Massachusetts invited me to a bris and delegated me to bring proper food from New York—smoked fish from Russ & Daughters, oven-fresh bagels and bialys from Kossar's, pickles from Guss, and corned beef from the Second Avenue Deli—that I got turned on to corned beef. I began nibbling it at the bris, and I've never looked back, though the Deli is the only place in the universe I'll order it.

I knew Abe first as a Deli customer, but in recent years we'd frequently chat at culinary events. He often lunched at Mesa Grill, where, despite his half-hearted and totally unbelievable protests that he was dieting, I always plied him with desserts.

Wayne Harley Brachman's Matzo Farfel Pancakes

SERVES 6

6 cups matzo farfel
¾ cup boiling water
6 large eggs
1 teaspoon coarsely ground black
    pepper
1 tablespoon unsalted butter

1 tablespoon canola or vegetable
    oil
Maple syrup
Blueberries, strawberries, or
    peaches

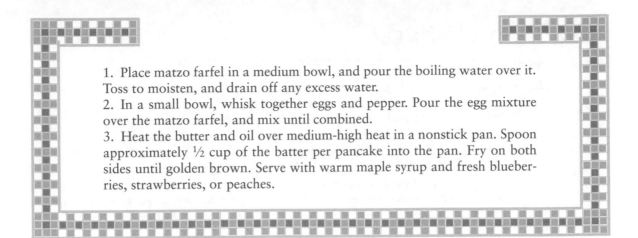

1. Place matzo farfel in a medium bowl, and pour the boiling water over it. Toss to moisten, and drain off any excess water.
2. In a small bowl, whisk together eggs and pepper. Pour the egg mixture over the matzo farfel, and mix until combined.
3. Heat the butter and oil over medium-high heat in a nonstick pan. Spoon approximately ½ cup of the batter per pancake into the pan. Fry on both sides until golden brown. Serve with warm maple syrup and fresh blueberries, strawberries, or peaches.

Noodle Kugel

In Eastern Europe, golden-crusted sweet *lokshen* (noodle) kugel—a variant of German bread pudding—was served as a Sabbath dessert. The heavy finale to a substantial midday meal, it ensured that Saturday would be a day of rest. In America, it evolved into a side dish that goes well with pot roast, fish, or chicken. Or it can be served as a lunch entrée, perhaps with soup or salad.

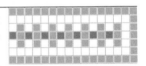

SERVES 8

1 pound medium noodles
5 eggs, beaten
⅛ cup fresh-squeezed lemon juice and grated rind from 1 lemon
1 teaspoon vanilla
1½ cups sugar
½ cup golden raisins

¾ cup finely chopped pineapple chunks (if canned, drain thoroughly)
1 cup water
½ teaspoon salt
Shortening for greasing pan

1. Preheat oven to 350 degrees. Fill a large pot three-quarters full with water, and bring to a rapid boil. Toss in noodles, and boil 5 to 7 minutes until al dente. Rinse in cool water, drain, and set aside.
2. Mix all other ingredients except shortening in a large bowl. Pour in noodles and combine thoroughly.
3. Pour mixture into a greased baking pan, and bake for 1 hour and 15 minutes, or until top is golden brown. Serve hot.

Noodle-Apple Kugel

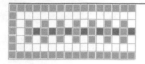

SERVES 8

Another variation on the above theme, this kugel uses a different mix of fruit as well as cheese and sour cream.

1 pound medium noodles
4 cups peeled, cored McIntosh
    apples sliced into 1-inch pieces,
    ¼ inch thick
1¼ teaspoons cinnamon
3 tablespoons unsalted butter
½ cup golden raisins

2 tablespoons sugar
1 cup sour cream
1 cup creamed cottage cheese
2 eggs, beaten
1 teaspoon salt
Shortening for greasing pan
Butter for dotting top of kugel

1. Fill a large stockpot three-quarters full with water, and bring to a vigorous boil. Toss in noodles, and cook 5 to 7 minutes until al dente. Rinse in cool water, drain, and set aside.

2. Preheat oven to 350 degrees. Toss apple slices with cinnamon. Melt butter in a large skillet, and sauté apples on moderate heat for 6 minutes, stirring occasionally. Add raisins and sugar, and sauté for 1 minute more. Refrigerate mixture to cool.

3. In a large bowl, combine sour cream, cottage cheese, eggs, and salt. Gently fold in noodles and apple-raisin mixture.

4. Pour noodle mixture into a greased baking pan, dot with butter, and bake for 1 hour or until top is golden brown.

Potato Kugel

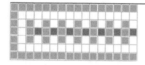

SERVES 8

Like all Jewish kugels, this makes for heavy eating (starches like mashed potatoes or rice go down like celery sticks by comparison). So what's the problem? You were planning to go dancing after the Seder, maybe? Heaviness notwithstanding, a good kugel should be soft and moist, not dense, with a crisp crust.

Note: This is the Deli's recipe. Some people like to grate in a few vegetables to add color, and cookbook author Ruth Kanin makes cute crusty individual kugelettes in a greased muffin pan.

2½ pounds potatoes, peeled and
    quartered
2 large onions (use 1½ cups grated;
    don't tamp down)
3 eggs, beaten
1 teaspoon baking powder
¾ cup corn oil

1 cup flour
2½ teaspoons salt
¼ teaspoon pepper
1 cup matzo meal
Corn oil for drizzling and greasing
    pan

1. Preheat oven to 400 degrees. In a food processor, fine-grate potatoes (don't liquefy; leave some texture), and strain to eliminate excess liquid. Don't overdo it; just let the water drain out. Fine-grate onions, and mix in a large bowl with potatoes. (If you don't have a food processor, you can grind the potatoes and onions in a meat grinder.)

2. Add eggs, baking powder, ¾ cup corn oil (most of it cooks out), flour, salt, and pepper; mix well. Fold in matzo meal, making sure that everything is very well blended.

3. Pour batter into a greased baking pan (your kugel should be about 2 inches high), and drizzle top with corn oil from a flatware tablespoon. Bake for 55 minutes, or until top is golden brown (check occasionally to see). Serve hot.

Broccoli Kugel

Though generally served hot as a vegetable side dish, this kugel is also good cold (take it out of the refrigerator about 30 minutes before serving). Cold, we like to serve it with mayo-mustard sauce on the side (mix 1 part Dijon mustard to 3 parts Hellmann's mayonnaise, and sprinkle with a little paprika).

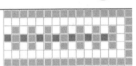

SERVES 6 TO 8

8 cups broccoli, chopped into ¼-inch to ½-inch pieces (cut into ¾-inch florets; then pulse a few times in a food processor)
½ teaspoon baking soda
1 tablespoon olive oil
2½ teaspoons salt
4 tablespoons corn oil
2 cups chopped onion
1 tablespoon finely chopped or crushed fresh garlic
6 eggs, beaten
¾ cup matzo meal
¼ teaspoon pepper
Shortening for greasing baking dish
Paprika

1. Preheat oven to 350 degrees. Pour 8 cups water into a large stockpot, and bring to a rapid boil. Add broccoli, baking soda, olive oil, and 1 teaspoon salt, and cook until broccoli is tender. Rinse in cold water, drain, and set aside.

2. While broccoli is cooking, heat 2 tablespoons of the corn oil in a large skillet, and sauté onions until browned. Add garlic, and brown very lightly and quickly. Remove onions and garlic to a large bowl with a slotted spoon. Let cool for 5 minutes.

3. Add eggs, matzo meal, 2 tablespoons corn oil, 1½ teaspoons salt, and pepper to the onions and garlic; combine thoroughly. Add broccoli, and stir in.

4. Pour mixture into a well-greased baking dish (approximately 9 inches square and 2 inches deep), and bake 30 minutes (or until top is lightly

browned and kugel is firm). Remove from oven, and sprinkle lightly with paprika.

Variation: You can make a spinach kugel pretty much the same way. Use 20 ounces of fresh spinach, thoroughly washed and finely chopped (use your food processor). Cook the spinach in boiling water for only 2 to 3 minutes, omitting the baking soda. Baking time will be a bit longer (35 to 40 minutes).

Matzo Kugel

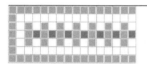

SERVES 6

Matzo kugel is often served at Seders. A hearty side dish, it's delicious with roast chicken or brisket and goes well with red Passover wines.

4 tablespoons corn oil
3 cups chopped onion
1 cup celery, chopped into ¹/₂-inch pieces
1 cup carrots, chopped into ¹/₈-inch pieces (this is most easily done by chopping them into ¹/₂-inch pieces and pulsing them a few times in a food processor)
3 cups scrubbed mushrooms, chopped into ¹/₂-inch pieces, ¹/₄ inch thick

6 squares matzo
2 tablespoons fresh dill
4 eggs, beaten
3 tablespoons schmaltz (optional)
1 tablespoon poultry seasoning
1 teaspoon salt
¹/₄ teaspoon pepper
Shortening for greasing baking dish

1. Preheat oven to 350 degrees. Heat 2 tablespoons of the corn oil in a large skillet, and sauté onions until nicely browned. Remove with a slotted spoon to a very large bowl. Add 1 tablespoon corn oil to skillet, and sauté celery and carrots until crisp and lightly browned, stirring occasionally. Remove with a slotted spoon to bowl with onions. Add 1 tablespoon corn oil (or more if needed) to skillet, and brown mushrooms. Remove with a slotted spoon to bowl with onions.
2. Crumble the matzos in a colander, run cool water over them to soften, and squeeze out excess liquid. Add matzos and all other ingredients except shortening to bowl with sautéed vegetables, and mix thoroughly.
3. Pour mixture into a greased baking dish (approximately 9 inches square and 2 inches deep), and bake 35 to 40 minutes, until top is lightly browned and crunchy and inside is firm.

"During the war, when my father was doing hard labor in Siberia, and my mother and I were deported to Kazakhstan, we had to leave all our possessions behind. So, at Pesach, we would recite the Haggadah as best we could from memory. One year, we held a Seder with an old woman and her daughter, but, of course, we weren't able to prepare the ritual dishes; all we had to eat was soup and potatoes. Later, in the DP camps, we held large communal Seders. There wasn't usually enough food to eat, but we did have an enormous shipment of matzos from Israel. We ate matzo so much over the next few months, we began to feel like it was coming out of our ears."

—Abe Lebewohl

PROMOTIONS, PITCHES . . . AND PITCHING NO-HITTERS

Get a Horse

IN 1973, AN OPEC-engineered oil shortage led to an alarming energy crisis in the United States. Gasoline rationing was instituted, there were long lines at the pumps, and the price of a gallon of gas jumped from about 30 cents to over a dollar. Abe was unfazed: he simply began making his food deliveries via horse and buggy. It was a charming and picturesque commentary on a serious problem—one typical of Abe, who always saw the bright side of any situation.

Creamy Matzo-Apple Kugel

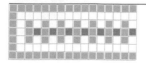

This sweet and creamy kugel makes an impressive centerpiece for a Passover brunch. You can also serve it for dessert.

2 tablespoons plus 2 teaspoons
  unsalted butter
4 McIntosh apples, peeled, cored,
  and cut into ³/₄-inch slices,
  ¹/₄ inch thick
¹/₂ cup raisins
¹/₂ cup sliced blanched almonds
10 squares plain unsalted matzo

4 eggs, beaten
2 cups sour cream
¹/₂ cup whipped cream cheese
³/₄ cup sugar
1 teaspoon cinnamon
¹/₂ teaspoon salt
Softened butter for greasing pan
Confectioners' sugar

1. Melt 2 tablespoons of the butter in a large skillet and sauté apple slices on high heat, stirring occasionally, until soft and lightly browned. Remove to a large bowl with a slotted spoon. Add 2 teaspoons butter to the skillet, lower heat to medium, and quickly sauté raisins and almonds, stirring constantly. Be careful not to burn them. Add to bowl with apples, and set aside.
2. Preheat oven to 350 degrees. Place matzo squares in another large bowl, and run cool water over them to soften. Crumble the matzo, and drain in a colander. Return drained matzo to bowl.
3. Combine eggs with matzo, and stir well. In another bowl, mix sour cream and cream cheese thoroughly. Then add it to the matzo mixture, along with sugar, cinnamon, salt, and fruit-nut mixture. Mix all ingredients thoroughly.
4. Grease a 10-inch square Pyrex baking pan (or similar) with butter (use quite a bit), pour mixture into pan, and bake for 50 minutes or until top is a light golden brown. Let cool on counter. Loosen sides with a knife, place a large platter over the baking pan, and carefully turn the kugel out onto the platter. If any pieces stick in the pan, just put them in place. When cooled, sprinkle top with confectioners' sugar (best done through a sieve or sifter). You can serve this kugel warm (not hot) or at room temperature, but we like it best chilled in the refrigerator with the confectioners' sugar added just prior to serving.

Matzo Kugel with Spicy Beef

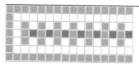

The matzo kugel above is a creation of Eastern European Jews. This version is based on an Indian recipe; most of the ingredients—not the matzos, of course—are those used for filling samosas (meat turnovers).

2 tablespoons olive oil
1 cup finely chopped onions
1 tablespoon finely chopped or
   crushed fresh garlic
1 pound chopmeat
10 squares plain unsalted matzo
4 eggs, beaten
1 large tomato, chopped into
   ½-inch pieces (remove seeds)
½ cup finely chopped fresh parsley

1 teaspoon dried mint leaves
2 teaspoons curry powder
⅛ teaspoon chili powder
1 teaspoon salt
Shortening for greasing baking
   dish

1. Preheat oven to 350 degrees. Heat 2 tablespoons olive oil in a large skillet, and brown onions well. At the last minute, add garlic and brown quickly. With a slotted spoon, remove onions and garlic to a large bowl, and set aside.

2. In remaining oil, sauté chopmeat, stirring frequently and breaking up lumps with a fork, until meat is fully browned and in loose pieces. Remove to bowl with onions and garlic, and mix thoroughly.

3. Place matzos in a colander, run cool water over them to soften, and squeeze out excess liquid. Crumble the matzos, and drain. Return drained matzos to a separate large bowl.

4. Combine eggs with matzos, and stir thoroughly. Add meat-onion-garlic mixture, tomato, parsley, mint, curry powder, chili powder, and salt; mix well.

5. Place mixture in a 10-inch square, lightly greased Pyrex baking pan (or similar) and bake for 40 minutes, until top is lightly browned and crunchy and inside is firm. Serve immediately.

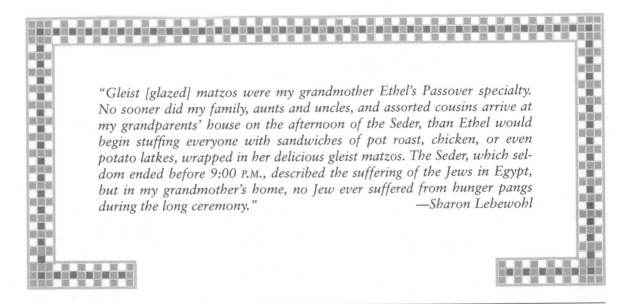

"Gleist [glazed] matzos were my grandmother Ethel's Passover specialty. No sooner did my family, aunts and uncles, and assorted cousins arrive at my grandparents' house on the afternoon of the Seder, than Ethel would begin stuffing everyone with sandwiches of pot roast, chicken, or even potato latkes, wrapped in her delicious gleist matzos. The Seder, which seldom ended before 9:00 P.M., described the suffering of the Jews in Egypt, but in my grandmother's home, no Jew ever suffered from hunger pangs during the long ceremony."
—Sharon Lebewohl

Gleist Matzos

MAKES 4 SLICES

The key to this recipe is very careful handling of the matzos. The squares should remain intact. When they're fried, they're pliable, and you can stuff them, like Ethel did, with pot roast, chicken, or anything else that appeals to you. For a dairy meal, they're great with sour cream.

3/4 cup very, very finely chopped onion—almost grated (use a food processor)
2 large eggs, beaten

1/2 teaspoon salt
1/4 teaspoon freshly ground pepper
4 squares plain unsalted matzo
Corn oil

1. Place onion, eggs, salt, and pepper in a large bowl, and beat until the eggs are frothy.
2. Lay out 4 squares of paper towel on your counter. One at a time, run the matzos under cold water for about 15 seconds on each side (if you break a square, discard it, and start again), and place them side by side on the paper toweling.
3. Carefully place a matzo square in a shallow dish with sides at least 1 inch high. Spread one-fourth of the onion-egg mixture on top of it. Pile the other matzos on top, spreading each square with one-fourth of the onion-egg mixture. Let sit for 5 minutes.
4. Heat a thin layer of oil in a large skillet. Fry the matzos, one at a time, until well browned on each side. Drain on paper towels.

TOM BIRCHARD is the owner of Veselka, a Ukrainian coffee shop located a block away from the Deli and an East Village institution in its own right. We're delighted that he's shared his famous pierogi recipe with us.

I started out working for my father-in-law at Veselka in the 1960s, and Abe often stopped in to chat with him in Ukrainian. In those pregentrification days, the Deli wasn't much more than a hot dog stand, and

Veselka, another neighborhood deli.

we were barely a candy store. When my father-in-law died, and I took over Veselka, I was immensely touched by the interest Abe took in my well-being and in the success of the place. I once asked him why he was so generously helping me out, when we were actually competitors. Abe waved away my question. "The more successful businesses on the block," he assured me, "the more business there'll be for all of us." Later, he was instrumental in forming a Second Avenue Merchants' Association to further his theory that cooperation produced more capital than competition. His stamp is on all the booming businesses along this section of Second Avenue today.

Of course, as all who knew him are aware, Abe's generosity extended far beyond valuable free advice. When a grocery store across the street from Veselka had a bad fire one summer, and much of its interior and stock was destroyed, Abe was one of the first on the scene. I watched as he pulled a wad of bills from his pocket and peeled off thousands of dollars to tide the unfortunate grocers over until repairs could be made and merchandise replenished.

In recent years, Abe dropped by almost daily for breakfast—a midmorning break from business (his day started about 4:00 A.M.) and a chance to read the paper in peace. When he died, my waiters wept. Though he came in to get away from work for a brief spell, he still took the time to chat with my staff and form some kind of relationship with them.

His bigheartedness remains an ongoing source of inspiration in both my business and my personal life.

Veselka's Potato Pierogi

MAKES 65 TO 70

These Polish-style dumplings have been a signature dish at Veselka since 1954. Though this recipe makes quite a large number, they can be frozen for about 3 weeks—a time period during which you're sure to crave them again.

4 tablespoons (half stick) butter
5 cups onion, chopped into ¼-inch
    pieces
2 egg whites

2 tablespoons water
Flour
Sour cream

FILLING

4 cups cooked Idaho potatoes,
    mashed very smooth (this is best
    done in a food processor)
4 ounces farmer cheese
4 tablespoons instant mashed
    potato granules

¾ cup sautéed onion (taken from
    5 cups listed above; see step 1)
2 teaspoons salt
¼ teaspoon pepper

WRAPPINGS

1 egg yolk
1 cup milk
½ cup water

1 tablespoon vegetable oil
3¼ cups all-purpose flour

1. Melt butter in a large skillet, and sauté onions very slowly (on moderate heat), stirring occasionally, until well browned. Separate out ¾ cup to use in potato filling, and set the rest aside in a bowl (do not refrigerate).

2. Combine all filling ingredients in a large bowl, and mix very thoroughly. Set aside.

3. For the wrappings: In a bowl, combine egg yolk, milk, water, and vegetable oil. Whip with a fork for 1 minute. Place flour in a large bowl, and pour wet ingredients into the center, about one-third at a time. Using your hands, gently fold everything together. If too sticky, add a little more flour, but only what is necessary to get your dough out of the bowl in one piece. Turn the dough out onto a well-floured pastry board, and knead for 3 minutes, once again dusting with flour if your dough is too sticky. Form dough into a ball, place in a bowl covered with plastic wrap, and refrigerate for 20 minutes.

4. In a small bowl, mix 2 egg whites with 2 tablespoons water, and keep it handy on your worktable, along with a pastry brush, rolling pin, flatware teaspoon and fork, 2¾-inch round cookie cutter (or similarly sized jar lid), and floured board (in addition to the one on which you are rolling out your dough; a large platter will do as well). Divide your dough into 3 sections. Place 1 section on a well-floured board, and roll out dough to $\frac{1}{16}$-inch thickness. Cut circles of dough with cookie cutter. Put a heaping flatware teaspoon of filling in the center of each circle (be careful not to get it on the edges, or it will make crimping difficult). You want to use the maximum amount of filling that still allows you room to seal the edges tightly. Brush some of the egg white mixture on half of the outer edge of your circle (it will work like envelope glue), and fold the dough over into a half-moon shape. Crimp the edges together with your fingers, or use a fork to do more-decorative crimping on both sides. Place finished pierogis on a floured board or platter. Do not stack them. Repeat with remaining dough and stuffing.

5. Fill a large stockpot about three-quarters full of salted water, and bring to a vigorous boil. Place pierogis, a few at a time, into the rapidly boiling water, and cook for 4 minutes. Drain, and serve, topping each portion with some of the remaining sautéed onion (heated up, of course) and a big dollop of sour cream. Or if you prefer them fried, boil for 2 minutes, then sauté in butter until golden brown.

Note: You can make pierogis in advance by boiling them for 2 minutes, draining, and coating with vegetable oil to keep from sticking. Refrigerate for use within the next day or two; otherwise freeze them. Reheat in boiling salted water or sauté as described above.

Matzo Brei

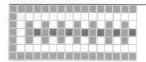

SERVES 1 OR 2

This is probably the world's simplest recipe. You can, however, get creative with it. For instance, try adding grated onions or finely chopped scallions and ¼ teaspoon pepper to the matzo-egg mix. Or add ½ teaspoon cinnamon, omit the salt, and serve your matzo brei with a side dish of peach or apple slices sautéed in butter. Nuts (we've tried almond slivers and pistachios) are another possibility. And you might also want to sift some powdered sugar on top.

Note: Increase all ingredients proportionately for additional servings.

2 slices matzo
1 egg, beaten
½ teaspoon salt

2 tablespoons corn oil or butter
Applesauce, jam, and/or sour cream

1. Crumble matzos to pieces no larger than 1¼ inches in a colander, and run under cold water until softened. Press out excess water.
2. Transfer matzos to a large bowl, and mix well with egg and salt. Let mixture sit on counter for 5 minutes.
3. Heat oil or butter in a skillet (don't use too large a skillet, or you'll end up with nothing but crust). Pour in matzo mixture, and cook on low heat until the bottom is golden brown and the matzo brei turns easily. Brown the other side. Alternatively, you can use a bigger pan, and scramble the matzo brei like eggs.
4. Serve with applesauce, jam, and/or, if preparing a dairy meal, sour cream.

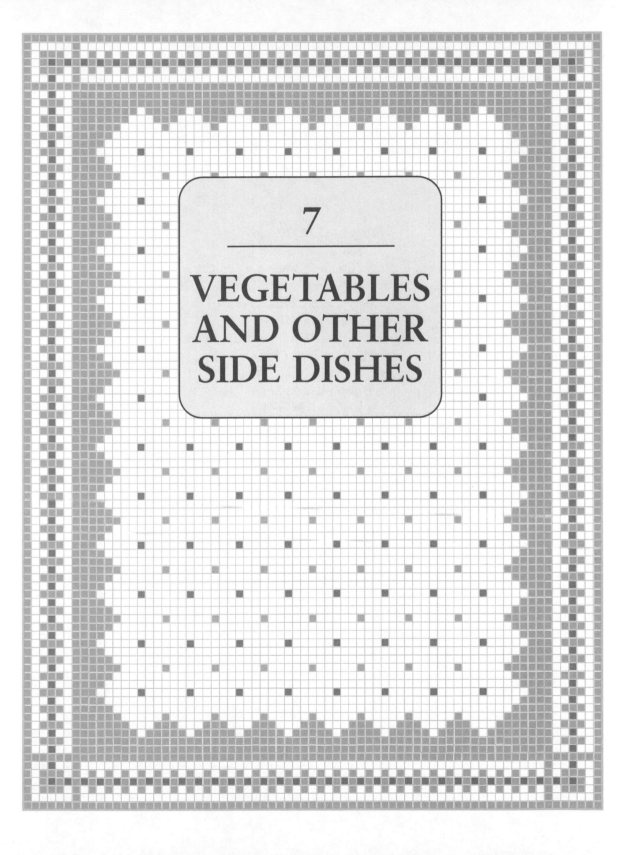

7

VEGETABLES AND OTHER SIDE DISHES

Farfel and Mushrooms
Kasha Varnishkes
Grandma Blanche Salter's Macaroni and Cheeses
Noodles with Cabbage, Raisins, and Almonds
Carrots with Honey, Fruit, and Nuts
Carrot Pudding
Art and Avital D'Lugoff's Vegetable Cholent
Cauliflower au Gratin
Garlic-Rosemary Roast Potatoes
Home-Fried Potatoes
French Fries
Mashed Potatoes
Meat and Potato Knishes
Grandpa's Fettuccine with Roasted Garlic, Tomatoes, and Artichokes
Herbed Rice
Herbed Rice with Dried Fruit
My Mother's Famous Spaghetti Recipe
Red Cabbage and Apples
Vegetable Croquettes
Vegetable Lo Mein
Roz Perry's Shtetl Sauerkraut
Tzimmes

WE'D AS SOON EAT an entrée without a vegetable and starch as a stack of pancakes without butter and syrup. Here you'll find diverse side dishes to complement your meals, from the Deli's famed farfel and mushrooms to golden vegetable latkes and croquettes.

Farfel and Mushrooms

Dishes made with egg barley, or farfel, are generally eaten at Rosh Hashanah; the grain-shaped pasta symbolizes the seeds of an abundant harvest in the year ahead.

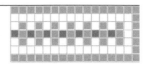

SERVES 6

3 tablespoons corn oil
2 cups chopped onions
2 cups scrubbed mushrooms, chopped into ¾-inch slices, about ³⁄₁₆ nch thick
2 cups uncooked egg barley

3 cups clear chicken soup or stock
Salt (the amount will depend on how much salt is in the chicken stock you use; if it's salty, you may not need any)
¼ teaspoon pepper

1. In a large skillet, heat 2 tablespoons of the corn oil, and sauté onions until lightly browned. Remove with a slotted spoon to a bowl. In remaining oil (add a bit more if needed), brown the mushrooms, stirring occasionally. Add to the bowl with onions, and set aside.
2. Preheat oven to 325 degrees. Pour egg barley into a baking pan (approximately 10 by 12 by 3 inches high), add 1 tablespoon of corn oil, and mix well. Place pan in the oven, and bake for 20 minutes, stirring at 10 minutes so that it browns evenly. While egg barley is baking, put the chicken soup in a pot with salt (if needed) and pepper, and warm on the stove.
3. Remove the baking pan from the oven. Stir in the onion-mushroom mixture and add the soup.
4. Lower the oven to 300 degrees, and bake for another 30 minutes or until all soup is absorbed. Stir after 15 minutes. Remove and serve.

Kasha Varnishkes

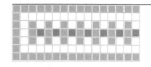

Kasha—today a classic of Jewish cuisine—was a mainstay of poor nine-teenth-century Russian and Polish Jews—the hearty grain that provided sustenance in the long, cold winter months. For holidays, it was stuffed with fried onions into kreplach or eaten with shell- or bow-tie-shaped pasta noodles.

1½ cups uncooked kasha
2 eggs, beaten
¼ cup corn oil or schmaltz
5 cups chopped onions

¾ pound bow tie noodles
  (varnishkes)
2½ teaspoons salt

1. Preheat oven to 350 degrees. Mix kasha and eggs thoroughly, and bake mixture in a shallow pan for 20 minutes.
2. Heat corn oil in a large skillet, and sauté onions, stirring occasionally, until well browned. Remove to a bowl, retaining cooking oil with onions.
3. Boil 6 cups of water in a large stockpot. Remove kasha from oven, stir into the boiling water, and simmer for 15 to 20 minutes (until all water has evaporated). When you're through cooking the kasha, break up clumps with a fork.
4. At the same time you're cooking the kasha, in a separate pot, boil bow ties for 15 to 20 minutes, until fully cooked. Drain and rinse.
5. Mix everything together, including salt, and serve.

TWO-TIME OSCAR WINNER and six-time nominee Dustin Hoffman was a very young-looking thirty-year-old in 1967, when Mike Nichols discovered him, Mrs. Robinson seduced him, and his shy smile turned on all of America. After *The Graduate* (his first Best Actor nomination), he went on to star in a mind-boggling number of first-rate Hollywood films. A noted stage actor as well, Hoffman made his first Broadway appearance in 1961 (a walk-on part in *A Cook for Mr. General*). He returned to the Broadway stage in 1984 (playing Willy Loman in an award-winning revival of Arthur Miller's *Death of a Salesman*), and in 1990, he received a Tony nomination for his portrayal of Shylock in *The Merchant of Venice*.

Though everyone thinks of Hoffman as the archetypal New York actor (and as a Deli habitué, he is, of course, an honorary Gothamite), he actually grew up in Los Angeles.

The Second Avenue Deli is where I ordered nonprescription remedies for myself, family, and friends. If one of us became ill, we didn't call a doctor, we called Abe Lebewohl and asked for a container of chicken soup with matzo balls. If the illness persisted, a potato knish or a noodle pudding was immediately called for.

On one occasion, I recall curing my brother-in-law, Leeroy, of a migraine headache by having a pastrami sandwich, coleslaw, potato salad, and sour pickles delivered to him.

Abe didn't allow me to pay for anything. He always promised to "send a bill." It never arrived.

We all miss Abe greatly and think of him often.

Grandma Blanche Salter's Macaroni and Cheeses

SERVES 4 TO 6 AS A SIDE DISH

The following dish was submitted by Lisa and Dustin Hoffman.

2 tablespoons butter
8 ounces elbow macaroni, cooked
   and drained
8 ounces mozzarella cheese, grated
8 ounces Swiss cheese, grated

8 ounces Gouda or Edam cheese,
   grated
Pepper
Parmesan cheese

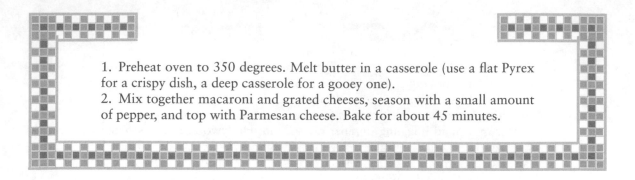

1. Preheat oven to 350 degrees. Melt butter in a casserole (use a flat Pyrex for a crispy dish, a deep casserole for a gooey one).
2. Mix together macaroni and grated cheeses, season with a small amount of pepper, and top with Parmesan cheese. Bake for about 45 minutes.

Noodles with Cabbage, Raisins, and Almonds

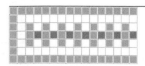

SERVES 6

This Austro-Hungarian recipe makes a nice lunch entrée or a combination starch and vegetable side dish for a meat (especially pot roast) or fish meal. Some people like to sprinkle poppy seeds in at the end.

Note: It's okay to substitute margarine for the schmaltz in this recipe; for a dairy version, use unsalted butter.

1 medium head green cabbage	*½ cup golden raisins*
1 teaspoon salt	*½ cup sliced blanched almonds*
¼ teaspoon pepper	*2 cups chopped onion*
½ teaspoon sugar	*4 cups egg noodles*
⅜ cup plus 2 teaspoons schmaltz	*Salt and pepper to taste*

1. Coarsely shred cabbage with a large knife, and toss with salt, pepper, and sugar in a large bowl. Set aside.
2. Heat 2 teaspoons of the schmaltz in a very large skillet, and quickly brown raisins and almonds, stirring constantly. Remove to a small bowl, and set aside.
3. Add the remaining ⅜ cup of schmaltz to the skillet, and sauté onions until lightly browned. Add cabbage (you may have to do this a bit at a time; as it cooks, you can add more), mix well, cover, and continue cooking on low heat for 30 minutes, stirring occasionally.
4. While cabbage is cooking, bring water to a vigorous boil in a large stock-pot, toss in the noodles, and cook for 5 to 7 minutes until al dente. Drain, return noodles to pot, and cover to keep warm.
5. Uncover skillet, turn up heat, and, stirring very frequently, continue cooking until cabbage is lightly browned.
6. Add cabbage mixture, raisins, and almonds to noodles, and cook on low heat for a minute or two. Remove to a large bowl, and toss ingredients, adding salt and freshly ground pepper to taste.

Carrots with Honey, Fruit, and Nuts

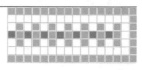

1½ pounds carrots, peeled and sliced into 1-inch sticks, about ⅜ inch wide

2 tablespoons butter or margarine

8 pitted prunes, chopped into ½-inch pieces

½ cup raisins

¾ cup coarsely chopped pecans or walnuts

¼ cup honey (if you grease your measuring cup with vegetable oil, the honey will slide right out)

1 teaspoon finely grated lemon rind

1 tablespoon sugar

½ teaspoon salt

SERVES 6

1. Place carrots in a saucepan, cover with water, and bring to a boil. Reduce heat, and simmer for 15 minutes.

2. While carrots are simmering, melt butter in a large skillet and sauté prunes, raisins, and nuts on moderate heat for 2 minutes, stirring constantly.

3. Drain carrots and return them to saucepan. Add fruit-nut mixture and all other ingredients, stir to thoroughly combine, and cook for 2 more minutes, stirring frequently. Serve hot.

Carrot Pudding

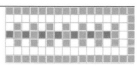

This dessertlike recipe comes from Iran (they call it a halvah), where a still-extant Jewish community dates back to 538 B.C.E.

2 pounds cooked carrots

2 tablespoons unsalted butter

¾ cup golden raisins

¾ cup sliced blanched almonds

1 cup heavy cream

1 teaspoon cinnamon

¾ teaspoon salt

¼ cup sugar

Butter for greasing pan and dotting top of casserole

SERVES 6

1. Preheat oven to 350 degrees. Mash carrots smooth (use a food processor or blender if you have one), and place in a large bowl.

2. Melt 2 tablespoons butter in a large skillet, and, stirring constantly, brown raisins and almonds (they brown very quickly, so be careful not to burn them). Set aside, with butter from pan, in another bowl.

3. Add cream, cinnamon, salt, and sugar to carrots, and mash in thoroughly. Add almond-raisin mixture and stir in well.

4. Grease baking pan with butter, and spoon in carrot mixture. Dot top with small pieces of butter. Bake for 25 minutes. Serve hot or cold.

ONE OF AMERICA'S most noted music impresarios, Art D'Lugoff founded the Village Gate in 1958 on Bleecker Street. At that famed nightspot—and in other clubs and concert halls throughout the United States—he hosted every major name in jazz, folk, blues, and gospel, as well as comedy and cabaret shows. Aretha Franklin made her first New York appearance at the Gate, and, over the years, D'Lugoff presented such legendary performers as Paul Robeson, Duke Ellington, Pete Seeger, Nina Simone, Dizzy Gillespie, Thelonius Monk, John Coltrane, and Billie Holiday.

His interest in music dates to his days at the Yeshiva of Flatbush, where he was inspired by his teacher, Cantor Moshe Nathanson, who composed "Hava Nagila." D'Lugoff is currently working on his autobiography and organizing an International Jazz Museum/Hall of Fame to be located in New York City.

I first met Abe at a picnic he catered in Central Park for the Friars Club, of which I'm a member. Over the years, I often ran into him at Jewish events (he donated food and services to dozens of charities), and, though we disagreed politically—especially about Israel—we became good friends. However heated our discussions, I always knew that his generosity and concern for others were paramount. He was an important presence in New York, and the creator of the city's finest deli.

Art and Avital D'Lugoff's Vegetable Cholent

SERVES 6

As a traditional Sabbath dish, this cholent needs to bake in the oven overnight. Plan ahead. See other cholent recipes on pages 86 and 111.

4 tablespoons corn oil
3 cups chopped onions
3 cups mushrooms, preferably portobellos, chopped into ³/4-inch pieces
2 quarts clear vegetable broth or stock (you can buy this at the supermarket or make your own; see recipe on page xxiii)
3 pounds large red potatoes, peeled and chopped into ³/4-inch pieces

1 cup Yankee beans
1½ cups barley
¼ cup water
10 dried prunes
½ cup derma stuffing, chopped into ½-inch pieces (optional)
2 teaspoons salt
¼ teaspoon pepper
1 teaspoon curry or paprika
6 eggs in the shell

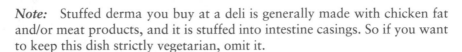

Note: Stuffed derma you buy at a deli is generally made with chicken fat and/or meat products, and it is stuffed into intestine casings. So if you want to keep this dish strictly vegetarian, omit it.

1. Heat 2 tablespoons of the corn oil in a large skillet, and sauté onions until browned. Remove onions—with cooking oil—to a bowl, and set aside. Add 2 more tablespoons corn oil to skillet, sauté mushrooms, and, with cooking oil, add to bowl with onions.
2. In a large stockpot, bring vegetable stock to a rapid boil. Toss in potatoes, beans, barley, onions, and mushrooms. Cover, and simmer for 1½ hours, stirring occasionally.
3. Add ¼ cup water, prunes, derma stuffing, salt, pepper, and curry or paprika, and mix well. Transfer about half the mixture to a Dutch oven or covered casserole (if you don't have either, a disposable aluminum baking dish tightly covered in aluminum foil will do). Place the eggs atop the mixture, and cover with the rest, so that they are completely buried. Bake overnight at 225 degrees.

Note: If you're not preparing the cholent as a Sabbath dish, you can reduce baking time to 1 or 2 hours. The less you bake it, the more individual ingredients will keep their texture and integrity. If you do this, however, boil the eggs for about 20 minutes before you bake them.

Cauliflower au Gratin

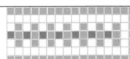

1 large head (or 2 small heads)
    cauliflower, divided into florets
    no larger than 2 inches
3 tablespoons plus 2 tablespoons
    unsalted butter, melted
3 tablespoons flour
¾ cup milk
¾ cup sour cream

1 egg yolk
1 teaspoon salt
¼ teaspoon pepper
⅓ cup seasoned bread crumbs
Butter for greasing pan
⅓ cup grated Parmesan cheese
Paprika

SERVES 6

Note: In gauging the amount of cauliflower to use, you should have enough florets to serve 6 people. If you want to make less (say, enough for 4 people), use ½ cup milk and ½ cup sour cream. Everything else can remain the same.

1. Pour water (you'll need enough to cover your cauliflower) into a large stockpot, and bring it to a rapid boil. When water is bubbling, toss florets into the pot, lower heat, and simmer for 10 minutes. Drain in a colander, and transfer to a large bowl. Set aside.

2. Preheat oven to 375 degrees. Place 3 tablespoons of the melted butter in a second bowl. Using a wire whisk, stir in flour until smooth. Add milk, sour cream, egg yolk, salt, and pepper, and blend thoroughly.

3. Toss cauliflower with bread crumbs. Butter a Pyrex or similar baking dish, and transfer cauliflower into it. Pour sauce over the cauliflower. Distribute Parmesan cheese evenly over the top, and, using a flatware teaspoon, drizzle evenly with the remaining 2 tablespoons of melted butter. Bake for 10 minutes.

4. Turn up oven temperature to broil, and place baking dish in the broiler for 2 to 3 minutes, until the top is nicely browned. Keep an eye on it; there's only a small margin of time between browning and burning.

5. Sprinkle lightly with paprika, and serve.

Garlic-Rosemary Roast Potatoes

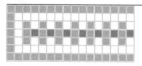

SERVES 6 TO 8

¼ cup vegetable oil
¼ cup schmaltz
6 large potatoes, peeled and
    chopped into 2-inch chunks
2 tablespoons finely chopped or
    crushed fresh garlic
6 peeled garlic cloves (optional)

2 cups coarsely chopped onion
2 teaspoons salt
¼ teaspoon pepper
1 tablespoon rosemary
Paprika
Fresh parsley for garnish

Note: You can use more or fewer potatoes, depending on how many people you're serving. It's easy to divide the chopped raw potatoes into portions and determine how many you'll need. Roasted garlic cloves are a plus if you like them.

1. Preheat oven to 350 degrees. Place all ingredients (except paprika and parsley) in a large bowl, and mix to thoroughly coat potatoes. Pour everything into a large baking dish, so that potatoes are all on one layer. Sprinkle with paprika, and bake 1 hour and 15 minutes or until tender and golden-crusted. (Every 30 minutes, check that potatoes are cooking evenly; if they're not, turn the pan around.) Garnish with chopped parsley.

Home-Fried Potatoes

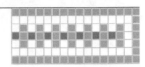

Home fries are so American. We add a bit of schmaltz to make them Jewish.

SERVES 6

3 pounds large red or Yukon gold
   potatoes, peeled but whole
3 tablespoons corn oil
3/4 cup green pepper, chopped into
   3/4-inch pieces
1 1/2 cups chopped onions
2 teaspoons finely chopped or
   crushed fresh garlic

3 tablespoons schmaltz or olive oil
2 teaspoons paprika
1/4 teaspoon cayenne pepper
1 1/2 teaspoons salt
1 teaspoon pepper

1. Bring a large stockpot of water to a vigorous boil, add potatoes, and simmer for 35 minutes or until potatoes are fully cooked (cooking time will depend on size). When potatoes cool sufficiently to handle, cut them into pieces approximately 1 inch by 1/2 inch. Place them in a large bowl, and set aside.

2. Preheat oven to 375 degrees. Heat corn oil in a large skillet, and sauté green peppers for 2 minutes. Add onions, and continue to sauté until brown. Add garlic at the last minute to brown quickly. Pour contents of skillet into bowl with potatoes, add schmaltz, and toss gently to mix.

3. Combine paprika, cayenne, salt, and pepper in a bowl. Mix thoroughly, and sprinkle evenly over potatoes. Toss gently to further distribute ingredients.

4. Transfer contents of bowl to a baking dish, and bake for 30 minutes, stirring every 10 minutes.

French Fries

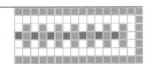

Idaho potatoes (as many as
   needed)

Corn or peanut oil
Salt

1. Cut potatoes into rectangles to create equal-sized fries. Then, using a sharp knife, cut fries about 2 inches long and 3/8 inch wide. Place the cut fries in cold water, and refrigerate for 2 hours. Rinse in cold water, and drain.

2. Heat oil (to 325 degrees if you have a candy thermometer) in a deep fryer or a tall stockpot. Place the potatoes in the basket of the deep fryer (or directly into the hot oil). Fry them for about 4 minutes; do not let them get browned. Remove potatoes to a bowl (use a slotted spoon if you don't have a basket), and refrigerate until cooled.

3. Heat oil again (to 375 degrees if you have a thermometer), and fry until golden brown and crisp. Toss into a bowl lined with paper toweling, blot excess oil, and salt to taste.

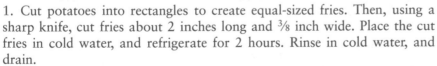

Mashed Potatoes

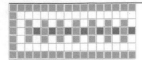

The Deli's mashed potatoes aren't very complicated. Each pound of potatoes serves about 3 people.

Potatoes (any kind are good; we
 like Yukon gold)
1 teaspoon salt

Schmaltz (3 tablespoons per pound
 of potatoes)
Salt and pepper to taste

1. Peel potatoes, and cut them into 2-inch pieces. Place them in a bowl covered with cold water, and soak for 10 minutes to remove starchiness; drain.
2. Fill a large stockpot about three-quarters full with water, and bring to a boil. Add potatoes and 1 teaspoon salt; cook until tender (about 18 minutes). Drain thoroughly in a colander. To further remove moisture (no one wants watery mashed potatoes), return potatoes to the pot on medium to high heat for a minute or two, turning them constantly so they don't burn.
3. For the smoothest results, put them through a ricer. If you don't have one, apply a lot of elbow grease to a potato masher. Do not mash them in a food processor or blender; it ruins the fluffy texture. Add 3 tablespoons schmaltz per pound of potatoes, and season with salt and pepper to taste.

Optional additions: Sautéed finely chopped onion or roasted garlic. For the latter, preheat oven to 350 degrees, chop tip off garlic head to expose cloves, and pull off loose peel. Drizzle with 1 tablespoon olive oil, sprinkle with fresh pepper, and bake, wrapped in tin foil, for 45 minutes. Squeeze garlic head to release cloves, mash them up, and mix them into the potatoes. Alternately, you can simply sauté large chunks of garlic in olive oil.

Variation: If you're making mashed potatoes as an accompaniment for fish, you might substitute unsalted butter for schmaltz and whip in some heated cream or half-and-half (about ⅜ cup per pound of potatoes).

Meat and Potato Knishes

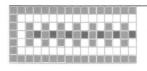

These Deli knishes (a variation on the real thing, since they're not wrapped in pastry) are substantial enough to make complete meals in themselves with a salad or vegetable on the side.

MAKES 8

FOR THE PATTIES

2 pounds potatoes, peeled and cut
 into chunks
2 tablespoons corn oil
1 cup finely chopped onions
1 tablespoon finely chopped or
 crushed fresh garlic
¼ pound corned beef

¼ pound pastrami
2 scallions, finely chopped
3 eggs
1 teaspoon sugar
¼ teaspoon salt
½ teaspoon pepper
1 cup seasoned bread crumbs

FOR THE CRUST AND COOKING
2 eggs　　　　　　　　　　　　*2 cups seasoned bread crumbs,*
3/8 cup water　　　　　　　　　　　*placed in a shallow pan or dish*
　　　　　　　　　　　　　Corn oil for frying

1. Set a pot of water to boil, and cook potatoes 15 to 20 minutes, until tender. While the potatoes are cooking, heat corn oil in a large skillet, and sauté onions. At the last minute, add garlic, and brown quickly. Remove onions and garlic to a large bowl with a slotted spoon. Drain potatoes, add them to bowl, and refrigerate while chopping corned beef and pastrami very fine (for best results, use a food processor).
2. Mash potatoes and onions (use a hand masher, not a food processor or blender) to a smooth consistency. Add all the remaining patty ingredients, except the bread crumbs, stir them in thoroughly with a fork, and then continue working them together with your hands. Still using your hands, mix in the cup of bread crumbs.
3. Form the potato mixture into 3-inch patties (about ¾ inch high), and place them on a cookie sheet covered with wax paper. Place in freezer for 1 hour.
4. Remove patties from freezer. Beat eggs and water together in a bowl. Dip each patty to coat completely, then dredge in bread crumbs, covering thoroughly. Return patties to wax-papered cookie sheet, and refrigerate 15 minutes.
5. Heat an inch of corn oil (it must be high enough to completely cover the knishes) in a deep skillet (unless you cook them in batches, you'll probably need 2 skillets). Carefully place knishes in the pan and cook for 5 minutes. Using a spatula and a fork, turn and cook for another 2 minutes until deep golden brown on both sides. Remove, and drain on paper toweling before serving.

Note: You can make your patties in the morning, refrigerate them, and fry them up any time within about 3 days.

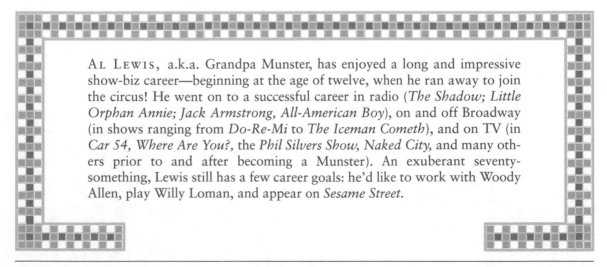

AL LEWIS, a.k.a. Grandpa Munster, has enjoyed a long and impressive show-biz career—beginning at the age of twelve, when he ran away to join the circus! He went on to a successful career in radio (*The Shadow; Little Orphan Annie; Jack Armstrong, All-American Boy*), on and off Broadway (in shows ranging from *Do-Re-Mi* to *The Iceman Cometh*), and on TV (in *Car 54, Where Are You?*, the *Phil Silvers Show, Naked City,* and many others prior to and after becoming a Munster). An exuberant seventy-something, Lewis still has a few career goals: he'd like to work with Woody Allen, play Willy Loman, and appear on *Sesame Street.*

I have many fond memories of Abe Lebewohl. One day, he and I were schmoozing over lunch at the Deli with pornmeister Al Goldstein (a mutual friend). High on chicken soup, or perhaps otherwise inspired, Goldstein blurted out, "Hey, I've got a great idea. Let's fly out to Nevada after lunch and go to a high-class brothel." Abe and I, both happily married men, just looked at each other. Finally, Abe said, "We'll go if you can find one that will accept corned beef and pastrami sandwiches as payment." Of course, we stayed right where we were.

I was at home with my wife when I heard the news about Abe's death. "It's not possible," I said. "I know Abe. If a guy tried to rob him, he'd not only give him all his money but offer him a couple of sandwiches and soup for the long ride home, and insist he take a soda as well."

Al Lewis

Of the recipe below, Grandpa says, "If you eat this dish three times a week, you'll live to be eighty-seven."

Grandpa's Fettuccine with Roasted Garlic, Tomatoes, and Artichokes

SERVES 6

1 large head garlic
3 tablespoons olive oil
Fresh-ground pepper
1½ pounds spinach fettuccine
1 large onion, thinly sliced
10 plum tomatoes, seeded and chopped into ½-inch pieces
2 6-ounce jars artichoke hearts, marinated in olive oil, drained and chopped into ¾-inch pieces

1 tablespoon chopped fresh thyme
¾ cup vegetable stock (you can buy this at the supermarket or make your own; see recipe on page xxiii)
Salt
Grated Parmesan or Romano cheese

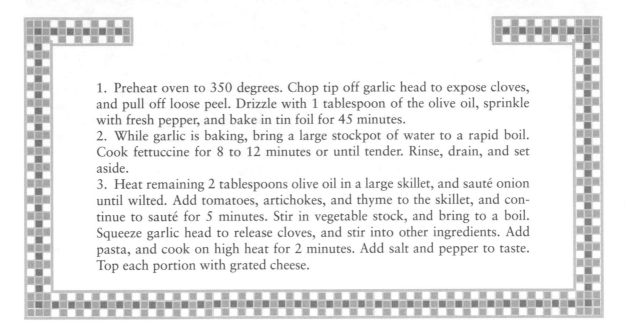

1. Preheat oven to 350 degrees. Chop tip off garlic head to expose cloves, and pull off loose peel. Drizzle with 1 tablespoon of the olive oil, sprinkle with fresh pepper, and bake in tin foil for 45 minutes.

2. While garlic is baking, bring a large stockpot of water to a rapid boil. Cook fettuccine for 8 to 12 minutes or until tender. Rinse, drain, and set aside.

3. Heat remaining 2 tablespoons olive oil in a large skillet, and sauté onion until wilted. Add tomatoes, artichokes, and thyme to the skillet, and continue to sauté for 5 minutes. Stir in vegetable stock, and bring to a boil. Squeeze garlic head to release cloves, and stir into other ingredients. Add pasta, and cook on high heat for 2 minutes. Add salt and pepper to taste. Top each portion with grated cheese.

Herbed Rice

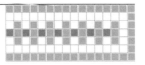

Iranian Jews—and non-Jews, for that matter—slowly steam their rice in a pot with butter or oil. It makes the rice very fluffy and forms a delicious golden crust. Since the first time we tried this method, we've never cooked rice any other way again.

SERVES 6

Note: For a dairy version, use vegetable stock instead of chicken soup and butter in place of margarine.

4 cups plain chicken soup or stock
2 cups water
2 cups long-grain white rice
6 tablespoons olive oil
2 cups chopped onions
1 tablespoon finely chopped or
    crushed fresh garlic
1 cup scrubbed mushrooms, sliced
    into ¹/₂-inch pieces, ¹/₈ inch thick
¹/₂ cup coarsely chopped walnuts or
    pecans

¹/₂ cup golden raisins
1 teaspoon rosemary
1 teaspoon thyme
¹/₄ teaspoon pepper
Salt (the amount will depend on
    how much salt is in the chicken
    stock you use; if it's salty, you
    may not need any)
3 tablespoons margarine

1. In a large stockpot, bring chicken soup and water to a boil. Add rice, and simmer for 18 minutes. (Hint: A teaspoon of cooking oil in the water keeps the rice from sticking.)

2. While rice is cooking, heat 2 tablespoons of the olive oil in a large skillet and sauté onions until nicely browned. Add garlic at the last minute, and brown quickly. Remove to a large bowl with a slotted spoon, add 1 table-spoon olive oil to skillet (use a little more if needed), and sauté mushrooms. Remove with slotted spoon to the same bowl. Sauté nuts and raisins (these brown very quickly) in the remaining oil, stirring very frequently, and re-move to same bowl with slotted spoon. Set bowl aside on counter.

3. Drain rice, but do not rinse, and place it in a different large bowl. Mix rosemary, thyme, pepper, and, if needed, salt into the rice.

4. In a clean wide-bottomed stockpot, melt margarine with remaining 3 ta-blespoons olive oil, swishing a bit on the lower sides of the pot. Return rice to pot, pour onion-mushroom-nut-raisin mixture on top, and cover com-pletely with a folded terry-cloth towel secured by a lid. Turn heat very, very low, and cook for 30 minutes.

5. Gently stir to combine all ingredients, including the crust from the bot-tom of the pot.

Herbed Rice with Dried Fruit

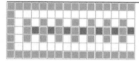

A variant of the above, this Iranian recipe adds dried fruit, a common in-gredient of Middle Eastern cuisines. Once again, use vegetable stock and butter for a dairy version.

SERVES 6

4 cups plain chicken soup or stock
2 cups water
2 cups long-grain white rice
6 tablespoons olive oil
2 cups chopped onions
1 tablespoon finely chopped or crushed fresh garlic
⅓ cup coarsely chopped dried apricots
½ cup coarsely chopped walnuts or pecans

½ cup golden raisins
½ cup coarsely chopped pitted prunes
1 teaspoon rosemary
1 teaspoon thyme
¼ teaspoon pepper
Salt (the amount will depend on how much salt is in the chicken stock you use; if it's salty, you may not need any)
3 tablespoons margarine

1. In a large stockpot, bring chicken soup and water to a boil. Add rice, and simmer for 18 minutes. (Hint: A teaspoon of cooking oil in the water keeps the rice from sticking.)

2. While rice is cooking, heat 2 tablespoons of the olive oil in a large skillet and sauté onions until nicely browned. Add garlic at the last minute, and brown quickly. Remove with a slotted spoon to a bowl. Add 1 tablespoon olive oil to skillet, and sauté apricots, nuts, and raisins (these brown very quickly; make sure they don't burn). Remove with a slotted spoon to the bowl with onions and garlic. Add prunes. Set aside on counter.

3. Drain rice, but do not rinse, and place it in a different large bowl. Mix in rosemary, thyme, pepper, and, if needed, salt.

4. In a clean wide-bottomed stockpot, melt margarine with 3 tablespoons olive oil, swishing a bit on the lower sides of the pot. Return rice to pot, pour onion-fruit-nut mixture on top, and cover completely with a folded terry-cloth towel secured by a lid. Turn heat very, very low, and cook for 30 minutes.

5. Gently stir to combine all ingredients, including the crust from the bottom of the pot.

NOTED GRAPHIC DESIGNER Milton Glaser was the founder of Pushpin Studios, an organization so influential in its field that it merited an exhibition at the Louvre. In 1968, along with Clay Felker, he founded *New York* magazine, where, in addition to being president and design director, he reviewed restaurants as the Underground Gourmet. Subsequently, at his firms WBMG and Milton Glaser, Inc., his design projects have included: the graphic revamping of dozens of major magazines; over three hundred posters; the famous I ♥ New York logo; public spaces ranging from the Observation Deck of the World Trade Center to the Sesame Place theme park; restaurants (most notably, the exterior, interior, and all graphic elements of New York's Trattoria dell'Arte); and the logo for the play *Angels in America*.

In the late fifties, my wife, Shirley, and I returned from a one-year honeymoon adventure in Italy. We found a spacious floor-through apartment on St. Mark's Place just about the time the area was beginning its transformation into the East Coast's prototypical sixties enclave. It was a turbulent and exciting time. Along with St. Mark's Church, the Second Avenue Deli provided some stability to the neighborhood. We didn't know Abe very well, but he always greeted us warmly when we stopped by for a brisket on rye.

We were having lunch at the Deli one day, when Abe stopped at our table. "What are you kids doing for Passover?" he inquired in his usual genial way. "We have no plans," I admitted, slightly embarrassed for overlooking the holiday. "Don't do a thing," Abe said. "What time will you be home?" "At six or so," I answered, with no idea of what he had in mind.

Promptly at 6:00 P.M., a delivery boy rang our doorbell and handed us an enormous brown shopping bag whose sides were hot to the touch. It yielded an enormous container of chicken soup, still simmering and replete with a whole quartered chicken, carrots, celery, and four baseball-sized matzo balls. The package also contained a slab of potato kugel, coleslaw, ruby-red horseradish, half-sour pickles, and a stack of carefully wrapped matzos—in short, everything needed for a complete Passover banquet.

At the time, we hardly knew Abe, but this kind of expansive generosity was characteristic of his behavior. He was a good man.

My Mother's Famous Spaghetti Recipe

SERVES 6

4 quarts salted water
1 pound Mueller's spaghetti (my mother was fearful of names like Ronzoni and Buitoni)

1 cup Heinz ketchup
1/2-pound slab Velveeta, cut into 1/2-inch cubes
Butter

1. Bring water to a boil, toss in spaghetti, cook for 30 minutes, drain, and return to pot.
2. Add ketchup and Velveeta, and mix thoroughly. Continue to cook for 10 minutes, stirring frequently.
3. Allow mixture to cool, preferably in a rectangular container.
4. Demold, and cut into 1/4-inch slices. Fry in butter until a nice crust has formed on each side. Serve with a small salad.

Red Cabbage and Apples

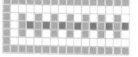

For a pareve version, substitute margarine for butter.

SERVES 6 TO 8

2 pounds red cabbage
4 tablespoons unsalted butter
2 McIntosh apples, peeled, cored, and sliced into 1-inch pieces, 1/4 inch thick
1/2 cup golden raisins

2 cups chopped red onion
6 tablespoons sugar
2 tablespoons white vinegar
3/4 teaspoon salt
1 cup water

FOR THE ROUX

2 tablespoons unsalted melted
  butter

2 tablespoons flour

1. Chop cabbage into large strips, and set aside in a bowl.
2. In a large skillet, heat 2 tablespoons of the butter, and sauté apple slices until browned. At the last minute add raisins, and sauté for about a minute more. Remove apples and raisins with a slotted spoon, and place in a large stockpot.
3. Add 2 remaining tablespoons of butter to skillet, and sauté onions until brown. Add sugar, lower heat, and continue to sauté while stirring for another minute. Place onion-sugar mixture in stockpot with apples and raisins, and gently toss to combine.
4. Add cabbage, vinegar, salt, and water to stockpot. Stir, cover, and simmer for 20 minutes, checking midway to make sure there's enough water and to stir ingredients.
5. Drain in a colander, and return to stockpot. Combine melted butter and flour in a small saucepan, stirring until very smooth; cook on low heat for 3 minutes, continuing to stir. Add roux to cabbage, and mix in thoroughly.

Vegetable Croquettes

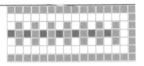

These tasty croquettes make a colorful and festive appetizer or vegetable side dish for Passover meals. But they're really too good to keep only for holidays; enjoy them any time of year.

1 tablespoon olive oil
½ cup red peppers, chopped into ¼-inch pieces
½ cup yellow peppers, chopped into ¼-inch pieces
2½ cups cooked potatoes, mashed
3 eggs, beaten
1¼ cups matzo meal
2 teaspoons salt
¼ teaspoon pepper

1 teaspoon paprika
⅛ teaspoon cayenne pepper
1 teaspoon crushed fresh garlic
¾ cup finely grated onion (squeeze out extra moisture)
¾ cup finely grated zucchini (peeled)
1 cup finely chopped fresh spinach
1 cup finely grated carrot
⅓ cup corn oil

MAKES
ABOUT 25

Note: Onions, zucchini, spinach, and carrots are best prepared in a food processor; pulse zucchini and carrots to the size of tiny pebbles, chop spinach fine, and reduce onions to a grated texture.

1. Heat olive oil in a skillet, and sauté red and yellow peppers until soft and light golden brown. Remove with a slotted spoon, and set aside to cool in a small bowl.
2. Place mashed potatoes in a large bowl. Add eggs, and mash in. Add

matzo meal, salt, pepper, paprika, cayenne, and garlic, and continue to mash in. Add onion, sautéed red and yellow peppers, and all other vegetables, and mix in thoroughly with a fork. Refrigerate for 1 hour.

3. Form patties 2½ inches in diameter and ¼ inch high. (If you have a ¼-cup measuring scoop, you can create very uniform patties by filling it, turning out the filling as from a mold, and flattening each patty to ¼-inch height with the palm of your hand.) Arrange patties, without stacking, on a cookie sheet or large platter covered with wax paper, and place in the freezer for 30 minutes.

4. Heat corn oil in a large skillet, and fry patties in batches on medium heat until golden brown on both sides. Drain on paper towel, and serve.

Vegetable Lo Mein

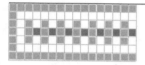

SERVES 6

Why does a Jewish deli serve lo mein? Chinese chef Pou Chun Cheng, a luminary of the Deli's kitchen since 1974, once prepared it for a private party at the Lebewohls' home. Abe loved it, and added it to the menu, where it's been a popular item ever since.

Note: Some of the items used in this recipe (notably fresh bean sprouts and lo mein noodles) may be a bit difficult to find. A Chinese grocery store is your best bet, but some Chinese restaurants will also sell you the necessary ingredients if you ask nicely.

¼ *cup plus 3 tablespoons plus 1 teaspoon corn oil*

2 *teaspoons salt*

1 *pound lo mein noodles (if you can't find them anywhere, substitute spaghetti)*

2 *cups onion, chopped into 2-inch strips, ½ inch wide (peel off a layer at a time and cut it into strips)*

1½ *cups broccoli, chopped into ¾-inch florets*

1 *tablespoon finely chopped or crushed fresh garlic*

½ *cup scallions, chopped into 1-inch pieces*

2 *cups (tamped down) shredded green cabbage*

¾ *cup carrot, chopped into ⅛-inch matchsticks, 1½ inches long*

½ *cup red peppers, chopped into 1-inch strips, ¼ inch wide*

½ *cup celery, chopped into 1-inch strips, ¼ inch wide*

1 *cup scrubbed mushrooms, chopped into ¾-inch pieces*

2 *cups fresh bean sprouts (if not available, use the canned variety, thoroughly drained)*

¼ *cup canned bamboo shoots (optional)*

1 *teaspoon Kitchen Bouquet (a browning sauce/gravy base available in supermarkets)*

3 *tablespoons soy sauce*

2 *tablespoons sesame oil*

Salt to taste

1. Fill a very large stockpot with water, add 1 teaspoon of the corn oil and 1 teaspoon of the salt, and bring it to a vigorous boil. Throw in lo mein noodles and cook, stirring once or twice, until al dente. Rinse, drain, and set aside in a large bowl.

2. Pour 3 tablespoons of the corn oil into a large skillet or wok, and, on high heat, sauté onions and broccoli until nicely browned, stirring occasionally. Add garlic at the last minute, and brown it quickly. Remove everything with a slotted spoon to a separate bowl, and set aside.

3. Use the oil left in the pan to sauté scallions until lightly browned. Remove with a slotted spoon to its own small bowl, and set aside.

4. Add remaining ¼ cup of corn oil to skillet, and toss in cabbage, carrots, red peppers, celery, mushrooms, and 1 teaspoon salt. Sauté on high heat, stirring frequently, until nicely browned. Remove with a slotted spoon to a colander, and press out excess liquid. Place drained vegetables in a large bowl, and set aside.

5. Add lo mein, bean sprouts, bamboo shoots, and Kitchen Bouquet to skillet, toss, and cook over high heat for 3 minutes, stirring frequently. Add onion-garlic-broccoli mixture, and continue to toss for about a minute. Add remaining vegetables, scallions, soy sauce, and sesame oil. Continue to stir-fry for about a minute longer, tossing to mix ingredients well.

6. Remove to a large bowl, toss ingredients even more thoroughly, add salt to taste if desired, and serve.

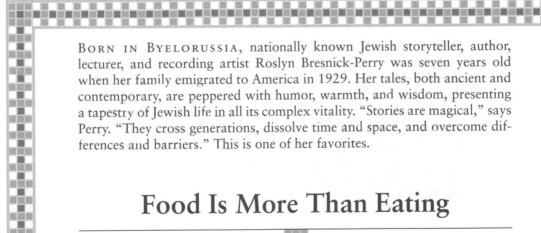

BORN IN BYELORUSSIA, nationally known Jewish storyteller, author, lecturer, and recording artist Roslyn Bresnick-Perry was seven years old when her family emigrated to America in 1929. Her tales, both ancient and contemporary, are peppered with humor, warmth, and wisdom, presenting a tapestry of Jewish life in all its complex vitality. "Stories are magical," says Perry. "They cross generations, dissolve time and space, and overcome differences and barriers." This is one of her favorites.

Food Is More Than Eating

"Food is more than eating," my grandfather used to say. "Food is for remembering who you are, what you are, and where you came from. And what is more important, with food you follow God's Commandments and celebrate His name."

Life in the shtetl revolved around religious observances and festivals in which food played a very important part. When we left Europe, my mother—who had a difficult time acclimatizing herself to her new life in America—held on to the Old Country ways, especially the ways of serving food for the holidays. She followed the routine her mother and her mother's mother had followed.

Every holiday had its own special menu. We knew what holiday we were celebrating by the delectable aromas emanating from the kitchen. My mother kept the Old Country alive for us by her meticulous adherence to what she called "her duty." This consisted not only of food preparation, but reciting, with great pleasure, the reasons we ate certain foods on particular holidays.

"You should always remember" (every lecture on holiday food began with that phrase) "that we eat hamantaschen, because it is a mitzvah to thank God that the Jews were saved by the beautiful Queen Esther and her wise uncle Mordecai from the terrible wrath of that arch-villain Haman." "But why are they called hamantaschen, and why are they shaped that way?" I asked. "I don't know," replied my mother. "They were always shaped that way."

On Simchat Torah, my mother piled kreplach high on our plates, adding her usual sermon. "*You should always remember* that we eat kreplach on Simchat Torah, because we are happy that God gave us the Torah." "Why kreplach, Momma?" I asked. "Because," chanted my father, "kreplach are good and the Torah is good."

"*You should always remember,*" intoned my mother on Chanukah, "we eat latkes on this day to celebrate the great victory of the Jewish heroes, the Maccabees, over the mighty Syrian legions." "Why latkes?" I asked. "I really don't know," my mother snapped, "and I don't think it's so important that you should always want to know *fun vanen di fis vaksn* [from where your legs start to grow]. Why must you understand everything?" My father, noting my disappointment over this rebuff, compounded my indignation by adding, "Chanukah is the season for lighting candles, and it deals with fire; we eat latkes so that the burning of the candles on the outside should correspond to the heartburn you get from eating them on the inside." In a Jewish family, everyone's a comedian.

His silly answer drove me to find a source of information outside the immediate family. After asking many relatives and neighbors without getting anywhere, I finally found a landsman who said he could explain it all to me. His name was Yudl-Leybke. He was a favorite of all us children—the only one of our parents' friends who deemed us important enough to talk to. "So," said Yudl-Leybke, "you really want to know why we eat latkes on Chanukah, do you? So sit yourself down, and I'll tell you a story.

"In the spring, all the little animals are born. The baby cows, the baby horses, goats, and geeses. In America, they call these baby geeses goslings, but in Europe we call them *gendzelakh*. So all summer these *gendzelakh* swim around with their momma, they eat little fishes and all kinds of grasses, and they grow up to be beautiful geeses."

"Geese," I corrected him.

"All right," he said, "geeses.

"What are you going to do with so many of them, because the winter is coming? So you take them to the *shecht* [ritual slaughterer] and slaughter them. The nights are getting longer, and what is there to do in the shtetl? So the young girls sit around the stove and pluck the geeses, using the beautiful white down to make feather beds and pillows for their trousseaus. Then the geeses are roasted for Shabbos, and their fat is rendered and made into delicious goose schmaltz.

"By now, it's already Chanukah. Everyone likes to go out to visit each other on Chanukah, to play cards, spin the dreidel, light the candles, sing songs; so what are you going to serve them? Potatoes, we got plenty. So you grate the potatoes, grate in some onion, add salt, pepper, an egg, a little bit of flour or matzo meal, then fry the latkes in wonderful goose fat. Oy, oy, oy! I can still feel the taste of those latkes in my mouth today. Nobody knows who started serving latkes on Chanukah, but if you ask me, whoever did it was a very smart person."

I must tell you, I was not at all pleased with his answer. I wanted something much loftier. But as I got older, I realized that customs arise for very practical reasons. People, however, need a little romance, a few miracles—and the myth, the legend, the story comes into being.

So why do we eat latkes on Chanukah? We eat them because we have always eaten them. So tell me, would you have it any other way?

Roz Perry's Shtetl Sauerkraut

MAKES 5 QUARTS

When I was a little girl in Russia, every year at Succoth, I used to watch my grandmother and aunts make sauerkraut, which I loved. They always made vast quantities, which we stored in barrels and ate throughout the winter. Especially thrilling was my part in the procedure. My grandmother would pick me up and place me on top of the large stone which was used as a weight to bring the brine to the surface. Then she'd say, "*Yets mamele tanz*" (Now, little mother, dance)—"dance and pack the cabbage down firmly so it can ferment and become sour." She and my aunts would all clap their hands and sing, and I would dance with all my might—for Succoth, for sauerkraut, and for pure joy.

5 pounds firm green cabbages   *1 teaspoon sugar*
1¾ tablespoons kosher salt

1. Purchase medium to large firm green cabbages, and keep them at room temperature for a day.
2. Wash well, and remove the outer leaves and cores with a knife. Reserve several large leaves. Shred cabbages to about a ⅛-inch thickness, and place in a large bowl. Add salt and sugar, and mix very thoroughly.
3. Place cabbage in a wooden keg, crock, or sterile glass jar, packing it firmly but not tightly. Cover with large cabbage leaves, topped with a piece of cheesecloth. Invert a large plate on top of the cloth, leaving at least 1 inch of cloth around the plate. On the plate, place a substantial weight, such as a heavy stone or chunk of wood, to bring the brine to the surface.
4. Store the crock in a cool, dark room (about 65 degrees) for 10 to 15 days (or longer), depending on the flavor desired. Start tasting after the seventh day to determine the amount of sourness (the longer it stays, the more sour it gets). The scum that begins to form after a few days must be skimmed off daily. When the desired taste has been achieved, transfer the sauerkraut to covered glass jars, and refrigerate. For hot sauerkraut, add 1 pint water per quart and a teaspoon of salt; boil to desired softness.

Tzimmes

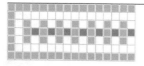

Not only is this sweet dish a Rosh Hashanah tradition (the blessing asks, "May it be Thy will to renew us a good and sweet year"), it is also served at the meal breaking the Yom Kippur fast—a joyous time celebrating that our sins have been forgiven (see also page 73).

MAKES I QUART

3 medium carrots, peeled and
 sliced into 1/4-inch coins
2 bay leaves
1/2 lemon, including peel, pitted
 and chopped into 1/2-inch pieces
1/2 juice orange, including peel,
 pitted and chopped into 1/2-inch
 pieces
1/4 cup honey (if you rub your
 measuring cup with vegetable
 oil, the honey will slide right out
 of it)

1/4 cup sugar
1/4 teaspoon cinnamon
2 cups mixed dried fruit (prunes,
 pears, apricots, and apples),
 chopped into 1-inch pieces
1/2 cup raisins
1/2 cup water
1 teaspoon cornstarch
1 teaspoon cold water

1. Place carrots in a large pot with bay leaves and just enough water to cover. Bring to a boil, then reduce heat, and simmer for about 20 minutes until carrots are al dente.

2. Remove carrots with a slotted spoon and set aside, retaining cooking water in the pot. Add lemon and orange pieces to pot, and simmer for 10 minutes.

3. Add honey, sugar, and cinnamon, and stir in until dissolved. Return carrots to pot, and simmer for 5 minutes.

4. Add dried fruit and raisins, along with 1/2 cup water. Simmer for 10 minutes, stirring occasionally so that everything cooks evenly.

5. In a small bowl, mix cornstarch with 1 teaspoon cold water, and stir until fully dissolved. Add cornstarch mixture to the tzimmes, stir in, and simmer for 10 more minutes or until everything is fully cooked and the liquid is almost completely absorbed. Serve hot as a side dish with chicken or beef.

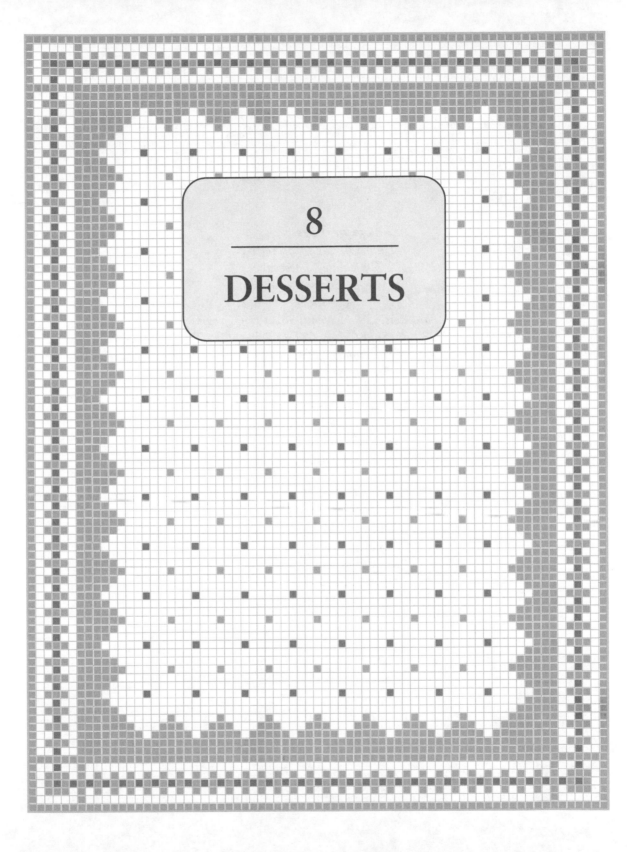

8

DESSERTS

Creamy Cheesecake
Fannie Abzug's Cheesecake
Chocolate Cheesecake
Cream Cheese Rugalach
Strudel
Paul Reiser's Fourteenth Street Egg Cream
Sour Cream Coffee Cake
Bundt Coffee Cake
Butterscotch Coffee Cake
Honey Chiffon Spice Cake
Lemon Bars
Lemon Cheese Pie
Abe's Double-Chocolate Ice Cream
Hamantaschen
Apple Squares
Challah Bread Pudding
Rice Pudding Brûlée
Brownies
Peach-Blueberry Crunch
Mandelbrot
Citrus Cake

In addition to desserts featured on our restaurant and catering menus, we've collected recipes from friends and relatives who are immensely talented bakers. This section includes excellent pareve desserts (which can be difficult to come by), the world's best hamantaschen, new takes on rice and bread puddings, and divinely decadent cakes . . . plus comedian Paul Reiser's formula for the ideal egg cream.

Creamy Cheesecake

Ever wonder why photos of pinup girls are called cheesecake? According to Martin Elkort in *The Secret Life of Food*, cheesecake dates back to ancient Greece, where it was baked in the shape of a woman's breast! Hence, the erotic-culinary connection. Ours, however, is best prepared in a springform pan. Who has a breast-shaped cake pan, anyway?

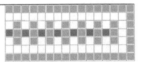

SERVES 8 TO 10

CRUST

1½ cups graham cracker crumbs
¼ cup sugar
4 ounces (1 stick) butter, softened
   to room temperature

½ teaspoon cinnamon

Shortening for greasing pan

FILLING

1 pound cream cheese, softened to
   room temperature
3 eggs, beaten
3 cups sour cream

1 cup sugar
2 teaspoons vanilla
¾ teaspoon almond extract
¼ teaspoon salt

TOPPING

2½ cups sour cream
¼ cup sugar

1¼ teaspoons vanilla
Fresh strawberries (optional)

1. Preheat oven to 375 degrees. Thoroughly combine crust ingredients in a bowl, and press along sides of greased cake pan.

2. Using an electric mixer or food processor, beat cream cheese smooth. Add eggs, and continue beating. Add all other filling ingredients, and mix well. Your batter should be perfectly smooth.

3. Pour batter into pan, and bake for 45 minutes, or until a toothpick inserted in center comes out dry. Remove, and let cool slightly, but leave oven on.

4. Combine all topping ingredients except strawberries, and when cake is slightly cooled, spoon topping evenly over it. Bake for another 5 minutes. Cool on counter.

5. If using strawberries, halve them vertically, and place aesthetically around the circumference of the cake. Refrigerate, and serve well chilled.

Pareve Cheesecake

At the Deli, we offer a wonderfully light and fluffy pareve cheesecake. Not only is it a boon to observant Jews; friends of ours who are lactose intolerant also adore it. For the crust, substitute margarine for butter. We know of two brands of pareve graham crackers, Lieber and Kemach (Nabisco graham crackers are baked in dairy ovens. Hence, though they contain no actual dairy ingredients, they are classed as dairy by observant Jews). For the filling, use Tofutti cream cheese and sour cream. Also add 1 teaspoon of flour, ½ teaspoon cornstarch, and 2 teaspoons lemon zest to your batter. Bake for 1 hour or until a pin inserted in the center comes out clean. Skip the topping, but decorate with fresh berries if you like.

For more than four decades, the late Bella Abzug was one of the nation's most dynamic leaders, civil rights activists, and advocates for the rights of women worldwide. As a Columbia Law School graduate (one of a handful of women in the class of '44), she specialized in labor and civil liberties law, going on to defend Hollywood actors targeted by the McCarthy witch hunts of the 1950s. After helping to organize Women Strike for Peace (a major force in protesting the Vietnam War) in 1961, she ran for Congress with the slogan "This woman's place is in the House—the House of Representatives." Winning the election, she served as a member of Congress from 1971 to 1977. In her later years, Bella devoted most of her time to international women's issues, serving as president of the Women's Environment and Development Organization and maintaining a busy law practice and public speaking schedule. We all miss her exuberant presence, both on the political scene and as a Second Avenue Deli regular.

I always enjoyed Abe, not only his food, but also his personality. Often we talked about life in general, the East Side specifically, and even about Russia—when he was trying to establish a business there. Always he was friendly, generous, and involved. I miss him, as I'm sure many, many do.

Fannie Abzug's Cheesecake

SERVES 6 TO 8

This is my grandmother's recipe.

CRUST
1 cup graham cracker crumbs
⅓ cup butter, softened to room
    temperature

¼ cup sugar

1½ pounds pot cheese
¼ pound cream cheese
6 eggs (separated)
1 teaspoon vanilla
2 tablespoons cornstarch

½ cup butter, softened to room
    temperature
½ pint sour cream
1 cup sugar

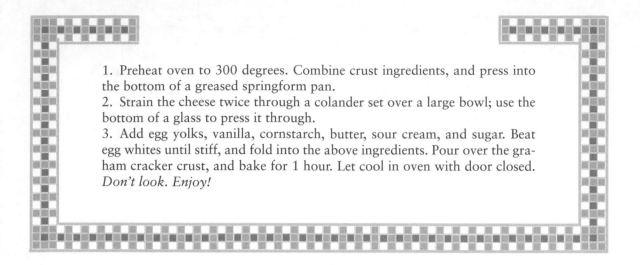

1. Preheat oven to 300 degrees. Combine crust ingredients, and press into the bottom of a greased springform pan.
2. Strain the cheese twice through a colander set over a large bowl; use the bottom of a glass to press it through.
3. Add egg yolks, vanilla, cornstarch, butter, sour cream, and sugar. Beat egg whites until stiff, and fold into the above ingredients. Pour over the graham cracker crust, and bake for 1 hour. Let cool in oven with door closed. *Don't look. Enjoy!*

Chocolate Cheesecake

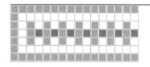

SERVES 8 TO 10

CRUST

1 cup graham cracker crumbs	*¼ cup sugar*
⅓ cup (5⅓ tablespoons) unsalted butter, softened to room temperature	*½ teaspoon cinnamon*
	Shortening for greasing pan

CAKE FILLING

1⅓ cups semisweet chocolate chips	*1 cup sugar*
3 tablespoons heavy cream	*2 eggs*
1½ pounds (3 8-ounce packages) cream cheese, softened to room temperature	*1 cup sour cream*
	½ teaspoon cinnamon
	1 teaspoon vanilla

Note: Though you can use any 9- or 10-inch cake pan (at least 2½ inches high) for this cake, a springform pan with removable sides will allow for the best presentation.

1. Preheat oven to 350 degrees. Thoroughly combine crust ingredients in a bowl, and press into the bottom of a greased cake pan.
2. Melt chocolate chips in the top of a double boiler (if you don't have one, use a small saucepan on very low heat). Add heavy cream, and stir.
3. In a large bowl, combine cream cheese and sugar, and beat with an electric mixer until smooth. One by one, fold in eggs, chocolate mixture, sour cream, cinnamon, and vanilla, mixing each in thoroughly. Batter should be completely smooth. Spoon evenly over crust, and bake for 50 minutes or longer—until a toothpick inserted in center comes out dry. Cool on counter and refrigerate. Serve chilled.

Cream Cheese Rugalach

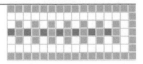

This is one of our favorite pareve desserts, because it tastes just as good as the version using dairy products. If you'd like to make the latter, substitute real cream cheese for Tofutti cream cheese and unsalted butter for margarine.

MAKES 32

8 ounces Tofutti pareve cream cheese, softened to room temperature
8 ounces (2 sticks) margarine, softened to room temperature
2 cups unbleached flour

⅛ teaspoon salt
½ cup sugar
½ cup raisins
½ teaspoon cinnamon
1 cup chopped walnuts
Confectioners' sugar

1. Place cream cheese, margarine, flour, and salt in a large bowl, and work it together with your hands until smoothly blended. Form into a ball, wrap well with plastic wrap, and refrigerate for at least 1 hour.
2. While dough is chilling, mix sugar, raisins, cinnamon, and walnuts in a bowl. Set aside.
3. When dough is chilled, dust your work surface with confectioners' sugar, and roll out half the dough at a time, leaving the remainder in the refrigerator. Roll into a circle about ¹⁄₁₆ inch thick, giving the dough quarter turns as you roll. Sprinkle with a bit of confectioners' sugar to prevent sticking. Work quickly; when the dough loses its chill, it's hard to work with.
4. Cut the circle of dough like a pie into 16 equal wedges. Place a little more than a flatware teaspoon of the mixture on each wedge, and roll from the wide edge to the point into a crescent. Place crescents on an ungreased cookie sheet, and refrigerate for at least 30 minutes. Repeat with the second half of the dough. Preheat oven to 350 degrees.
5. Bake 15 to 20 minutes until lightly browned. Do not overbake; the rugalach will be soft when done.

Strudel

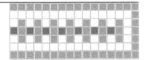

Strudel originated in Austria (where it was stuffed with cabbage or fish) and spread, via Hungary, to the rest of Eastern Europe. Usually filled with apples or cheese, it became, and remains, a staple in Jewish bakeries and restaurants. Flaky, paper-thin strudel dough has long been one of the many tests of a great Jewish cook, but if you don't care to take on the challenge, frozen phyllo dough is available in many supermarkets and Middle Eastern groceries.

SERVES 10

FOR THE DOUGH
2 cups sifted flour
*1 cup (8-ounce container) sour
    cream*

*4 ounces (1 stick) unsalted butter,
    softened to room temperature*
¼ teaspoon salt

OTHER INGREDIENTS
Flour
¾ stick unsalted butter, melted
Unseasoned bread crumbs

*Shortening for greasing cookie
    sheet*
Confectioners' sugar
Various fillings (see below)

1. Combine all dough ingredients and blend thoroughly, first with a fork, then using your hands. Roll dough into a ball, and refrigerate in a covered bowl for at least 3 hours (it's okay to refrigerate it as long as 2 days ahead).
2. Prepare one of the fillings listed below and set aside in refrigerator.
3. Preheat oven to 375 degrees.
4. Cover your kitchen table with a sheet or cloth, and rub it very liberally with flour. To secure the cloth, you may want to tape it under the table. Have your melted butter, filling, bread crumbs, pastry brush, and greased cookie sheet near at hand. Lightly flour your rolling pin. Roll out the dough in all directions, working it toward a rectangular shape (at least 12 by 17 inches, after you've trimmed the edges) and getting it as thin as you can without tearing. You can pull the edges gently with your hands. Trim the sides of the rectangle to create straight lines, and reserve the dough you snip off to roll into a smaller strudel. Using a pastry brush, brush the dough (only the side facing up) generously with melted butter. (Don't worry if you get a little tear in your dough. You can just pull a little over the hole to mend it.)
5. Now you want to create a 3-inch band of bread crumbs (don't use too many—just a moderate sprinkling) on one side of your dough, over which you'll place your filling. Start about 2 inches from the top (shorter end) of your rectangle and about 1 inch from the side over which you will place your filling. Distribute the filling evenly over the bread crumbs. (Reserve a bit of filling for your small strudel made of leftover dough.) Roll up, lengthwise, like a jelly roll, beginning on the side with filling. Seal the ends well, and place completed roll, seam-side down, on your greased cookie sheet. Brush the top of the roll with melted butter and, with a sharp knife, make neat diagonal slashes every ¾ inch along the top. This creates a nice decorative touch and also keeps your strudel from swelling up like a beached whale.
6. Repeat process with leftover dough and filling.
7. Bake for 45 minutes (check after 38) or until top is a light golden brown. Remove strudel to a rack or plate, and, when it has cooled a bit, use a sieve or sifter to sprinkle the top with confectioners' sugar. Serve slightly warm or chilled.

APPLE FILLING

3 cups peeled, cored, and very
   thinly sliced McIntosh or
   Granny Smith apples
1/2 cup chopped pecans

1/2 cup golden raisins
3/4 cup sugar
1 teaspoon cinnamon

1. Combine all ingredients in a large bowl, mix thoroughly, and spread on the strudel dough as indicated above.

CHEESE FILLING

1 pound farmer cheese
8 ounces whipped cream cheese
3/8 cup sugar

1 egg, beaten
1 teaspoon vanilla

1. Combine all ingredients in a large bowl, blend thoroughly, and spread on the strudel dough as indicated above.

RASPBERRY FILLING

1 12-ounce jar raspberry preserves
2/3 cup chopped pecans

1 cup raisins

1. Spread raspberry preserves along the band of bread crumbs (see above), and sprinkle evenly with nuts and raisins.

Mad About You star Paul Reiser was born and raised in New York City, where, as a teenager, he haunted Village comedy clubs. In college, summer breaks were spent doing stand-up at places like Catch a Rising Star and The Improv; as a result, he was already well established on the comedy-club circuit by the time he graduated. Paul's first big break came in 1982, when he accompanied a pal to a movie audition; director Barry Levinson unexpectedly asked him to read, then cast him in the movie *Diner*. Other films followed (*Aliens, Beverly Hills Cop II, The Marrying Man,* and *Bye, Bye Love,* among others), as did the TV sitcom *My Two Dads* (1987–90).

Mad About You is largely based on Reiser's life (like his alter ego, Paul Buchman, he's married, with a baby and an almost-human dog), with further documentation in two best-selling books: *Couplehood* and *Babyhood.* A Deli regular when he's in town, Paul has used Second Avenue Deli shopping bags and mugs as archetypal New York props on *Mad About You.*

My favorite image of Abe is him standing outside the restaurant, serving complimentary "tastes" of chopped liver to the people waiting on line to come in. And while taking care of them, he would also oversee

Paul Reiser and Helen Hunt working in a plug for the Second Avenue Deli on Mad About You.

the loading and unloading of several Second Avenue Deli vans that were preparing to deliver more food to yet more about-to-be-happy customers all across town. He would step into traffic (in his shirt-sleeves—I don't know if I ever saw the man wear a coat) and proceed to guide the vans safely on their way, halting and directing traffic in four directions with effortless skill and good cheer. It was as if all the wonderful, nurturing chaos of his kitchen was spilling out onto the street, on its way to enveloping the entire city in a warm blanket of pastrami and love.

Paul Reiser's
Fourteenth Street Egg Cream

SERVES I

Step one: Play basketball, and get real sweaty. Like rosy-cheeked, out-of-breath sweaty.

Step two: Go home.

Step three: Take a glass (a *glass* glass, not a plastic glass), and pour in a bunch of Fox's U-Bet chocolate syrup.* (It doesn't matter how much.)

Step four: Pour in some seltzer. (It doesn't matter how much.)

Step five: Add a little milk. (It doesn't matter how much, but too little is better than too much.)

Step six: Get a *metal* spoon. Now this is the only important part of the whole thing: stir vigorously and increasingly quickly, until your wrist is a blur, and the spoon is actually moving *vertically.* You should hear a very strong, rapid clanking of metal on glass.

Step seven: When the ferocious whirlpool has subsided, drink the egg cream very fast—in fact, a little faster than is reasonably healthy.

Step eight: Emit a long sigh, stressing the letters *a* and *h.*

Step nine: Go out and play basketball some more.

*Although purists would disagree, I say Hershey's chocolate syrup is just as good.

Comedy corner: Jack hanging out with Jerry Seinfeld and Paul Reiser in a Deli booth.

Sour Cream Coffee Cake

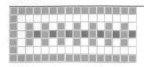

SERVES 12

2 cups sifted flour
1½ teaspoons baking powder
¼ teaspoon salt
2 cups coarsely chopped pecans
1 tablespoon cinnamon
¼ cup brown sugar
8 ounces (2 sticks) butter, softened to room temperature (use margarine for a pareve version)

2 cups sugar
1 teaspoon vanilla extract
2 eggs, at room temperature
1 cup sour cream, at room temperature (use Tofutti sour cream for a pareve version)
Shortening for greasing pan

1. Preheat oven to 350 degrees. In a large bowl, combine flour, baking powder, and salt. Set aside.
2. In another bowl, combine pecans, cinnamon, and brown sugar. Set aside.
3. Place butter and sugar in a third bowl, and, with an electric mixer, cream until light and fluffy. Using a rubber spatula, fold in vanilla and eggs, blending thoroughly. Alternately, stir the sour cream and the flour mixture, a bit at a time, into the other ingredients.
4. Put half the nut mixture in the bottom of a greased Bundt pan, pour batter over it, and sprinkle remaining nut mixture over the top.
5. Bake for 50 minutes or until a toothpick inserted in the center comes out dry. Let the cake cool for 20 minutes before turning it onto a rack or plate.

Bundt Coffee Cake

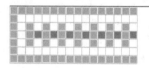

SERVES 8

1½ cups sifted flour
4 ounces (1 stick) plus 3 tablespoons unsalted butter, softened to room temperature
1½ teaspoons baking powder
¼ teaspoon salt
1 cup sugar
2 eggs
½ cup heavy cream

1 teaspoon vanilla
2 teaspoons grated lemon rind
1 teaspoon fresh lemon juice
½ cup brown sugar
¾ cup finely chopped pecans
½ teaspoon cinnamon
¼ cup graham cracker crumbs
Shortening for greasing pan
Confectioners' sugar

1. Preheat oven to 350 degrees. In a large bowl, combine flour, ¼ pound of the softened butter, baking powder, and salt; stir with a fork until it assumes a crumbly texture. Add sugar, and mix thoroughly.
2. Add eggs, beaten, one at a time, followed by cream, vanilla, lemon rind, and lemon juice. Blend all ingredients very thoroughly, first by hand, then using an electric mixer for 7 full minutes.

3. In another bowl, combine brown sugar, pecans, cinnamon, graham cracker crumbs, and 3 tablespoons softened butter. Mix thoroughly. Press into the bottom and slightly up sides of a well-greased Bundt pan. Spoon in batter evenly atop this nut–graham cracker mixture, and bake for 1 hour or until a toothpick inserted in center comes out clean.

4. Turn out of pan immediately, let cool for 10 minutes, and sprinkle with confectioners' sugar (best done through a sieve or sifter).

Butterscotch Coffee Cake

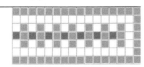

We both love this cake and frequently make it for company. It always gets raves.

SERVES 15

FOR THE BATTER

2 cups sifted flour
1½ cups sugar
8 ounces (2 sticks) unsalted butter, softened to room temperature
2 eggs, beaten
8 ounces sour cream

2 teaspoons grated lemon rind
1 tablespoon vanilla
2 teaspoons baking powder
1 teaspoon baking soda
⅛ teaspoon salt
¾ cup butterscotch chips

FOR THE FILLING

¾ cup brown sugar
½ cup finely chopped pecans
½ teaspoon cinnamon

Shortening for greasing pan
Confectioners' sugar

1. Preheat oven to 350 degrees. In a large bowl, combine all batter ingredients except butterscotch chips, and beat until smooth. Fold in chips.

2. In a separate bowl, mix brown sugar, pecans, and cinnamon. Spoon two thirds of the batter into a well-greased tube pan. Evenly distribute the brown sugar–pecan mixture on top of the batter in the pan, and spoon the remaining batter on top. Bake 45 minutes or until a toothpick inserted in the center comes out clean. Let the cake cool completely before removing it from the pan. If a few pieces stick to the bottom of your baking pan (this is a very dense, moist cake that doesn't come easily out of the pan), just stick them on top of the cake; the confectioners' sugar will camouflage the problem.

3. Using a flour sifter or sieve, dust cake with confectioners' sugar.

Variation: This cake is also fabulous made with chocolate chips instead of butterscotch chips. With chocolate chips, omit the brown-sugar-pecan-cinnamon filling.

Honey Chiffon Spice Cake

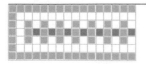

SERVES 8

Honey cake is the most traditional of sweet Rosh Hashanah dishes, harking back to the land of milk and . . . Generally, we don't get excited about honey cake. But this light and fluffy version, given to us by Lynn Kutner—who has taught baking and kosher cooking at the New School since 1974—is a delight. Lynn is the author of two cookbooks of her own, *Bountiful Bread* and *A Pocketful of Pies*.

7 extra-large eggs, separated
½ cup honey (if you rub a dab of oil into the measuring cup, the honey will slide right out)
½ cup hot coffee (you can use 2 teaspoons instant coffee granules dissolved in boiling water)
¾ cup packed dark brown sugar
2 cups sifted all-purpose flour

3 teaspoons baking powder
½ teaspoon baking soda
¼ teaspoon salt
¾ teaspoon cinnamon
¾ teaspoon ginger
¼ teaspoon allspice
¼ teaspoon nutmeg
¼ cup granulated sugar
½ cup sunflower oil
Confectioners' sugar

1. Preheat oven to 325 degrees. Using an electric mixer, beat egg yolks with honey. Slowly beat in hot coffee, followed by brown sugar. Allow mixture to cool.
2. In a large bowl, mix flour, baking powder, baking soda, salt, and spices. Set aside.
3. In another bowl, beat egg whites until soft peaks form. Gradually beat in granulated sugar, and continue beating until whites are very stiff.
4. Make a well in the flour mixture. Pour in egg yolk mixture and sunflower oil. Blend with a whisk until smooth.
5. Fold in one-quarter of the egg whites. Turn this batter over the rest of the egg whites, and gently fold (this procedure should take about 1 minute).
6. Bake for 50 minutes in an ungreased 10-inch angel-food pan, set on top of a cookie sheet. Turn heat up to 350 degrees; bake for 10 minutes more.
7. Invert pan on a rack to cool. When cake is cooled, remove from pan, and dust with confectioners' sugar.

Lemon Bars

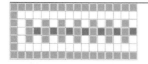

MAKES 12

8 ounces (2 sticks) softened butter (for a pareve version, substitute margarine)
1⅔ cups plus 3 tablespoons sifted flour
⅜ cup confectioners' sugar
¼ teaspoon salt

Shortening for greasing pan
1⅔ cups granulated sugar
3 eggs, beaten
¼ cup fresh lemon juice
¾ teaspoon baking powder
Confectioners' sugar

1. Preheat oven to 350 degrees. In a large bowl, use a fork to combine softened butter with 1⅔ cups of the flour, ⅜ cup confectioners' sugar, and salt. When the mixture is crumblike, press it into the bottom of a well-greased 9-inch square (or similar) baking pan, and bake for 15 minutes or until the edges are just starting to brown.

2. In another bowl, beat granulated sugar and eggs until the mixture is fluffy. Add lemon juice, and fold in 3 tablespoons flour and baking powder. Pour topping over crust, and bake for 20 minutes or until topping is firm. Serve chilled (cut squares from pan), sprinkled with confectioners' sugar.

Lemon Cheese Pie

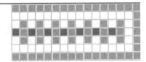

SERVES 8

CRUST
1½ cups graham cracker crumbs
4 ounces (1 stick) unsalted butter,
  softened to room temperature
¼ cup sugar
½ teaspoon cinnamon
⅛ teaspoon salt

FILLING
1 pound farmer cheese
½ pound whipped cream cheese
1 cup sugar
3 eggs, beaten
1 teaspoon vanilla
1 tablespoon lemon juice
2 teaspoons lemon rind

TOPPING
2 cups (a 16-ounce container) sour
  cream
¼ cup sugar
1¼ teaspoons vanilla

Shortening for greasing pan

1. Preheat oven to 350 degrees. Thoroughly combine crust ingredients (use your hands), and press into a greased 10-inch deep-dish pie pan. Bake 4 minutes, and set aside. Raise oven temperature to 375 degrees.

2. Combine filling ingredients in a large bowl, and beat to a smooth consistency with an electric mixer. Fill pie shell, and bake for 35 minutes or until the entire pie has a firm (not liquidy) custardlike consistency. Remove, and let cool slightly, but leave oven on.

3. Combine topping ingredients, and spoon evenly over pie. Bake for another 5 minutes. Cool on counter, and refrigerate. Serve chilled.

JOE FRANKLIN, an early innovator of the TV talk show format, started out as a radio DJ in the 1920s. *The Joe Franklin Show,* which debuted in the early 1950s, showcased many of today's biggest celebrities—Woody Allen, Bill Cosby, Dustin Hoffman, Barbra Streisand, and others—at the beginning of their careers. At one time, his in-house singer was Bette Midler, and her accompanist was Barry Manilow!

When I had my talk show on WOR, Abe was a frequent guest. His first appearance was on a show about famous people who grew up on the Lower East Side—celebrities like Eddie Cantor, Georgie Jessel, and Jimmy Durante. Abe was passionate about the area's rich Jewish history. We became chummy, and he was such a relaxed and enjoyable guest that I asked him back again and again. On later shows, he bantered with Bill Cosby, Otto Preminger, Sally Kirkland, Rudy Vallee, and Tiny Tim, among others.

Sometimes I had him on to do cooking demonstrations. Most memorable of these was the time he and Anna Moffo, the great operatic soprano, almost burned down my television studio preparing a flambé dessert.

One summer I invited Abe to be a guest the same night Vincent Price was appearing. I happened to mention to Abe that Price loved ice cream. Abe arrived with an ice cream recipe and the necessary ingredients, and he proceeded to make the richest possible double-chocolate ice cream for Price. That program was the beginning of a ritual: every time afterward, when Abe was a guest on my show, he and I would retreat to the station's test kitchen the minute we went off the air . . . to make vast quantities of ice cream. This is his recipe.

Abe's Double-Chocolate Ice Cream

MAKES ABOUT 2 QUARTS

2 cups semisweet chocolate chips
6 egg yolks, beaten
2 14-ounce cans sweetened
    condensed milk
¼ cup water
⅓ cup vanilla extract

2 pints heavy cream
¼ cup sugar
2 cups finely crushed Oreo or
    Hydrox cookies (Oreos are
    finally kosher)

Note: The easiest way to crush the cookies is in a food processor.

1. In a double boiler, melt the chocolate chips (if you don't have a double boiler, use a small saucepan), and stir frequently until very smooth.
2. In a large bowl, blend egg yolks, condensed milk, water, vanilla, and melted chocolate chips.
3. Combine heavy cream and sugar in a blender to make whipped cream. Fold cookies and whipped cream into other ingredients. Pour this mixture into lidded plastic quart containers (or a baking pan lined with tin foil), and freeze overnight.

Hamantaschen

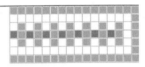

On Purim—which celebrates the victory of the Persian Jews over their enemy and King Ahasuerus's chief adviser, Haman—Jews eat a triangular-shaped pastry called hamantaschen. The reason: Haman, who had ordered that all Persian Jews were to be massacred, wore a tricorne, which, on Passover, we devour while gloating in triumph. At least that's one explanation. Others say the pastries resemble Haman's ears . . . or the purse he was going to fill with Jewish gold. Sephardic Jews do eat deep-fried crescent-shaped pastries called "Haman's ears" on Purim. Gingerbread man–like images of Haman are also devoured on this slightly cannibalistic holiday. For further details of the story, consult the Book of Esther.

We've provided a choice of two different hamantaschen doughs, both of them scrumptious. The first is pretty much a traditional dough, with extra citrus zip. The second is almond-flavored. Have your filling prepared before you begin to make the dough.

DOUGH NO. 1
4 cups flour
2 teaspoons baking powder
½ teaspoon salt
3 eggs
1 cup sugar
½ cup vegetable oil
Juice and zest (very finely grated rind) of 1 whole orange

Juice and zest (very finely grated rind) of 1 whole lemon
1 teaspoon vanilla
Sugar to sprinkle over hamantaschen before baking
Shortening to grease cookie sheet

FOR THE GLAZE AND SEALER
1 egg, beaten and diluted with 1 teaspoon water and 1 tablespoon heavy cream (use
nondairy creamer to make a pareve version)

1. In a large bowl, sift flour, baking powder, and salt. Set aside.

2. In another large bowl, beat eggs with an electric mixer until fluffy, and set aside.

3. In a third bowl, combine sugar, vegetable oil, orange and lemon juices and zests, and vanilla. Add this juicy mixture to the eggs and blend well. Then add flour–baking powder–salt mixture, and continue mixing until your dough forms a ball and pulls away from the sides of the bowl. Turn dough out onto a well-floured board, and knead until it no longer sticks to your fingers.

4. Divide dough into 4 sections. On a well-floured board, using a floured rolling pin, roll out the dough to a ⅛-inch thickness. Have filling, egg glaze, sugar, cookie cutter, flatware teaspoon, pastry brush, and greased cookie sheet close at hand.

5. Preheat oven to 375 degrees. Use a cookie cutter (or jar lid) to create circles about 4 inches in diameter. Place about 1 teaspoon (a flatware teaspoon, not a culinary measuring spoon) of the filling in the center of the circle, fold in sides, and press dough to seal, creating two sides of a triangle. Use a little of the egg glaze mixture as "glue" if you need it. Then fold the bottom of the circle up to form the third side of your "tricorne," leaving a little of the filling visible in the center. Brush top side of each pastry well with egg glaze mixture, sprinkle with sugar, and place on the greased cookie tray. Since cutting circles leaves a lot of marginal dough, you'll have to gather scraps in a ball and roll them out again. Bake for 20 minutes or until your hamantaschen are a light golden brown (check after 15 minutes to see how they're doing). Let hamantaschen cool before you remove them from the baking pan with a spatula.

ALMOND-FLAVORED DOUGH NO. 2

The almond dough may require a little less baking time than the citrus. Check your oven after 13 minutes.

3 cups flour
2 teaspoons baking powder
½ teaspoon salt
1 cup finely pulverized blanched almonds (you can do this in a food processor or by hand with a mortar and pestle)
3 eggs

1 cup sugar
4 ounces (1 stick) softened butter (use margarine for a pareve version)
1 teaspoon vanilla
1 teaspoon almond extract
Shortening to grease cookie sheet

FOR THE GLAZE AND SEALER
1 egg, beaten and diluted with 1 teaspoon water and 1 tablespoon heavy cream (or nondairy creamer)

Sugar to sprinkle over hamantaschen before baking

1. In a large bowl, sift flour, baking powder, and salt. Add almonds, and mix thoroughly. Set aside.

2. In a separate bowl, beat eggs with an electric mixer until fluffy, and set aside.

3. In another large bowl, cream sugar and butter with your electric mixer until completely blended. Add eggs, vanilla, and almond extract, and mix thoroughly. Add almond-flour mixture, and, using your hands, blend until the dough begins to form a ball and pull away from the sides of the bowl. Turn out onto a well-floured board, and knead the dough until it no longer sticks to your fingers.

4 and 5. Steps 4 and 5 are the same as in previous recipe.

THE FILLINGS

Prune and poppy seed are the classic fillings, but you can use others. We've included apricot and apple fillings as well. If you want to invent your own, you'll need about 1½ cups. These recipes give you a tad more fruit filling than you'll need. For one thing, it's better to have a little extra than too little. For another, they're delicious, and you'll want to nibble a bit while you work.

Notes: The reason for adding nuts last in the recipes below is that you don't want them completely pulverized in the mixing process; fruit fillings are tastier if nuts retain a bit of texture.

If your dried fruits (prunes, apricots, raisins) have become hard, soak them in warm water until soft but firm.

FOR THE PRUNE FILLING

Poppy seeds (see below) were the original hamantaschen filling; the use of prunes, which has today become the most popular, dates to eighteenth-century Europe.

1 cup pitted prunes
½ cup plum jam
2 teaspoons fresh-squeezed lemon juice
¼ cup brown sugar

2 teaspoons finely grated lemon rind
¼ teaspoon orange extract or 1 teaspoon orange zest
⅜ cup finely chopped pecans

1. Purée all ingredients except nuts in a blender or food processor. Transfer mixture to a bowl, and thoroughly blend in finely chopped nuts.

FOR THE POPPY SEED FILLING

The poppy seed filling commemorates Queen Esther's three-day fast, during which, subsisting on seeds, she prayed to God to repeal Haman's evil decree. Another explanation is that the Yiddish word for poppy seeds is *mohn*, which sounds like Haman; like his hat, he gets devoured.

¾ cup poppy seeds
3 tablespoons honey
¼ cup brown sugar
⅔ cup dark raisins, finely chopped

2 teaspoons finely grated lemon rind
½ cup finely chopped pecans

1. Pour boiling water over the poppy seeds and set aside for 15 minutes. Drain and grind (or put them in your food processor with the honey, brown sugar, raisins, and lemon rind). Transfer mixture to a bowl, and thoroughly blend in finely chopped nuts.

FOR THE APRICOT FILLING
¾ cup dried apricots
½ cup mixed dried fruit (apples and pears, not prunes)
½ cup apricot jam

1 tablespoon grated lemon rind
2 tablespoons brown sugar
½ cup finely chopped pecans

1. Purée all ingredients except nuts in a blender or food processor. Transfer mixture to a bowl, and thoroughly blend in finely chopped nuts.

FOR THE APPLE FILLING

This is a basic strudel filling that is also delicious in hamantaschen.

⅔ cup peeled and cored McIntosh apples, diced into ¼-inch pieces
⅛ cup unseasoned bread crumbs
¼ cup finely chopped raisins

¼ cup sugar
¼ teaspoon cinnamon
¼ cup finely chopped pecans

Combine all ingredients in a bowl and mix thoroughly. Put in a blender or food processor and pulse for a few seconds to make mixture a little moister and easier to use.

Apple Squares

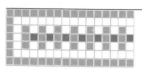

MAKES 9

For a pareve version, use margarine in place of unsalted butter.

½ cup blanched slivered almonds
½ cup raisins
1 tablespoon butter
4 ounces (1 stick) melted butter
1 cup sugar
1 egg, beaten
3 McIntosh apples, peeled, cored, and cut into 1-inch slices, ⅛ inch thick

1 teaspoon vanilla
1 cup sifted flour
½ teaspoon baking powder
½ teaspoon baking soda
¾ teaspoon cinnamon
⅛ teaspoon salt
Shortening for greasing pan
Confectioners' sugar

1. Preheat oven to 350 degrees. In a large skillet, sauté almonds and raisins in 1 tablespoon of butter; stir very frequently, and be careful not to burn them. Set aside in a small bowl.

2. In a large bowl, combine melted butter and sugar. Mix in egg, followed by apples, vanilla, almonds, and raisins.

3. In a separate bowl, combine flour, baking powder, baking soda, cinnamon, and salt. Gradually add this flour mixture to the apple-nut mixture, stirring to combine thoroughly.

4. Turn into a greased 9-inch square (or similar) pan, and bake for 45 minutes, or until a baking pin inserted in center comes out clean. Serve chilled (cut squares from pan), sprinkled with confectioners' sugar (best done through a sieve or sifter).

Challah Bread Pudding

Bread pudding originated as a peasant dish designed for using up leftovers. This is a lavish upscale version, featuring rich ingredients.

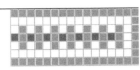

SERVES 6 TO 8

3 cups milk
4 eggs, beaten
1 teaspoon vanilla
¾ teaspoon salt
1 pound stale challah bread (an 8-inch rectangular loaf, not a twist)
4 tablespoons (½ stick) unsalted butter, softened to room temperature
½ cup golden raisins

¾ cup sugar
½ cup chopped pecans
2 McIntosh apples, peeled, cored, and sliced into 1-inch pieces ¼ inch thick
2 teaspoons cinnamon
2 teaspoons lemon rind
Butter for greasing pan
⅓ cup brown sugar
⅓ cup melted butter

1. Preheat oven to 375 degrees. Combine milk, eggs, vanilla, and salt in a large bowl, and mix thoroughly.

2. With a sharp knife, cut challah into 1-inch slices, and butter each slice with softened butter on one side. Dice buttered challah into 1-inch cubes, put them into the milk-egg mixture, and mix them thoroughly to soak up moisture. Let bread cubes soak for at least 15 minutes, tossing them occasionally.

3. In another bowl, combine raisins, sugar, pecans, sliced apple, cinnamon, and lemon rind, and mix thoroughly. Toss into bowl with soaked bread cubes and mix thoroughly.

4. Butter a 10-inch square (or similar) baking dish, at least 3 inches high, and transfer the bread pudding into it. Crumble brown sugar on top, and, using a flatware tablespoon, drizzle melted butter evenly. Bake for 45 minutes. Serve hot.

Rice Pudding Brûlée

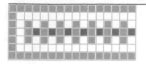

SERVES 8

Rice pudding goes from everyday ordinariness to impressively elegant when you make it with a brûlée topping. And it's so easy to do!

3 cups cooked long-grain rice, drained
2½ cups heavy cream
2½ cups milk
⅔ cup sugar
1½ cups raisins

3 tablespoons unsalted butter
2 eggs plus 1 yolk, well beaten
1 teaspoon vanilla extract
1 teaspoon cinnamon
½ teaspoon ground nutmeg
Sugar for brûlée topping

1. Place rice, heavy cream, milk, and sugar in a large saucepan, and stir to combine ingredients. Cook on medium heat for 35 minutes, stirring occasionally.
2. While rice is cooking, sauté raisins in butter for 1 or 2 minutes (brown, but don't burn), and leave in pan.
3. In a bowl, combine eggs (including extra yolk), vanilla, cinnamon, and nutmeg. Using a flatware tablespoon, add 8 spoonfuls, one spoon at a time, of the liquid from the cooking rice, and stir in immediately to keep the eggs from solidifying.
4. Pour egg mixture into rice pot, add raisins (retaining the cooking butter), and stir to combine ingredients. Pour mixture into individual ovenproof serving dishes or one large dish. Let cool at room temperature until the pudding begins to solidify and a film forms on the top.
5. Set oven to broil. Sprinkle top of pudding with sugar (cover entire surface), and place in broiler for 2 to 3 minutes until it caramelizes and forms a golden-brown crust. Check once or twice to make sure it doesn't get too burned. Refrigerate, and serve cold.

Brownies

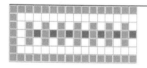

MAKES 12

Pareve brownies are a favorite dessert with our Deli customers. You'll find these as rich, moist, and chocolaty as any brownies you've ever tasted. Of course, you can also make them nonpareve by substituting butter for margarine and milk for the ¼ cup water.

½ cup flour
½ teaspoon baking powder
⅛ teaspoon salt
3 ounces (¾ stick) margarine
2 ounces unsweetened baking chocolate plus ¾ cup semisweet chocolate chips

1¼ cups sugar
2 eggs, beaten
¼ cup water
1 teaspoon vanilla
½ cup chopped walnuts or pecans (optional)
Shortening for greasing pan

1. Preheat oven to 350 degrees. Sift flour, baking powder, and salt into a medium-sized mixing bowl.
2. Melt margarine and chocolate in the top of a double boiler (use a small saucepan on very low heat if you don't have one). Stir thoroughly.
3. While chocolate and margarine are melting, in a large bowl, add sugar to beaten eggs and stir thoroughly.
4. Pour margarine and chocolate into sugar-egg mixture, and blend thoroughly. Fold in flour mixture. Add water, vanilla, and nuts, and mix well.
5. Grease an 8- or 9-inch square baking pan. Pour in batter, and bake for 35 minutes, or until a baking pin inserted in center comes out dry. Let cool on counter. Cut squares directly from pan.

Peach-Blueberry Crunch

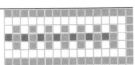

4 cups peeled fresh peaches, cut into 1-inch slices, ¼ inch thick
1 cup fresh blueberries (make sure your berries are well rinsed, and pick through for stems and smushy ones)
½ cup brown sugar, tightly packed
1 cup plus 3 teaspoons flour
½ teaspoon cinnamon

1 cup granulated sugar
¼ teaspoon nutmeg
1 teaspoon baking powder
¼ teaspoon salt
1 egg, beaten
4 ounces (1 stick) unsalted butter, melted (for a pareve version, use margarine)
Shortening for greasing pan

SERVES 8

1. Preheat oven to 375 degrees. Mix peach slices and blueberries in a large bowl (stir in a little sugar if your fruit isn't sweet enough). Fill the bottom of a well-greased 2-quart baking dish with fruit mixture.
2. Blend brown sugar, 3 teaspoons of the flour, and cinnamon in a different bowl, and distribute mixture evenly over fruit.
3. In another bowl, sift 1 cup of the flour, granulated sugar, nutmeg, baking powder, and salt. Add egg, and beat with a fork to a crumbly texture, making sure all ingredients are well integrated. Distribute this mixture evenly on top of the brown sugar mix, and spoon melted butter evenly over it.
4. Bake 35 minutes or until top is lightly browned. Let cool on counter for 30 minutes before adding topping.

FOR THE TOPPING

The topping is optional. This dessert is also great with a scoop of vanilla ice cream accompanying each portion; for a pareve version, you can use nondairy topping.

1½ cups whipped cream cheese
3 tablespoons confectioners' sugar
1 teaspoon finely grated orange peel

1 teaspoon finely grated lemon peel
2 tablespoons freshly squeezed orange juice

1. In a large bowl, combine cream cheese and confectioners' sugar, beating with a fork until fluffy. Add other ingredients, and continue beating. Chill until ready to use. Serve dessert chilled, cutting squares from pan.

Mandelbrot

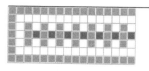

SERVES 12 TO 15

This easy-to-make breakfast bread (Yiddish for almond bread, but you can make it, as we do, with other nuts as well) tastes best toasted and buttered. A cross between a cake and a cookie, it's Eastern Europe's answer to Italian *biscotti*. Italians dunk it in espresso, Jews in a glass of tea.

2½ cups flour
1 teaspoon baking powder
⅛ teaspoon salt
3 eggs, beaten
¾ cup sugar
¾ cup (1½ sticks) softened
   margarine or butter

¾ cup chopped pecans or walnuts
½ cup raisins
1 teaspoon vanilla
⅛ teaspoon orange extract
Shortening for greasing pan

1. Preheat oven to 350 degrees. Sift flour, baking powder, and salt into a large bowl. Add all other ingredients except for shortening and mix thoroughly.
2. Grease a 9- by 9-inch (or similar) baking pan, pour in batter, and bake for 35 minutes or until a toothpick inserted in center comes out clean.

Variation: For a crisper version of mandelbrot, let cool, carefully cut into diagonal slices with a very sharp knife, and bake on a clean cookie sheet for 5 to 7 minutes on each side. Check after a few minutes to make sure the slices are browning evenly.

Citrus Cake

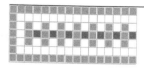

SERVES 10

4 tablespoons (½ stick) unsalted
   butter, softened to room
   temperature
1 cup sugar
1 egg, beaten
2 cups flour
¼ teaspoon salt

1 teaspoon baking soda
1 teaspoon baking powder
1½ cups sour cream
2 teaspoons grated lemon rind
3 tablespoons grated orange rind
1 teaspoon vanilla
Shortening for greasing pan

Note: Your dough will look thick and scant, but it will rise and become a light, moist, and fluffy cake.

1. Preheat oven to 350 degrees. In a large bowl, use a fork to cream butter and sugar. Add egg and beat in.

2. Sift flour, salt, baking soda, and baking powder in a separate bowl.

3. Alternately, about one-third at a time, add sour cream and flour mixture to butter-sugar mixture, and blend thoroughly. Stir in lemon rind, orange rind, and vanilla.

4. Grease and flour a 10-inch tube pan, spoon in batter, and bake for 35 minutes—or until top is a light golden brown and a baking pin inserted in the center comes out dry. Let cool before carefully loosening edges with a knife and removing from pan.

FOR THE ICING

3 ounces (¾ stick) unsalted butter, softened to room temperature

1½ cups sifted confectioners' sugar

2 tablespoons heavy cream

1 teaspoon vanilla

2 teaspoons very finely grated orange rind

2 teaspoons fresh-squeezed lemon juice

2 teaspoons fresh-squeezed lime juice

1. Place butter in a bowl, add confectioners' sugar, and mix thoroughly with a fork. Add all remaining ingredients, and continue to mix until icing consistency is smooth. Refrigerate for 15 minutes before spreading on thoroughly cooled cake after it has been removed from the pan. Your icing should be of a firm-enough consistency not to melt, but smooth enough to spread easily.

ACKNOWLEDGMENTS

MANY CONTRIBUTORS added zest, spice, and flavor to *The Second Avenue Deli Cookbook*. We'd like to thank those who took time from their busy schedules to write personal reminiscences of Abe Lebewohl, most of whom also shared their favorite recipes with us: Bella Abzug, Tom Birchard, Wayne Harley Brachman, Roslyn Bresnick-Perry, Patrick Clark, Senator Al D'Amato, Art D'Lugoff, Mark Federman, Raoul Felder, Bobby Flay, Joe Franklin, Mayor Rudolph W. Giuliani, Milton Glaser, Rozanne Gold, Al Goldstein, Dustin Hoffman, Grandpa Al Lewis, Drew Nieporent, Antonio Pagán, Alfred Portale, Helen Reiser, Paul Reiser, Morley Safer, Mimi Sheraton, Curtis Sliwa, Adam Tihany, José Torres, Tim and Nina Zagat.

We'd also like to thank these talented cooks and bakers for their valuable

The Deli's team.

contributions: Lucille Feenberg, Dottie Griss, John Holmes, Lynn Kutner, Eleanor Lebewohl, Ethel Lebewohl, Felicia Lebewohl Rosen, Jenny Lebewohl, Terry Lebewohl, Susan Leelike, Lisa Legarde, Esther Marcus, Everett McCourt, Judy Morris, Israel Moskowitz, Frieda Rockman, Sylvia Rudolph, Tzipora Said, Gili Tsabari.

Warmest thanks to: literary agent and cookbook maven Jane Dystel, whose enthusiasm and expertise have lovingly guided this project through the publishing process.

Our delightful and very talented editor, Mollie Doyle, for her brilliant creative input.

The grandchildren and nephews: Eli and Tzvi Barax for sharing in-depth interviews with Abe; Ayalah Barax for her help and encouragement in the kitchen; Evan and Eitan Rosen and Josh and Jeremy Lebewohl for their enthusiastic participation as food tasters. These seven children were responsible for the constant glimmer in Abe's eyes.

Arlene Bluth, whose extensive research into Second Avenue Deli history was invaluable.

And Pushpin people Seymour Chwast and Phyllis Rich Fader.

Finally, many, many thanks to the Deli kitchen staff, whose work we daily interrupted while creating this cookbook: "Doctor" Pou Chun Cheng, Michael Gladstone, "Captain" Sam Clayton, and Sylvester Mitchell. Ditto Deli managers Steve Cohen and Tony Sze; all the countermen; and Deli office staffers Karen Glasser and Pat Communiello.

INDEX

ABOUT THE AUTHORS

Born with a soupspoon in her mouth, SHARON LEBEWOHL grew up in the deli business, working at the restaurant and learning her father's secret recipes firsthand. Since her father's death in 1996, Sharon has worked with Abe's brother, Jack, to oversee the Deli's daily operations and to ensure that Abe's spirit is kept alive. She remains deeply rooted in the Jewish community and is active in many Jewish women's groups. Sharon is also the mother of three teenagers.

RENA BULKIN began her career in Paris, writing about European hotels and restaurants for *The New York Times* International Edition. Returning to her native Manhattan after several years abroad, she worked, respectively, at *The New Yorker* and *New York* magazines. She has written fifteen Arthur Frommer travel guides, as well as numerous magazine articles on travel, food, and other subjects. A close friend of the late Abe Lebewohl, she has a long history with the Second Avenue Deli, where she has worked on many public-relations campaigns.